Progressive Lawyers under Siege

Progressive Lawyers under Siege

Moral Panic during the McCarthy Years

Colin Wark and John F. Galliher

LEXINGTON BOOKS
Lanham • Boulder • New York • London

Published by Lexington Books
An imprint of The Rowman & Littlefield Publishing Group, Inc.
4501 Forbes Boulevard, Suite 200, Lanham, Maryland 20706
www.rowman.com

Unit A, Whitacre Mews, 26-34 Stannary Street, London SE11 4AB

British Library Cataloguing in Publication Information Available

Library of Congress Cataloging-in-Publication Data

Wark, Colin (Colin D.) author.
Progressive lawyers under siege : moral panic during the McCarthy years / Colin Wark and John F. Galliher.
p. cm.
Includes bibliographical references and index.
ISBN 978-0-7391-9560-4 (cloth : alk. paper) – ISBN 978-0-7391-9561-1 (ebook)
1. Law–United States–History–20th century. 2. Anti-communist movements–United States–History–20th century. 3. Lawyers–Political activity–United States–History–20th century. 4. Political crimes and offenses–United States–History–20th century. 5. Legal services–United States–History–20th century. 6. Political persecution–United States–History–20th century. 7. Left-wing extremists–Legal status, laws, etc.–United States–History–20th century. 8. Blacklisting, Labor–United States–History–20th century. I. Galliher, John F., author. II. Title.
KF371.W37 2015
340.0973'09045–dc23
2015002893

∞ ™ The paper used in this publication meets the minimum requirements of American National Standard for Information Sciences Permanence of Paper for Printed Library Materials, ANSI/NISO Z39.48-1992.

Printed in the United States of America

Contents

Prologue

This book deals with a very troubled period in American history, so much so that the era has been given names such as the period of the Red Scare or the McCarthy Era named after the junior U.S. senator from Wisconsin, Joseph McCarthy. McCarthy claimed to have proof positive that many high-ranking officials in the U.S. State Department and in the U.S. Army were either Communists or Communist sympathizers. Senator McCarthy was ultimately censured by the U.S. Senate. In this strange political environment federal and state legislation often provided harsh treatment for liberals, Jews, African Americans, and drug addicts. The high water mark for federal drug penalties occurred during this period. This legislation was enthusiastically enforced by the FBI.

Those who complained to the FBI about racial discrimination were also subjected to the agency's scrutiny. Professor Laud Humphreys complained to the FBI about illegal racial segregation in a Memphis restaurant and as a consequence had a file opened on him (Galliher, Brekhus, and Keys 2004). Those who criticized the FBI and its director were also targets, especially if they were women. For example, Professor Mabel Elliott chided Hoover for his claims that prisons were like country clubs (McGonigal and Galliher 2009) and thus a file was opened on her as well. Academics who sympathetically studied marginalized groups were targeted. Professor Alfred Lindesmith studied drug addiction and drug addicts. He claimed that addiction was a sickness rather than a crime and as a consequence, the FBI pressured the Indiana University administration to terminate him and also asked the University not to publish his books. Both requests were ignored by Indiana University President Herman Wells (Keys and Galliher 2000). Alger Hiss was a prominent State Department officer who was hounded by the FBI for several decades (Jacoby 2009). During this time many Americans were blacklisted and forced out of their employment by the FBI.

This book deals with attorneys in one San Francisco law firm, two Jews (only one of whom was active in the local temple) and a secular protestant. Two of the partners graduated from elite law schools and one did not. While differences abound, these attorneys were linked by the fact that they represented labor union leaders and members, and thus were considered radicals by the FBI.

In sum this book deals with what is, what could be, and what should be. Our research relies on descriptive materials, but also includes implied predictive information and prescriptive data. The implication clearly is that all people could be and should be free from attacks by the FBI and the federal government.

Acknowledgments

This book is largely based on information obtained from FBI files including those of Richard Gladstein, George Andersen, Norman Leonard, and Harry Bridges. These materials provide the reader with a glimpse into the culture of the Bureau during the height of the McCarthy Era. The files were obtained by submitting FOIA requests to the FBI.

Thanks are due to Nancy Myers for steering us in the direction of some relevant literature. We are also grateful to Raymond Michalowski and Peter Mickulas for a careful reading of an earlier draft of the manuscript and for their intelligent comments. Michele Welsing, Raquel Chavez, and the staff at the Southern California Library Archives were generous with their direction, as were Catherine Powell and Ben Blake at the San Francisco State University Labor Archives. Rob Remar at the Leonard Carder law firm in San Francisco (the current incarnation of the Gladstein, Andersen, and Leonard firm) provided us with documents not held elsewhere. The same was true of Robin Walker at the ILWU archives. Tami Suzuki, Jeff Thomas, Wendy Kramer, and Christina Moretta at the San Francisco History Center were generous with their time and expertise. Dorothy Lazard of the Oakland Public Library was very helpful in offering intelligent advice on the location of relevant information. The family and colleagues of Gladstein, Andersen, and Leonard also provided valuable insights including attorneys Jed Gladstein, Ben Andersen, David Andersen, William Carder, and Richard Patsey. Kathy Herman mailed documents pertaining to her late father Aubrey Grossman. We also acknowledge a research leave granted to John Galliher by the University of Missouri that enabled completion to this research. Most of all we are indebted to Ann Fagan Ginger for her intelligent and compassionate leadership in this research.

Chapter One

Introduction

Because a pattern of repression has occurred during almost every major crisis in U.S. history it is not "a temporary aberration, but rather . . . a normal part of American political life" (Schrecker 2008, 68). This was definitely true during the McCarthy Era—the late 1940s and 1950s (Schrecker 2008). The U.S. government's irrational fear of communism resulted in the persecution of many innocent people who were accused of being Communist sympathizers. For example, during this time period a concern for the safety of New York City's water supply prompted a rule requiring those who applied for a permit to fish in the city's reservoirs to first take a loyalty oath. In 1957 the state's "commissioner of water, gas and electricity actually refused to grant fishing permits to two Communist Party . . . leaders" (Schrecker 2008, 69). FBI Director J. Edgar Hoover was "astute" and "cunning" (Weiner 2012, xvi) and had learned the basics of "mass arrests and detentions during his first year at [the] Justice [Department]" in 1919 when nearly 100 Germans living in the United States had been jailed (Weiner 2012, 13). By 1940 the FBI had begun creating a list with thousands of names of people who were to be jailed in advance of conviction (Weiner 2012, 86) and by the late 1940s Hoover developed plans for a massive crackdown on American Communists.

GETTING STARTED WITH HELP FROM A LAW FIRM

In December 2007 (Weiner), we learned that FBI Director J. Edgar Hoover sent a plan to jail 12,000 Americans to the White House on July 7, 1950. The plan was never implemented and it was declassified on December 21, 2007. We contacted the National Archives and asked for a copy of this proposal. The National Archives confirmed that the list of names was declassified and suggested that we contact the U.S. State Department. On February 12, 2008, we filed a FOIA (Freedom of Information Act) request with the State Department and they suggested that we look at their website before ultimately telling us to contact the FBI (Federal Bureau of Investigation). Soon after filing our request with the FBI we received a letter from the Kansas City Field Office telling us that they were unable to find the requested information in their records. However, they said that we had the option of filing an "administrative appeal" with the Office of Information and Privacy in Washington, D.C. Soon after receiving this letter we filed an appeal and requested help from a law firm in Columbia, Missouri.

On May 15, 2008, approximately 5 weeks after we filed the administrative appeal, the Associate Director of the Office of Information and Privacy sent us a letter affirming the Kansas City Field Office's decision. She invited us to submit an appeal to FBI Headquarters and/or file a lawsuit. Finally, in September of 2008, with the help of the lawyer who was working on our behalf, we obtained the records that we had requested—10 months after our initial request. Nearly all of the names of individuals were removed, or redacted.

ORIGINS OF THE RESEARCH PROJECT

Once we received the FBI records we saw that between August 2, 1950, and February 4, 1955, the Bureau designated an increasing number of individuals as security risks. On August 11, 1950, there were 12,182 people listed as security risks and by February 4, 1955, this number had climbed to 26,705. But by November 4, 1955, the number had precipitously decreased to 12,863, or approximately where the numbers began. The increases are easily understandable as part of the "Red Scare," that is widely believed to have begun on February 9, 1950, with an infamous speech given by Wisconsin Senator Joseph McCarthy in Wheeling, West Virginia, where he warned of many Communists in government service (Greenberg 2008).

SAMPLE SELECTION OR PROBLEM SELECTION

The records we received indicated that the FBI targeted Jewish and union groups for arrest. The Jewish groups targeted included the Jewish Information Service—Los Angeles, the Jewish Cultural Association, Jewish Cultural Center, and the Jericho Temple-Detroit. The unions and union members targeted included the Baltimore Organizer for the United Electrical, Radio and Machine Workers of America-CIO, the labor union at the Kennecott Copper Co., and anyone with trade union "experience as picket captains, . . . [and those who participated] in violent strikes, riots or demonstrations" (2/10/55, Custodial Detention Sect. 4 [Comsab], 40). As we already noted, the names of individuals were redacted but there were actually files on more than 26,000 people. The only names of individuals that were not redacted were those of three attorneys: Richard Gladstein, George Andersen, and Norman Leonard, 240 Montgomery St., San Francisco (9/20/51, Custodial Detention Sect. 8, 50). We later learned that these three law partners had working class backgrounds. Leonard was the son of Jewish immigrants while Andersen was a gentile and an immigrant from Denmark. The law firm had two Jewish partners (Gladstein and Leonard), one born abroad (Andersen), and all three were deeply involved in defending labor union members including those who were picketing their employers.

Here we have included the page from the FBI's Security Index that lists the names of the law partners and the address of their office as well as the items that would be considered "contraband" in the event of a police raid.

Additionally, in the appendix we have included excerpts from the partners' FBI files. These pages will give the reader an idea of the culture that pervaded the FBI during the McCarthy Era.

One of Richard Gladstein's sons who is also an attorney wondered why the FBI singled out his father's firm for this public censure. One possibility is because the FBI considered the partners to be the worst of the worst. In an e-mail to Colin Wark (July 28, 2013) Gladstein's son put it this way: "Normally when someone is accorded special treatment there is a reason for it." Although we will never know with certainty, it seems likely that the release of these names was simply a human error or accident. This is not surprising since FBI analysts are expected to protect the identities of thousands of individuals, but the names of groups and organizations can be released. After selecting these partners and this firm for analysis we found not a single book or article written solely about them but we did find snippets of information such as a discussion of Gladstein's defense work in the New York Communist trial and subsequent prison sentence for contempt of court (See Brody 2010).

This law firm was "hidden from history" along with other marginalized groups including women (Rowbotham 1976), black radicals (Duffield 1988), gays and lesbians (Duberman, Vicinus, and Chauncey 1989), prostitutes (Frances 2007), and participants in the black labor movement (Ortiz 2005). Most recently (Glass 2013) a book was published on United States and British army deserters being "A Hidden History of World War II." This book is the most recent treatment of a hidden, marginalized group and it is set in roughly the same time period (around WWII) that the Gladstein partners came under scrutiny by the FBI. The book also shows that the U.S. military at that time, like the FBI, was riddled with anti-Semitism and a bias against immigrants.

San Francisco Division

Premises occupied by the law firm of
Gladstein, Andersen and Leonard
Entire Fifth Floor
240 Montgomery Street
San Francisco, California

Contraband:

1. Propaganda material of the enemy or insurgents.

2. Propaganda material which fosters, encourages or promotes the policies; programs, or objectives of the enemy or insurgents; and printing presses, mimeograph machines, or other reproducing media on which such propaganda aforementioned has been or is being prepared.

3. Any and all records, including membership and financial records, of any organization or group that has been declared subversive or may hereafter be declared subversive by the Attorney General.

4. Cash funds either in currency or coins, promissory notes or checks, or securities of any nature.

PLC:mjt

FBI's Security Index. ***09/20/51, Custodial Detention Sect. 8 (Detcom), 50.***

PURPOSE OF THE STUDY AND DATA SOURCES

The goal of this research was to learn about the culture provided by this law firm for its partners and its most famous and beleaguered client, International Longshoremen's and Warehousemen's Union (ILWU) President, Harry Bridges, himself an immigrant from Australia. During the 1940s and 1950s the law firm routinely defended accused Communists. The attorneys and their clients suffered through very difficult times in the late 1940s and early 1950s. Gladstein was sentenced to federal prison for legally defending Communists and Andersen was shot in his office by unknown intruders who were never captured nor identified by the police. We hasten to add that we have only indirect evidence of this legal culture, as our research is largely based on existing historical documents.

Newspaper articles from the *San Francisco Chronicle* were obtained from the clippings files of the North Baker Research Library of the California Historical Society in San Francisco. The Southern California Library in Los Angeles holds the Gladstein papers, the San Francisco State University Labor Archives and Research Center contains most of the George Andersen materials and the Norman Leonard and Richard Gladstein Oral Histories were found at the University of California, Berkeley. The San Francisco International Longshore and Warehouse Union (ILWU) Anne Rand Research Library also held various documents, as did the San Francisco History Center at the San Francisco Public Library. The San Francisco law firm Leonard Carder (the current incarnation of the Gladstein, Andersen, and Leonard law firm) also provided us with documents, especially photos. To ensure reliability the authors made two trips to California approximately 12 months apart to locate the Caroline Decker Gladstein oral history and other documents in Los Angeles and the Andersen materials in San Francisco. The authors also secured the FBI files of Gladstein, Andersen, Leonard, and Bridges through Freedom of Information Act (FOIA) requests. Finally, interviews were conducted with the children and former partners of these lawyers.

A recently published book that deals with the FBI, Ronald Reagan, and their war on students at UC Berkeley relies on many of the same sources that we used in studying the Gladstein firm (Rosenfeld 2012). Rosenfeld used FBI files on law-abiding citizens that were only grudgingly released after a protracted legal fight using the Freedom of Information Act. He also utilized interviews, news accounts, and many oral histories, none of which included those of the law partners studied here.

FBI FILES FOR OTHER PROMINENT AMERICANS

Keen (1999) found that the FBI kept files on many prominent American academics including Jane Addams, Herbert Blumer, C. Wright Mills, Thorstein Veblen, W.E.B. DuBois, E. Franklin Frazier, Alfred McClung Lee, Gunnar Myrdal, and Edwin Sutherland. These scholars were both sociologists and economists, African Americans and Anglos, and they represented all political stripes with Sutherland being the most politically conservative.

In addition the late Mabel Elliott had an active FBI file from 1938 to 1967 with no evidence of law violation. The FBI merely wanted to keep an eye on her every move since she was a criminologist with ideas on crime differing from those at the Bureau. Since Elliott's file involved no law violation there was no redacting necessary (McGonigal and Galliher 2009). The late Alfred Lindesmith also had an FBI file as early as 1946, within a year of his discharge from the U.S. Army (Keys and Galliher 2000). The government delayed four years before releasing the file and then sent only 19 very heavily redacted pages that revealed nothing except that Lindesmith was investigated for alleged espionage. Finally, there was little delay in releasing the 69-page file of the late Laud Humphreys in 2002 (Galliher, Brekhus, Keys 2004). This file was opened in 1966 when Humphreys complained to the FBI about illegal racial segregation in a Memphis restaurant. But the bulk of this file covers non-violent civil disobedience and law violation at an Illinois draft board.

Unlike actors and others who were blacklisted from employment the attorneys that we studied were employed throughout their blacklisting. Indeed, they always had employment *because* of FBI blacklisting.

AMERICAN UNIONS AND THE FBI

The labor union movement was revived by the Great Depression in every state and in every industry (Zieger 1994). The CIO as a leftist union experienced particularly rapid growth as did the International Ladies Garment Workers Union (ILGWU). During WWII the labor union movement continued to grow. Total labor union membership in the United States grew from approximately 8.9 million in 1940 to nearly 15 million in 1946 (U.S. Bureau of the Census 1950, 207).

There was especially significant growth in union membership from 1936–1939 and 1940–1945 (Cochran 1977). Maritime unions comprised nearly 18 percent of total union membership (Cochran 1977, 208–9). During this time victories were especially pronounced in the auto and steel industries.

THE COMMUNIST PARTY, UNEMPLOYMENT, AND STRIKES

The size and growth of the Communist Party in the United States was also phenomenal during the 1930s and 1940s with the greatest gains in influence and numbers occurring between 1935–1939, and 1941–1945 (Cochran 1977). Protests flared especially during the early 1930s, and they were often led by anti-capitalist radicals including Communists (Zieger 1994). Unemployment was a typical problem. And during the Great Depression most new members of the Communist Party were predictably unemployed (Cochran 1977).

By the fall of 1930, during the height of the Great Depression, government officials acknowledged that unemployment was over 15 percent. Many millions required public relief. "Relief agencies were swamped" (Zieger 1994). In Chicago the black community formed an anti-eviction crowd that was opposed by the local police. Ford laid-off all except a small minority of its workers. General Douglas McArthur made war on 20,000 military bonus protestors in Washington, D.C., using 4 troops of cavalry, 6 tanks, and an infantry column.

Yearly strikes were commonplace. Undoubtedly significant for the FBI was the West Coast waterfront strike in 1934, which closed 2,000 miles of coastline from May 9 to July 27. This was one of many strikes that year (Cochran 1977). During WWII there predictably developed public opposition to strikes since they were seen as unpatriotic. But 1941 was a big year for strikes. Approximately 1 out of every 12 workers was involved in a work stoppage and in total there were approximately 2.4 million workers involved in 4,288 work stoppages (U.S. Bureau of the Census 1950, 208). The 1950 Statistical Abstract of the United States indicates that yearly work stoppages nearly doubled from 1940–1945 to 4,750 (U.S. Bureau of the Census 1950, 207). There were long strikes in 1943 at Goodyear and Firestone (Cochran 1977). Labor strikes grew rapidly after the end of the war in 1945 (Zieger 1994).

JEWS AND THE FBI

The relationship between Jewish unions and the U.S. government was very troubled. This is because the American labor movement became more radical as Jewish activists were inspired by the Russian Revolution. The International Ladies Garment Workers Union is one example of what was a predominantly Jewish union. In 1920, 80 percent of the union's members were Jewish (Wenger 1999) and by World War II Jewish membership was still at 60 percent (LeMay 2013). From the 1880s to the 1920s Jewish immigrants flooded into the United States with more than 2.5 million coming from Eastern Europe (Library of Congress 2010). Many of these new immigrants became members of the ILGWU.

The FBI was not only facing Jewish trade unionists, but also women and black Americans who were entering the workforce. WWII brought many women into work outside the home. By 1945 19 million of the nation's 54 million civilian workers were women. At this time black workers also made significant gains (Zieger 1994). So the FBI from its perspective had a lot to fear from unions—long and bitter strikes, war, the Great Depression, the unemployed, the Soviet Union as an ally during WWII, and as an opponent afterwards during the Cold War. Soviet immigrants who were suspected Communists and Jews were also at the top of the FBI list, not to mention black and women workers. All of this fits with the targeting of the Gladstein law firm.

THE SMITH ACT AND THE RED SCARE OF THE 1950S

During the Cold War the Gladstein firm routinely defended those charged with violating the Smith Act of 1940 that prohibited supporting the overthrow of the U.S. government (Tedford and Herbeck 2009). In 1949 at the urging of FBI Director J. Edgar Hoover the Act was used in New York to try 11 accused Communists. The defendants "were not charged with any overt acts [but rather merely] 'advocating and teaching the principles of Marxism" (Smith 1998).

The Red Scare that began after WWII and lasted until the early 1960s is widely acknowledged to be a prime example of a moral panic (Cohen 1972). The witchcraft craze in the Massachusetts Bay Colony is another early example of a moral panic on American shores that created clear boundaries between good and law-abiding citizens and others who were considered beyond the pale (Erikson 1966). During the Red Scare following WWII Harvard educated attorney and prominent government official Alger Hiss was tried and sentenced to prison in 1950, serving nearly four years. In 1949 and 1950 Judith Coplon, a graduate of Barnard College, and another prominent victim of this witch-hunt, was tried as a Soviet spy but not convicted. Yet the worst of this persecution seemed reserved for working class Jews such as Julius and Ethel Rosenberg who were tried, convicted, and executed for being Soviet atomic spies in 1953. While Gladstein, Andersen, and Leonard were professionals and thus not working class, two of these attorneys were Jewish and all three law partners had clients who were largely working class and considered by government officials to be Communists.

ERVING GOFFMAN AND *STIGMA*

In his book *Stigma*, Goffman (1963, 5) notes: "The person with a stigma is not quite human. On this assumption we exercise varieties of discrimination." Goffman discusses stigma in various forms. One type involves "blemishes of individual character perceived as . . . treacherous and rigid beliefs," such as communism during the Cold War. Another includes "the tribal stigma of race, nation, and religion" (Goffman 1963, 4). In our research we studied two Jews and two men who were foreign born and all reflected some consequent stigma. Some who are stigmatized do not appear "to be impressed or repentant" (Goffman 1963, 6) and even create a subculture of "those who share this stigma" (Goffman 1963, 20), such as unions, their leaders, and the law firm that we studied. In addition those stigmatized "are likely to support agents and agencies who represent them" including law firms (Goffman 1963, 24). Finally, when "a person with a particular stigma attains [a] high occupational . . . position . . . a new career is likely to be thrust upon him, that of representing his category" (Goffman 1963, 26) and so it was with the Gladstein law firm. Most of the stigmatized clients that the Gladstein firm represented during the Cold War were not professionals and had lower social status and education than did the law partners.

Those known to have been blacklisted included during this era immigrants, labor union members and leaders, Jews, and actors. Those singled out often could not secure employment merely because they were accused of associating with Communists. Hollywood's Red Scare was another instance of moral panic, where activists stigmatized a group as immoral and deviant (Pontikes et al. 2010, 456–57). A courtesy stigma is a "taint that afflicts individuals associated with others who are blemished by . . . disreputable occupations" (Pontikes et al. 2010, 458). Goffman (1963, 29) described a courtesy stigma as involving those who work "in an establishment which caters either to the wants of those with a particular stigma or to actions that society takes in regard to these persons." The San Francisco law firm was just such an establishment. Schrecker (1994, 85) states that attorneys defending accused Communists were "particularly affected." They were hurt economically because potential clients turned to lawyers who were not associated with national disloyalty. Even more daunting were the threats of disbarment and jail time that these attorneys faced.

In our research those who worked in the disreputable occupations were labor union members, especially officers of the ILWU and the organization catering to their needs, the Gladstein law firm. We will demonstrate how a "courtesy stigma" overshadowed the Gladstein, Andersen, and Leonard legal practice merely due to their representation of Communists and Harry Bridges, the long-time head of the ILWU. No evidence was found indicating that these attorneys were Communists, nor for that matter was Bridges a Communist. But it is true that all four had Communist associates. Some members of the ILWU were Communists as were some of the firm's other clients.

CHAPTER SUMMARY

During the McCarthy Era, fears of communism were rampant and the U.S. government persecuted even those accused of associating with Communists. Under the leadership of J. Edgar Hoover, the FBI had assembled a list of thousands of individuals who were to be arrested and jailed prior to conviction. With the assistance of a law firm we obtained this list although with the exception of the attorneys studied here nearly all of the names were redacted. We learned that the number of individuals designated by the FBI as security risks more than doubled during the early 1950s before falling sharply in 1955. Additionally, the FBI targeted Jewish and union groups for arrest. We also learned that the law partners had working class backgrounds and they routinely defended labor activists. Further, there were no publications focusing solely on them. Thus the partners in this law firm were "hidden from history" in the same way as other marginalized individuals.

Our goal was to study the culture within the law firm and for this we utilized archival materials, personal interviews, and the FBI files of Gladstein, Andersen, Leonard, and Bridges. The FBI also kept files on other prominent Americans. Ironically the more the FBI pursued its blacklisting campaign the more work these attorneys had.

During the 1930s and 1940s both U.S. labor unions and the Communist Party experienced significant growth. Labor strikes were plentiful and during the Great Depression there was high unemployment. Jewish labor activists faced intense scrutiny as did black and women workers. The Gladstein partners defended many clients who were charged with Smith Act violations. The Red Scare that followed WWII was a moral panic that resulted in the persecution of accused Communists and even the lawyers who defended them. The sociologist Erving Goffman's concept of courtesy stigma is used to explain the harsh treatment that the Gladstein partners endured due to their two-decade representation of Harry Bridges and other accused Communists.

Chapter Two

Blacklisting During the Cold War

HOW BLACKLISTS WORKED

In this chapter we will consider how the U.S. government developed a blacklisting system in the late 1940s and 1950s. We will see how the long arm of the state extended to those who were union members, musicians, screen workers, broadcasting employees, the press, various corporations, the State Department and the Army, teachers and professors, scientists, and attorneys.

BLACKLISTING AND THE U.S. ATTORNEY GENERAL

The Attorney General's List of Subversive Organizations (AGLOSO) was the primary tool used by the federal government for blacklisting organizations. The AGLOSO was created on March 21, 1947, under Executive Order 9835 as part of President Truman's loyalty-security program (Goldstein 2006). A journalist claimed in 1947 that the development of the blacklist was an attempt by the Truman administration to remove the "Communist smear" from the Democratic Party (Aronson 1970, 38).

Once the U.S. Attorney General put an organization on the list it could not be contested. An organization was labeled as a "Communist front" if it had speakers who were fellow travelers, Communist sympathizers, and/or received favorable mention in Communist publications (Bontecou 1953). It was alleged that most members of Communist front organizations were non-communists who merely helped to advance Communist objectives (Bayley 1981, 5, 177). This shows how vague and general the blacklisting criteria were.

President Eisenhower's Attorney General Herbert Brownell (1953–1957) realized that the "loyalty oath was a powerful symbolic issue" (Auerbach

1976, 239). Brownell told the American Bar Association in 1953 that the National Lawyers Guild had leaders who were Communist Party members, or at least "fellow travelers" (Auerbach 1976, 235). However, as we will see later, the National Lawyers Guild was never placed on the AGLOSO. The three partners of the law firm considered here were all members of this progressive organization.

The loyalty oath was often used as a prelude to blacklisting. Corporations including GE and U.S. Steel publicly stated that they would fire any employee who invoked the Fifth Amendment when asked about their politics (Schrecker 1994, 77–78). The oaths were stretched to incredibly long lengths. "Pharmacists in Texas, professional wrestlers in Indiana, and people who wanted to fish in the New York City reservoirs all had to take loyalty oaths" (Schrecker 1994, 73) as did all New York State employees and all University of California employees at the direction of their Board of Regents (Schrecker 1994). Indeed the University of California terminated even tenured faculty if they refused to take a loyalty oath (Gardner 1967).

The primary punishment for refusing to take the loyalty oath was loss of employment, although alleged Soviet spies Ethel and Julius Rosenberg were executed and others were merely stripped of their passports. Yale law professor Ralph Brown (1958, 488) estimated that 11,500 lost their jobs in this way, including a whopping 3,800 who were dismissed for failing the security clearance in the Port Security Program. This figure demonstrates the centrality of the ILWU to this dispute (See also Gellhorn 1950, 135).

BLACKLISTING IN THE INTERNATIONAL LONGSHOREMEN'S AND WAREHOUSEMEN'S UNION (ILWU)

It appears that ILWU president Harry Bridges was the central figure in the port blacklisting program and thus we devote a separate chapter to his career. The 1957 Report of the Commission on Government Security gives a detailed look at the Port Security program. The report may have aggravated the public image of the ILWU and indeed may have been created due to the very threatening image of the union in the first place. The Port Security Program was created by the Coast Guard at the request of President Truman to identify potential security risks among maritime and waterfront employees thus guarding the country's "shipping, ports, [and] harbor installations . . . from destruction and crippling damage by saboteurs and subversives" (Commission on Government 1957, 351). Perhaps referring to ILWU President Harry Bridges the Commission noted that the circumstances which justified implementing the program still existed and these included the "substantial Communist control of certain maritime unions" (Commission on Government 1957, 352).

The screening of applicants was carried out at Coast Guard headquarters where an applicant's name was sent "from the district in which he requests clearance to the [Coast Guard] Commandant. After the requested information . . . [was] received, it . . . [was] analyzed by a three-member committee, which then . . . [made] a recommendation for action by the Commandant" (Commission on Government 1957, 357). Once an applicant was granted or denied clearance, this status could change at any time if the FBI received additional information and forwarded it to the Coast Guard.

The Commission noted that screeners had no formal background in "security matters" and the job required no unique qualifications (Commission on Government 1957, 357). Screeners were expected to utilize only their Coast Guard experience. Moreover, screening duties were carried out in addition to the screeners' primary Coast Guard duties (Commission on Government 1957). Even after noting the limited qualifications of the screeners the Commission defended the program. The Commission also recognized the hardship placed upon those who were blacklisted from the ports stating that "an adverse determination on loyalty in the case of a seaman in the port security program destroys his means of livelihood" (Commission on Government 1957, 470). Nevertheless, the Commission linked criticism of the port security program to "a general Communist offensive against the security policies of the United States Government" (Commission on Government 1957, 470).

Coast Guard clearance was needed for anyone who possessed "maritime credentials shipping on United States vessels of 100 gross tons or over, and all waterfront workers who may want jobs in restricted areas" (Commission on Government 1957, 346). Of those who applied for clearance 1,835 people were denied permission to work on ships and 1,935 were denied permission to work at the ports (Commission on Government 1957, 332).

MUSICIANS

Pete Seeger

Folk singer Pete Seeger (1919–2014) was of great concern to federal authorities. Seeger has been called "the most picketed, boycotted performer in American history" (Dunaway 1981, 2). The U.S. intelligence community considered Seeger a public menace and went out of their way to watch his every move. Seeger first came to the FBI's attention as a member of the folksong group the Almanac Singers, which he helped to establish in early 1941 (Dunaway 1981, 79). The FBI opened a file on Seeger after an informant attended an Almanac's show and reported on a song titled "The Ballad of Harry Bridges" which contained the lyrics "The FBI is worried, the bosses they are scared" (Dunaway 1981, 88). FBI officials believed that the Almanac Singers' music jeopardized the war effort and J. Edgar Hoover distributed a memo to law enforcement requesting information on the "Almanac gang" (Dunaway 1981, 102).

Following World War II Seeger helped to form an organization called People's Songs, Inc. (PSI) for the purpose of "publish[ing] a newsletter of union songs and form[ing] a national network, singing on picket lines and demonstrations" (Dunaway 1981, 112). U.S. Army intelligence gatherers reported that PSI was a "Communist front" and an informant testified before the HUAC that People's Songs "performed before Communist-led groups" (Dunaway 1981, 124).

In the late 1940s Seeger began singing with a group called the Weavers (Dunaway 1981, 137). Even though Seeger was the only Weaver listed in *Red Channels* (the entertainment industry's blacklist) the FBI worked diligently to keep the group off the air. With the help of the magazine *Counterattack* they were ultimately successful. Like most entertainers, the Weavers' prominence opened them up to criticism. Some of the information found its way into newspaper reports and the Weavers were soon being investigated by Senator Pat McCarran's Internal Security Subcommittee. The group's problems came to a head in early 1952 when an informant told the HUAC "that three of the Weavers were members of the Communist Party" (Dunaway 1981, 156).

In 1955 Seeger was subpoenaed by the HUAC. He entered the hearing room carrying his banjo and during testimony he offered to play a song for the committee to demonstrate his faith in America. The Committee refused to allow it and the House voted to cite him for contempt of Congress. When Seeger was tried on the contempt charge his lawyer argued that the HUAC had no right to question Seeger: "In no instance in this committee's investigation was the matter of national security, espionage, sabotage, or . . . advocating . . . the violent overthrow of the government involved" (Dunaway 1981, 200). The U.S. Court of Appeals ultimately dismissed Seeger's case.

Although he was never convicted of contempt, Seeger's career was affected by the HUAC ordeal. In the late 1950s the Detroit Labor Forum tried to give Seeger a chance to perform at the Institute of Arts auditorium but the city's Arts Commission would not allow it stating that the facilities "may not be rented for programs of a political or controversial nature" (Dunaway 1981, 192). The dispute ended up in court and the judge ruled that Seeger should be allowed to perform because he "would be singing ergo, he was a singer, and . . . singing songs isn't likely to start a riot'" (Dunaway 1981, 192). When Seeger was offered a chance to appear on the TV musical show Hootenanny, he was told that he would first have to sign a loyalty oath. "'Dear ABC,' he replied brusquely: 'I just finished a seven-year court battle to prove the principle that such oaths are unconstitutional, and I was acquitted and vindicated'" (Dunaway 1981, 217).

Leonard Bernstein

During the mid-twentieth century Leonard Bernstein (1919–1990) was considered America's premier conductor. In 1945 he conducted a concert devoted to Russian music (Freedland 1987). In 1949 his earlier opposition to fascism was made public. Since Bernstein was a person of the left who had many causes, in 1953 the U.S. State Department refused to renew his passport. His passport was returned only after he publicly renounced his earlier left-wing associations (Seldes 2009). Bernstein was never subpoenaed by the HUAC nor the Senate committee. Rather, temporary humiliation was all that was attempted. Bernstein's prominence on the American cultural scene likely prevented authorities from blacklisting him or seizing his passport for any length of time.

SCREEN WORKERS

Along with maritime workers and musicians, screen workers were primary targets of blacklisting (Schrecker 1994). The list included actors, composers, conductors, playwrights, writers, directors, and producers. The plethora of blacklisted screen actors was in part a consequence of Ronald Reagan's eagerness to turn over names to the FBI (Rosenfeld 2012).

Many of those targeted were listed in the 1950 publication *Red Channels* which (as we noted earlier) became the entertainment industry's blacklist (See for example Cogley and Miller 1971; Holden 2008; Schrecker 1994). *Red Channels* listed 151 people who worked ". . . in the radio-television industry whom, the editors claimed, were linked . . . with a variety of 'Communist causes'" (Cogley and Miller 1971, 1).

Judy Holliday was an actress blacklisted by Hollywood who was born in New York City in 1921 or 1922 and died there in 1965 (Barranger 2008; Hyman and Moore 1998; McMahon; *New York Times* 1965; Sicherman et al. 1980). She was type cast as a dumb blond though in reality she scored a 172 on the Otis intelligence test "which placed her in the genius category" (Barranger 2008, 10). She won the Best Actress Oscar in 1950 for her role in *Born Yesterday* (McMahon; *New York Times* 1965). Once she achieved this fame, allegations that she was a Communist surfaced (McMahon). In 1952 Holliday was subpoenaed to testify before the U.S. Senate Internal Security Subcommittee (Barranger 2008; McMahon; *New York Times* 1965; Sicherman et. al. 1980). There she used her dumb blond image to her advantage (Carey 1982). Her performance merely irritated her critics. She received death threats and was blacklisted by the film industry (McMahon). Her career was cut short by the ravages of breast cancer (Barranger 2008; McMahon; *New York Times* 1965). Another woman whose work as an actress was interrupted by her blacklisting was Gypsy Rose Lee. Gypsy Rose Lee was born in Seattle in 1911 and died in Los Angeles in 1970 (Frankel 2009). Since she worked in burlesque, early in her career she was arrested three times for obscenity but later was able to defend her work as art. In the late 1930s she provided aid to Republican Spain. Members of the HUAC accused Gypsy Rose Lee of being a Communist, but she responded in an innocent tone "Why I couldn't be, I voted the Democratic ticket" (Frankel 2009, 77). Gypsy Rose Lee was luckier than many of her contemporaries because she was able to "override" the blacklist. Even though she was listed in *Red Channels* and told that she "would never work again in radio or television" she soon began appearing on television (Barranger 2008, 32). Even after her blacklisting in the early 1950s Gypsy Rose Lee courageously defended racial integration.

Zero Mostel (1915–1977) was yet another actor blacklisted during the 1950s. According to his FBI file he attended Communist Party meetings in 1941. He was subpoenaed to appear before the HUAC in 1955. During his HUAC testimony Mostel claimed to work for 18th Century Fox and manipulated the committee members to make them look foolish. Yet his career was in ruins after the blacklisting (Brown 1989).

Charlie Chaplin was also blacklisted. Chaplin was born in London in 1889 and died in Switzerland in 1979. During the 1930s he became a strong supporter of the New Deal. In 1937 Chaplin made a film titled *The Great Dictator* demonstrating the dangers of fascism (Lynn 1997). After WWII the HUAC began to investigate him and in 1947 he was subpoenaed to appear before the Committee (though he was never asked to testify) and was blacklisted (Sbardellati and Shaw 2003; Spartacus Educational: Charlie Chaplin). Unlike many of his contemporaries, Chaplin was largely unaffected by the blacklist due to his partial ownership of United Artists. Indeed "he was simply too independent" (Sbardellati and Shaw 2003, 505).

After being blacklisted Chaplin made *A King in New York* showing how a deposed monarch is tormented by McCarthy style investigations. In 1954 the *Saturday Evening Post* severely criticized Chaplin for his support of black actor-singer Paul Robeson (McCabe 1978). To the press Chaplin asserted that he was not a Communist and indeed had never voted, but he admitted in a wire to the House Committee that he was a "peacemonger" (McCabe 1978, 216). Considering the HUAC charges, it is ironic that Chaplin's work was condemned in the Soviet Union for a "lack of progressivism" (McCabe 1978, 217).

Black men and women in the film industry, though less commonly implicated in the Communist threat, were nonetheless still present. African American singer and actor Paul Robeson (1898–1976) was blacklisted for his civil rights activities, (IMDB; Appiah and Gates 2004) which included a 1949 statement condemning the Korean War and asking black troops to stay home and fight domestic racism (Robeson 2010). He compared the United

States unfavorably with the Soviet Union where he saw no signs of racism, showing that socialism "represents an advance to a higher stage of life" (Robeson 1958, 39). Robeson rejected gradualism as essentially harmful to race relations. A multitalented person, he played professional football and earned enough money to attend Columbia University's law school after a distinguished academic and athletic career at Rutgers. Robeson was blacklisted in the United States and had his passport seized by the State Department. He was therefore unable to travel abroad for employment (Robeson 1958). Lena Horne was an African American actress who was born in New York City in 1917 and died there in 2010. Horne's friendship with Paul Robeson led to her being blacklisted for 10 years after her contract with MGM ended (BlackClassicMovies.com; Harmetz 2010; Kaufman and Kaufman 2009). Horne felt that the HUAC wanted to subpoena other blacks to target Robeson (Buckley 1986).

PLAYWRIGHTS

Playwright Arthur Miller was quoted as saying "I would use a man who was in complete disagreement with me politically if he was right for the part" (Cogley and Miller 1971, 211). Miller saw the Holocaust as a disaster not just for Jews but for all of humanity (Mason 2008). Miller was blacklisted by Hollywood for his "left-wing connections" (Miller and Roudané 1987) and for refusing to inform on fellow writers before the HUAC (*BBC* 2005) but this did not interfere with his plays being performed on stage (Spartacus Educational: Arthur Miller). Miller referred to the Committee as a "permanent kind of thought police" (Mason 2008, 9). Miller's 1956 subpoena and subsequent conviction for contempt of Congress resulted in a year's suspended sentence, a $500 fine, and cost him tens of thousands of dollars in attorney's fees (Miller 2000; Miller and Centola 2000). As with many of his contemporaries, Miller's contempt conviction was eventually overturned (*BBC* 2005). Miller achieved fame for writing many plays including *The Crucible* (1953) that ostensibly dealt with the 1692 witch trials but in reality spoke volumes about McCarthyism. Thus Miller had a foot in both worlds, Hollywood and the stage.

Lillian Hellman (1905–1984) was an American playwright who, like Arthur Miller, worked as a writer both for Hollywood and the stage. She was born in New Orleans but spent most of her life in New York City (Liukkonen and Pesonen 2008; Driscoll and Feeney 1984). During the Cold War she sympathized with dissident writers in the Eastern bloc of nations and early on became interested in racial equality (Martinson 2005). In 1946 she led an effort to desegregate theaters in Washington, D.C. (Newman 1989). When called to appear before the HUAC in 1952 she testified that she was not a member of the Communist Party (Newman 1989), but refused to provide the names of those who might be Communists. Unlike others Hellman was not charged with contempt of Congress because "After all, she's a woman" (Liukkonen and Pesonen 2008; *Time Magazine* 1952). Nevertheless, she was blacklisted until the 1960s.

Orson Welles (1915–1985) was a blacklisted screen and stage actor, director, and writer. He was politically progressive having directed a 1936 version of *Macbeth* set in Haiti and the next year a version of *Julius Caesar* set in fascist Italy (Walsh and Laurier 2009). Welles was blacklisted in Hollywood from the late 1940s until the mid-1950s. In 1946 he hosted a weekly radio show in which he delivered an impassioned speech condemning a South Carolina police officer who had severely beaten and blinded a decorated black WWII veteran who was innocent of all crimes except a demand for racial justice (Rosenbaum 2007).

BROADCASTERS

The broadcasting industry was targeted by the Roman Catholic Church and businessman Alfred Kohlberg. CBS initiated a loyalty oath and even hired a security officer (Schrecker 1994, 80). By 1946 Kohlberg created the magazine *Counterattack* which was devoted to fighting communism, and he was aided in this by the Catholic Welfare Conference (Keeley 1969). Newspapers also created blacklists, including the *New York Times* (Schrecker 1994, 84).

Roman Catholics gave considerable support to Wisconsin Senator Joe McCarthy because they considered him one of their own and agreed with his strident opposition to what some saw as Godless communism (Crosby 1978). In 1954 Edward R. Murrow was the first to publicly challenge McCarthy and seriously discredit the Senator and his obvious lies. The falsehoods included the claim that Murrow was a member of the Industrial Workers of the World and McCarthy's illogical reasoning that "The Communist Party opposes me, Murrow opposes me; Murrow is a transmission belt for communist propaganda" (Miller and Centola 2000, 198).

THE ARMY AND STATE DEPARTMENT

The U.S. Army was directly attacked by Senator McCarthy who argued that some Army leaders should be blacklisted. In a secret meeting in early 1954 Senator McCarthy "stabbed a finger at Brigadier General Ralph Zwicker saying: 'General, you are a disgrace to the uniform. . . . You're not fit to be an officer'" (Crosby 1978, 147). The general was the commanding officer of an army dentist who had been honorably discharged even with a questionable security record. In a later public hearing McCarthy said "General, you should be removed from command" (Crosby 1978, 148).

State Department officials (Schrecker 1994, 121) were targeted as well. One of the most infamous of these blacklisting cases involved the conviction of prominent State Department official Alger Hiss who was accused of being a Communist during a 1948 House investigation. Hiss' accuser, Whittaker Chambers, was curiously much less polished than Hiss who was a Harvard trained attorney and New England Brahmin who had served as Secretary General of the U.N. and President of the Carnegie Endowment for International Peace (Spartacus Educational: Alger Hiss). Within weeks of Hiss's perjury conviction where he was sentenced to five years in prison the McCarthy crusade was launched. Senator McCarthy stated in his infamous 1950 West Virginia speech that he held a list containing hundreds of Communist sympathizers including 57 State Department employees (Schrecker 1994, 210). Alger Hiss always maintained his innocence. His government pension was restored in 1972 and he was readmitted to the Massachusetts bar in 1974. Hiss died in 1996 at age 92.

SCHOOL TEACHERS AND PROFESSORS

Many public school teachers were fired during the McCarthy Era. Indeed "Hundreds of elementary and high school teachers lost their jobs" often after an appearance before the HUAC (Schrecker 1994, 84). Teachers were subjected to greater scrutiny than those who worked in most other occupations. Brown (1955) argues "that no profession, and no class of government employees, has been singled out for official loyalty tests the way teachers have been" (114). We will show that two public school teachers were accused of being Communist Party members and thus terminated. One of these teachers faced criminal charges related to the accusations and was defended by the Gladstein firm.

Nearly one hundred University Professors were terminated after "refusing to cooperate with anti-communist investigators" (Schrecker 1994, 84; See also Schrecker 1986). Sanders (1979) describes how in 1949 the Regents at the University of Washington terminated three tenured professors who had refused to testify before a Congressional investigating committee. The University President sided with the Regents in this dispute. Three other tenured professors were placed on probation.

In 1953 a prominent tenured Cornell physics professor was terminated because of his public defense of the Communist Party and his support for Julius and Ethel Rosenberg (Schrecker 1986, 152). That same year a tenured Ohio State physics professor was terminated after invoking the fifth amendment at a HUAC session (Schrecker 1986, 207). Similarly, a tenured economics professor from a private school, the University of Kansas City, was terminated for taking the fifth, as was a tenured professor at Temple in 1953 (Schrecker 1986). Also, in 1952 a distinguished full professor of neurophysiology at Tulane's medical school was fired for his radical politics. Finally, Jefferson Medical College in Philadelphia terminated three professors simply because they were Jewish (Schrecker 1986). This last example shows what a slippery slope these academic pogroms created.

The U.S. government not only revealed itself by those it blacklisted, but also by those it did not. One of the most radical scholars during this time period was African American, Marxist sociologist Oliver Cox (1901–1974). Cox earned a Ph.D. at the University of Chicago and later taught at Wiley College, the Tuskegee Institute, Lincoln University and Wayne State University (BlackPast.org; Hunter 1983). Following a bout with polio Dr. Cox walked with crutches. In the early 1950s while at Lincoln he was invited to Missouri University in Columbia by MU professor Noel Gist to give a public lecture on his research explaining the economic foundations of American racism in American capitalism. This public lecture caused great outrage at Missouri University. His Marxist explanations were ignored as long as he taught at the small, underfunded, predominantly black Lincoln University, but he raised concern once he spoke at predominantly white Missouri University. There is no evidence that Oliver Cox was blacklisted.

PROMINENT SCIENTISTS

Famed rocket scientist Tsien Hsue-Shen was also blacklisted by the U.S. government. Tsien Hsue-Shen was born in Shanghai, China, in 1911 and graduated from college there in 1934 (*IEEE Control Systems Magazine* 2010). In 1935 he came to the United States to attend graduate school. He completed his Master's degree at MIT in 1936 and received his PhD from Caltech in 1939. He later taught at both of these schools (Noland 2009).

While at Caltech, Tsien and colleagues founded the Jet Propulsion Laboratory "which became one of the first major centers for the study of missiles and rockets in the United States" (Pahl 2007, 171). Tsien served on the U.S. government's Scientific Advisory Board and became one of the country's top rocket scientists (Pahl 2007; Noland 2009). Following WWII Tsien was the primary scientist who helped the U.S. military transfer German rocket technology and German rocket scientists to the United States (Pahl 2007, 171). It was around this time that the FBI and various McCarthyists discovered that one of the key players in the U.S. military's missile program "was Chinese and therefore might be 'a communist'" (Pahl 2007, 171). Tsien's problems stemmed largely from his association with Sidney Weinbaum during the late

1930s. Weinbaum was a colleague of Tsien's at Caltech and a member of the Communist Party (Chang 1995).

Tsien Hsue-Shen was branded a Communist by the FBI, a charge which he adamantly denied (*IEEE Control Systems Magazine* 2010; Chang 1995). Tsien's government security clearance was soon revoked (*Caltech Today* 2009) and in August 1950, his scientific papers were seized (Harvey 2004; Chang 1995). The government claimed that some of Tsien's papers contained "secret codes" which were later shown to be merely logarithmic tables (Harvey 2004: 20). Tsien was arrested at his home by INS agents on September 7, 1950 (Chang 1995). He was accused of hiding his Communist Party membership thus entering the U.S. illegally upon returning from China in 1947 (Chang 1995). Tsien was held at the INS detention center in San Pedro, California, for 15 days before being released on an "unusually high" $15,000 bond (Chang 1995, 165).

Although the allegations that Tsien Hsue-Shen was a Communist were baseless, in October, 1950, the Immigration and Naturalization Service issued him a "delayed deportation order" under the Internal Security Act of 1950 (Chang 1995; *Caltech Today* 2009). Tsien did not challenge the deportation order. Over the next 5 years he and his family were closely watched by the U.S. government and placed under "partial house arrest" (*Caltech Today* 2009). Although Tsien was no longer allowed to work as a government rocket scientist he continued his research at Caltech (Pahl 2007). In September 1955 Tsien Hsue-Shen and his family were deported to China (Harvey 2004) where he continued his research becoming the "father of China's missile program," as well as a government leader and the country's "most honored scientist" (*Caltech Today* 2009).

Other highly prestigious, world-class scientists were blacklisted merely by having their passports seized to prevent them from traveling abroad. Linus Pauling (1901–1994) received the 1954 Nobel Prize in chemistry and later the 1962 Nobel Peace Prize for his crusade against nuclear weapons testing (Abrams 2001; Scitable 2011). Like Tsien Hsue-Shen Pauling was educated and spent most of his academic career at Caltech (Pauling et. al. 2001). He became a Democrat in 1936 and supported Roosevelt and was alarmed by escalating Nazi power in Europe. Due to an irrational fear of liberals Pauling was blacklisted in 1952 and not allowed to leave the country. He forcefully opposed McCarthyism "when many others were taking cover" (Goertzel and Goertzel 1995, 85).

Equally distinguished scientist J. Robert Oppenheimer (1904–1967) received his BA from Harvard in chemistry in 1925 and in 1928 joined the faculty at the University of California-Berkeley. At the time he was vaguely a liberal but the Nazi movement in Europe really got his attention (NNDB). During WWII Oppenheimer was asked to head the Manhattan Project that developed the atomic bomb. The scientific advances of this project were enormous but Oppenheimer's initial jubilation turned to deep unhappiness when he learned that the bombs had killed in excess of 200,000 people who were primarily civilians. By 1947 he was elected chair of the General Advisory Committee of the new Atomic Energy Commission. In 1949 Oppenheimer testified before an executive session of the HUAC that was closed to avoid embarrassing him (Schweber 2000). By 1953 Oppenheimer was stripped of his security clearance and forced to leave the Atomic Energy Commission based on his earlier liberalism. He did, however, remain a professor at Berkeley.

PRACTICING ATTORNEYS

The U.S. Supreme Court did not intervene in the government's blacklisting campaign and thus the program encountered few legal obstacles (Schrecker 1994, 89). Attorneys were severely impacted by the threat of jail and disbarment for contempt of court if they chose to represent accused Communists (Schrecker 1994, 96). However, litigation was clearly the most effective means of resisting the blacklisting machine and thus attorneys were central to the process (Schrecker 1994, 102). We will show in the following chapters that the senior partner of the law firm we are studying served a term in federal prison after working as the defense counsel in a New York trial of Communists and was also threatened with disbarment. Despite these obstacles attorneys were not blacklisted at the rate of screen or dockworkers and according to existing sources no prominent practicing attorneys were blacklisted.

WHY ATTORNEYS WEREN'T BLACKLISTED

Brown (1955) describes two possible reasons why attorneys were largely immune to blacklisting. First, attorneys were already held to stringent loyalty standards in that: a) they have done more than "any other profession in imposing loyalty standards on themselves" and b) those who represented accused Communists faced significant "popular pressures" (Brown 1955, 115). The loyalty standards for attorneys were supported by the bar associations and upheld by the threat of disbarment or (for bar applicants) the denial of membership. Of course those who were trying to obtain bar membership were subjected to greater scrutiny than existing members (Brown 1955, 115).

The second possible reason why attorneys weren't blacklisted is due to factors outside of the legal profession. Government officials may have feared that harassing attorneys would bring legal challenges that could threaten federal loyalty-security programs. The Department of Justice's (DOJ) decision to back away from adding the National Lawyers Guild (NLG) to the

Attorney General's List of Subversive Organizations (AGLOSO) illustrates this point.

The U.S. government's attempts to blacklist the NLG are not surprising considering that Guild lawyers represented "radicals" and the organization was critical of both FBI practices and federal government policies, especially the loyalty security program (Goldstein 2008). By 1948 the FBI was lobbying the DOJ to add the NLG to the AGLOSO and in 1950 the HUAC made a similar request. Initially the DOJ refused to add the NLG to the list but in 1953 Attorney General Herbert Brownell stated his intention to do so (Goldstein 2008; *American Bar Association Journal* 1955). The NLG spent five years trying to avoid the blacklist until the DOJ finally backed away fearing ". . . that AGLOSO might otherwise suffer a fatal legal rebuke" (Goldstein 2008, 242). Similar concerns about legal retaliation may have played a role in preventing the government from blacklisting attorneys generally.

CONCLUSION

The House Committee did not respond well to humor directed its way by those it was investigating. Screen actors were often blacklisted on the most flimsy of evidence, including opposition to American racism. Folk musician Pete Seeger particularly irritated federal authorities because his songs and singing called for racial justice, peace and unions, all anathema to American law enforcement. Port workers were also frequently barred from their employment as were grade school and high school teachers. World-class scientists and performers typically suffered from merely having their passports seized, if they were U.S. citizens. Those who were not U.S. citizens were subjected to jail and deportation. We will demonstrate that the U.S. government spent approximately 20 years attempting to deport ILWU President Harry Bridges and he seems to have been spared by the good offices of the Gladstein law firm. The chapters that follow will also answer some questions about why practicing attorneys do not make more of an appearance as victims of this political harassment and seemed less liable to blacklisting.

CHAPTER SUMMARY

During the late 1940s through the 1950s many different types of people were blacklisted by the U.S. government. Organizations were blacklisted by the Attorney General's List of Subversive Organizations (AGLOSO) and it was very easy for the Attorney General to put an organization on the list. Once an organization was placed on the list it could not be contested.

Many people were made to take a loyalty oath and those who refused often lost their jobs. People in a wide variety of occupations were targeted. In the maritime and shipping industry many lost their jobs for failing the Coast Guard's Port Security Program and Harry Bridges and the ILWU were central to this controversy. Many people in the entertainment industry were also blacklisted. Prominent figures in the music industry who were blacklisted include Pete Seeger and Leonard Bernstein. Many screen workers were blacklisted and their names often appeared in the publication *Red Channels*, which became the entertainment industry's blacklist. Targeted screen workers included Judy Holliday, Gypsy Rose Lee, Zero Mostel, Charlie Chaplin, Paul Robeson, and Lena Horne. Playwrights who were blacklisted included Arthur Miller, Lillian Hellman, and Orson Welles. Many who worked in the broadcasting industry were targeted by the Roman Catholic Church and businessman Alfred Kohlberg who created the magazine *Counterattack*. In 1954 the broadcaster Edward R. Murrow publicly confronted Joe McCarthy who then retaliated by accusing Murrow of spreading Communist propaganda. McCarthy and others also accused U.S. Army and State Department employees of disloyalty including Alger Hiss who was sentenced to prison but ultimately vindicated. Schoolteachers and professors were also blacklisted and even tenured professors were fired. Prominent scientists who were blacklisted include Tsien Hsue-Shen, Linus Pauling, and J. Robert Oppenheimer.

Although attorneys were less affected by blacklisting than other occupational groups, they still faced the threat of jail and disbarment for contempt of court if they represented accused Communists. The Department of Justice had considered blacklisting the National Lawyers Guild but ultimately backed away fearing possible legal repercussions.

Chapter Three

Lawyers and the Micro Environments in American Law Firms during the 1930s to the 1960s

In this chapter we will explore the stratification of American law firms and lawyers that existed from the 1930s to the 1960s to see where the Gladstein firm fits into this system. We begin at the top of the hierarchy and end at the bottom.

LARGE WALL STREET LAW FIRMS

The classic study of prestigious law firms was conducted in the 1950s by Smigel (1964). Their political ideology was uniform. They were primarily Republicans. Many accepted positions on their prestigious clients' boards of directors. Their standards for attire demanded jackets and ties.

Until the late 1960s associates at elite firms were paid the same or less than their counterparts in other areas of law (Wilkins and Gulati 1996). Yet between 1950 and 1965, 73 percent of young attorneys hired by the most prestigious New York law firms had earned their degrees from Harvard, Yale, or Columbia and 91 percent had graduated from a "top ten" law school (Sander 2006, 1778). These firms wanted the top students, law review members from elite law schools. As we will see Norman Leonard fits this profile nicely since he was on the law review at Columbia.

These law firms traditionally hired "white Christian males" (Galanter and Palay 1995, 24). They sought "Nordic" lawyers with "pleasing personalities" and "'clean-cut' appearances" from privileged social backgrounds (Smigel 1964, 37). Partners were often members of organizations such as the Yale

Club. The firms wanted WASPs and members of the Social Register and that was definitely not Norman Leonard. Prior to the late 1960s social connections were at least as important as academic achievements (Wilkins and Gulati 1996).

These firms represented corporate giants such as CBS, NBC, ABC, or the *New York Times* (Hoffman 1973). And attorneys with these firms would often come from, or go to, top government positions. Richard Nixon brought Pepsi-Cola and a lot of money with him when he joined a firm in 1963 after temporarily leaving politics. Some firms specialized in litigation and were known for being tough, as was true of Richard Gladstein. In these environments disbarment was rarely mentioned, unlike the experience of Gladstein and threats against his partners.

Another book dealing with these powerful firms was written by Ralph Nader, who was born in 1934 to immigrant parents (Nader and Smith 1996). Nader graduated from Princeton and then Harvard Law School. He was drafted in 1959 and afterwards briefly practiced law in Hartford, Connecticut. He soon became a full-time political activist.

Nader noted that in 1996 the world's largest law firm had 1,642 lawyers with more than 50 offices around the world. The clients of such firms include the largest corporations in the world. One mammoth law firm defeated the U.S. government in anti-trust litigation against IBM. The cases handled by such firms include President Nixon's refusal to release his office tapes of his phone conversations, the defense in the 1980s and 1990s of the savings and loan industry "con artists" (Nader and Smith 1996, 39), and defense of the fraudulent research of tobacco companies purporting to show that tobacco smoking was harmless. These firms also helped auto manufacturers delay government demands that air bags be installed. Clearly, such law firms are often more powerful than governments and have absolutely no scruples about the practices of their clients. Thus Nader believed that the common confidential settlement should be abolished since it shrouds corporate deals in secrecy.

SMALL AND SOUTHERN FIRMS

Carlin (1962) found that smaller cities do not have really large law firms (See also Nader and Smith 1996). The ABA was traditionally southern and small town oriented (Hoffman 1973). By the early twentieth century, however, the "independent country lawyer" was no longer dominant having been replaced by "corporate attorneys and . . . [urban] solo practitioners from ethnic minority groups" (Auerbach 1976, 52).

Small law firms in small towns typically engaged in a general practice rather than a specialty practice. If they were the only lawyers in town they felt obligated to take all types of cases. However white southern lawyers could not engage in civil rights law because of local prejudices and thus the late William Kunstler felt it was left to him to take up the slack (Kunstler and Isenberg 1994).

JEWISH ATTORNEYS: EVENTUAL, CONDITIONAL ACCEPTANCE

Even as Jews began to be accepted in the legal profession their names seldom appeared on firm shingles (Smigel 1964). Dramatic patterns were found in the responses to a questionnaire sent to all members of the Yale Law School classes of 1951 through 1962 who had worked in New York City since graduation (*Yale Law Journal* 1964, 630).

Jewish law school graduates typically found employment at smaller firms and those graduates who were below the top third of their class initially received less pay than Gentiles with similar class standing (*Yale Law Journal* 1964, 646, 648). Moreover the Jewish attorneys were less successful than Gentiles in landing their preferred jobs (*Yale Law Journal* 1964). The authors of the study reasoned that Jewish job applicants were hindered by earlier discriminatory policies and that their inability to compete may have been partly "self-erected"—rooted in the belief that they would face discrimination when applying to certain firms (*Yale Law Journal* 1964, 657).

Corporate law firms, for the most part, did not hire Jews until the late 1960s even though many Jewish applicants were highly qualified (Wilkins and Gulati 1996; See also Galanter and Palay 1995, 24). Jews were rarely promoted to partner in these top firms. During WWII many elite firms began to accept Jewish lawyers when "desirable" candidates were no longer available (Smigel 1964, 65; Galanter and Palay 1995, 48). The acceptance of Jews into positions at large law firms gained momentum after 1960 and accompanied "a general lessening of social exclusiveness" (Galanter and Palay 1995, 24).

During the Great Depression many young attorneys became interested in labor law because they supported unions and wanted to help workers. The labor activism of the 1930s convinced minority attorneys, especially Jews, to pursue labor law—a field that would allow them to combine "liberal reform or radical hope with professional fulfillment" (Auerbach 1976, 218). At the time there were very few attorneys in the country who represented labor unions. One lawyer remarked that prior to 1935: "if there were ten lawyers known as union lawyers I'd be surprised" (Auerbach 1976, 218). In this environment the Gladstein firm understandably specialized in labor law.

LAWYERS FOR THE POOR

Prior to the advent of public defenders and neighborhood legal services there were (in most states) attorneys who defended poor people accused of crimes or in need of other assistance (See Wood 1956). These attorneys typically had working class backgrounds and were using the law for upward mobility. Of course, public defenders provide legal aid to the poor who are charged with crimes. The low prestige and horrid working conditions of public defenders are legendary. Public defenders are very poorly paid, often work with many clients, and receive no respect from observers. Attorneys who serve the poor in civil practice face many of the same problems.

RADICAL PRACTICE

William Kunstler was a secular Jew (Kunstler and Isenberg 1994). His father and grandfather were physicians. He was a Yale undergraduate from 1937 to 1941 as well as an outstanding student and member of Phi Beta Kappa. He joined the Army as an enlisted man in 1941 and became a second lieutenant in 1942. By the time he was discharged in 1946 he was a major. Kunstler was in combat in 1944–1945 and received the Bronze Star for valor. He attended Columbia Law School from 1946 to 1949 and later formed a two-person firm with his brother Michael. There is no indication that he ever considered, or was recruited, by an elite law firm in spite of his distinguished military service and education.

During the 1960s and 1970s Kunstler changed from a liberal to a radical. And during this time his law partnership with his brother unraveled. He began representing numerous African Americans. H. Rap Brown (the 1960s chair of SNCC) became his friend and client. In 1967 he represented Harlem Representative Adam Clayton Powell. In 1992 Kunstler represented the beleaguered D.C. politician Marion Barry. In 1985 he represented Darrell Cabey who was shot and maimed by Bernard Goetz. Kunstler also represented a wide variety of dissident Americans. In 1968 he represented Roman Catholic priests Daniel and Phillip Berrigan on charges of disrupting a draft board. From 1987 to 1992 he represented organized crime boss John Gotti and in 1993 he became involved in gay rights litigation.

SOLO PRACTICE

From 1948 to 1970 the percentage of U.S. lawyers in solo practice dropped from 61 percent to 37 percent—a 24 percent decrease. The percentage of these lawyers is lower in large cities and they have little prestige (Heinz and Laumann 1994, xvii). According to Heinz and Laumann (1994, xvii), "The poles of the [legal] profession's prestige hierarchy [include] Wall Street lawyers at the top [and] criminal lawyers, personal injury lawyers, or solo practitioners, at the bottom."

The parents of solo practitioners were generally poor. Many of them were immigrants from Eastern Europe with little formal education. Solo practitioners typically attended a night law school (Wood 1956) and had difficulty starting their practice with a meager income and clients that were less than ideal. They relied on family, friends, and neighbors for referrals. They dealt with evictions, personal injury, criminal defense, and divorce cases. They also handled residential real estate closings, real estate tax foreclosing, debt collection, drawing up wills, and they worked as claims adjusters for insurance companies.

In the early twentieth century the Protestant lawyers who dominated the American Bar Association resented the influx of working class Jews and Catholics into their profession (Auerbach 1976). Thus they came up with a series of ethical guidelines or "Canons" to proscribe the behavior of these newcomers. These new attorneys were primarily "urban solo practitioners" and the children of Eastern and Southern European immigrants "whose behavior was unethical because established Protestant lawyers said it was" (Auerbach 1976, 50).

The Canons allowed WASP lawyers to express their belief that they were morally superior to these "unfit" newcomers. Moreover "traditional" lawyers resented the rise of corporate attorneys though these negative feelings were tempered by the WASP heritage that the two groups shared as well as a common desire to reserve the profession's top positions for those of their own ethnic background (Auerbach 1976, 52).

ACADEMIC LAWYERS

Shamir (1995) noted that elite lawyers as early as the 1930s were deeply suspicious of academic attorneys for their lack of patriotism toward the U.S. government. Law professors, of course, are not members of firms. This suspicion can be seen in the career of law professor William P. Murphy. When Galliher came to Missouri University (MU) and Columbia, Missouri, in 1967 he soon met MU law professor William P. "Bill" Murphy. Bill was Galliher's neighbor for approximately four years. Bill had come to MU from the University of Mississippi Law School where he taught constitutional law from 1953 to 1962. He felt forced to resign from "Ole Miss" because he feared that he and his family would be the targets of violence since he insisted on teaching that the U.S. Constitution requires the racial integration of schools—which it does. History records that Mississippi politicians, including Mississippi Governor Ross Barnett, took great exception to the U.S.

Constitution, to Bill Murphy, and to the way in which he taught constitutional law. He was charged with "atheism, communism, and subversion" (Boger 2008, 306).

Although Bill was far from being a political radical he soon got into trouble with Missouri politicians and MU administrators. A law school colleague recalled that Bill then "spoke out against the exercise of Presidential power in Vietnam" (Boger 2008, 306). That's not the entire story of Bill's problems at MU. In 1970 Bill was elected Chair of the campus Faculty Council. In that capacity and due to his skill as a professional labor arbitrator he was asked to mediate a conflict between antiwar faculty who had gone on strike to protest the war in Vietnam and senior campus administrators and Missouri politicians who felt that faculty as public employees had a patriotic duty to support the war. Campus administrators moved for summary punishment of the dissident faculty, but Bill objected since this violated principles of due process that Missouri Universities' own regulations stipulated. The law school dean was so outraged that he froze Bill's salary. As a matter of both principle and financial survival Bill resigned from MU in 1971 and moved to the University of North Carolina at Chapel Hill where he taught until his retirement in 1990.

WOMEN IN THE LAW

Harvard Law School did not admit women until after World War II (Auerbach 1976, 29). And prior to 1916 Harvard was the only law school that required applicants to have a college degree (Auerbach 1976, 28–29).

In 1963 less than 3 percent of attorneys in the U.S. were women (Auerbach 1976, 295). Although the number of female law students increased dramatically during the 1960s by the end of the decade female lawyers were still primarily limited to "low-status fields of specialty practice that were regarded as suitably feminine: domestic relations, juvenile and probate work" (Auerbach 1976, 295). Gender discrimination "kept the law a precarious and often demeaning profession for its female practitioners" (Auerbach 1976, 295).

From 1930 to 1960 female lawyers were highly marginalized. For example, it was not until 1934 that a woman, Florence Allen, became a federal judge (Smith 1999). Nowhere is this marginalization better demonstrated than in the case of Carol Weiss King (1895–1952) [Ginger 1993]. King was a native of Manhattan who graduated from Barnard in 1917 and New York University Law School in 1920. She practiced law in New York City until her death in 1952. The top law schools had a quota on Jewish students and none would accept her, even though she came from "an upper-middle-class, intellectual, New York Jewish family" (Ginger 1993, xiv). Her father and two brothers were very successful attorneys. In 1917 she married Gordon King and in 1925 she gave birth to a son. Gordon died in 1930.

Carol King began her practice in 1921 during desperate days for workers. Due to gender discrimination she was a solo practitioner for most of her career and could not be a courtroom litigator. Thus she prepared briefs for men to present in the courtroom. King worked as a volunteer for immigrants associated with the International Ladies Garment Workers Union. She represented Harry Bridges in 1938 and was appointed General Counsel for the American Committee for the Protection of Foreign Born in 1942. In 1948 the Committee scheduled a dinner in her honor. King was also a founding member of the progressive National Lawyers Guild. She did not know that the Immigration service was routinely allowing the FBI to intervene in her cases. King died in 1952 at the age of 56.

Helen Mathilde Cirese is a part of the same generation of female attorneys, but was a bit more integrated into the mainstream than Carol King (Helen Cirese Papers n.d.). Cirese was born in 1899 and was a Roman Catholic, the daughter of Italian immigrants. In 1921 she graduated from law school at DePaul University in Chicago and started her own solo practice (Helen Cirese Papers n.d.). She soon joined a small law firm and in 1930 began practicing with her brother while another brother joined this firm in 1943. Cirese was elected Justice of the Peace in 1945, 1949, 1953, and 1957. She participated in the Immigrants Protective League, Italian Committee, and was involved in Democratic Party politics. Cirese died in 1983.

Combining the problems of timing, gender, and radical politics Doris Brin Walker was a political radical and an attorney who fought Cold War blacklists. She died in August 2009 at age 90 (Egelko 2009). Walker's legal career initially did not go well. She was the only woman in her 1942 University of California Berkeley law school class. She recalled that she was fired from her first law firm position due to her gender and thus for a time left legal practice in the 1940s to become a labor organizer. She also held a series of menial jobs at canneries from which she was fired when it was learned that she was a Communist. Later things began to look up for her. Walker was the first female president of the National Lawyers Guild in 1970–1971 and also in the 1970s she headed a California law firm with Robert Treuhaft, husband of Jessica Mitford. Walker successfully defended UCLA Professor Angela Davis in 1972 on charges of murdering a judge and in 2004 sponsored a resolution asking the California State Bar to investigate George Bush and Dick Cheney for the wars in Iraq and Afghanistan. It is not an exaggeration to say that in the early 1940s there was no place in American legal practice for her, but by 1970 everything had changed.

Carol King's biographer Ann Fagan Ginger is a constitutional lawyer who graduated from the University of Michigan law school in 1947. Ginger is a prolific author who founded the Meiklejohn Civil Liberties Institute.

Ginger was born in 1925 into "an English Quaker, Irish Catholic, Lithuanian Jewish Midwestern socialist journalist family" and was immersed in social justice issues from an early age ("Ann Fagan Ginger" 2006). Ginger's mother was a social activist and member of the League of Women Voters and her father was a newspaper reporter. While attending law school Ginger aspired to become a labor lawyer. However, like her seven female classmates (including the class valedictorian) Ginger was unable to find work immediately upon graduation. Nevertheless, she soon began doing "legal work" for a labor union, yet they refused to call her an attorney. She then started taking clients including some who were made to appear before the Un-American Activities Commission of Ohio. One case lasted 8 years and Ginger ultimately prevailed when the case went to the U.S. Supreme Court in 1959.

AFRICAN AMERICAN ATTORNEYS

Perhaps the place to begin a discussion of African American attorneys who practiced between 1930 and 1960 is with the most prominent practioner, Thurgood Marshall. Marshall was born in 1908 in Baltimore and attended all black Lincoln University in Pennsylvania (Haskins 1992). In 1930 he applied to the University of Maryland Law School and was rejected because of his race (Thurgood Marshall, Supreme Court Justice). The law school dean told Marshall that even though he had earned top honors as an undergraduate, Maryland state law would not allow them to admit him because he was African American (Haskins 1992). Committed to becoming an attorney Marshall was accepted into law school at Howard University (Tushnet 1996). Soon after graduation he began working for the Baltimore NAACP.

Ironically Marshall's first major victory came in 1933 when he successfully sued the University of Maryland Law School to admit an African American student. In 1936 he became an assistant legal counsel and later the Chief Counsel to the NAACP. Thereafter he is remembered for winning 29 Supreme Court cases and attacking various aspects of racism. In 1954 he won the historic *Brown v. Board of Education* (of Topeka, Kansas) case that destroyed the practice of "separate but equal." Now Thurgood Marshall was clearly on his way, ultimately being appointed to the U.S. Supreme Court in 1967. Marshall was never a member of a law firm and he spent his career in solo practice. He died in 1993.

In 1960 African Americans comprised about 1.1 percent of all attorneys in the United States (Sander 2004). The first black president of the D.C. Bar recalled that in 1950 Washington, D.C., had over 150 black lawyers, nearly all of whom were in solo practice or members of small all black firms (Becker 2001). The clients of these attorneys were typically the poor such as a divorced woman seeking the enforcement of a child support order. Thus black male attorneys often needed financial support from their wives who worked as schoolteachers. The few black female attorneys were often confused by judges with the black men they represented. A central frustration of black attorneys was that the few financially secure black clients often used white attorneys. The first black woman lawyer was Charlotte Ray, a graduate of Howard University who passed the D.C. Bar in 1872 (Smith 1999).

Like Jews, blacks could not work for large law firms because these firms hired only "white, Christian males" (Galanter and Palay 1995, 24). Even with the gradual acceptance of Jews by large law firms following World War II African Americans and other people of color "were still hardly visible" in these environments (Galanter and Palay 1995, 24). Although few African Americans had the educational credentials necessary for employment in large law firms (Galanter and Palay 1995, 24) those who did "were systematically excluded" prior to the late 1960s (Wilkins and Gulati 1996).

NOTES ON THE NATIONAL LAWYERS GUILD

African American lawyers were attracted to the National Lawyers Guild (NLG) because the organization's "policy of racial equality stood in sharp and welcome contrast to the all-white ABA" (Auerbach 1976, 200). The NLG was founded in 1937 and was the first racially integrated bar association. Maurice Sugar was a progressive Detroit lawyer who first conceived of this association and developed an outline for its national organization (Sugar 1988). Guild lawyers were mainly poorly paid urban lawyers on the East and West coasts who had little prestige. The National Lawyer's Guild attracted ". . . professional outsiders, whose desperation for work encouraged experimentation" (Auerbach 1976, 209). The "outsider" character of the NLG is illustrated by the ethnic composition of the Philadelphia chapter's executive committee, which consisted of "eight Jews, three Catholics and one black" (Auerbach 1976, 209).

The NLG was known for ". . . its diffusion of professional participation, its sensitivity to contemporary social and legal problems, and its commitment to innovative means toward fulfilling obligations traditionally ignored" (Auerbach 1976, 209). Guild attorneys defended the rights of free speech and picketing for workers, opposed the 1947 federal Taft-Hartley Act, and represented Julius and Ethel Rosenberg (Auerbach 1976; Bailey 1982). Quite predictably, in 1985 the National Lawyers Guild held a dinner in honor of radical lawyer William Kunstler (Kunstler and Isenberg 1994).

Lawyers who defended "radical" labor activists risked their careers and sometimes their personal safety. Indeed, "Law practices were ruined since clients, frightened by an attorney's reputation, looked elsewhere for counsel; and lawyers [who defended labor activists] were threatened by the vigilante tactics of community and bar" (Auerbach 1976, 218). For example, George Andersen, one of Gladstein's law partners, was shot in his office by unknown assailants.

CONCLUSION

Auerbach notes that in the early twentieth century it was possible for ethnic minority and working class students who excelled in law school to make law review. The bigger question was whether they could gain admission to law school in the first place. Indeed, "[r]estrictions based upon sex, race, ethnicity, class, and family background permeated the admissions process" (Auerbach 1976, 29). Law school was effectively closed off to the poorest people in society among whom racial and ethnic minority groups were overrepresented (Auerbach 1976, 29).

A survey of attorneys in the 1970s showed that the social status of a law firm's clients made a significant impact on the prestige of the practice (Sandefur 2001). The Wall Street law firm is clearly at the top of this legal food chain. These firms represent powerful elites. A subtle anti-Semitism has settled in among these firms. Law firms in the Deep South tended to be smaller than Wall Street firms but certainly not without influence in the ABA. Politically radical lawyers on the left were often in solo practice no matter how distinguished their backgrounds. Those in solo practice also included graduates of night law schools and black attorneys who were at the very bottom of American legal practice. Law professors were also in a type of solo practice and were often looked down upon by attorneys in elite law firms.

CHAPTER SUMMARY

In the mid twentieth century, large Wall Street firms were at the top of the United States legal hierarchy. Until the late 1960s associates at these firms were paid the same as or less than their colleagues in other areas of law. These firms typically hired only white, upper class, Christian males who graduated from elite law schools. They often represented large corporations and, in these environments, the threat of disbarment was virtually non-existent. Further down were small and southern firms, Jewish attorneys, lawyers for the poor, radical lawyers, lawyers in solo practice, academic lawyers, women lawyers, and finally, African American lawyers. Minority lawyers often faced discrimination at the hands of the legal Establishment. Prior to the Great Depression very few attorneys specialized in labor law. Also, attorneys who had poor clients faced terrible working conditions and were often viewed with disdain. William Kunstler represented African Americans and dissidents and thus was considered a radical attorney. Attorneys who worked in solo practice also had very little prestige and their numbers declined significantly after midcentury. Academic lawyers often had their patriotism questioned by the legal Establishment and the few women attorneys were relegated to low status gendered fields of practice. African American attorneys faced tremendous discrimination and most often represented poor people.

The National Lawyers Guild was the first racially integrated bar association. Guild attorneys typically worked in urban environments and had little income or prestige. The organization attracted "professional outsiders" (Auerbach 1976, 209) such as the Gladstein partners who defended radical labor activists and risked their careers and personal safety by doing so.

In the United States at midcentury law school was reserved for the wealthy white majority. This was due to discriminatory admission standards combined with high tuition costs and the significant time investment needed for a legal education. Politically radical and African American attorneys often worked in solo practice as did those who graduated from night law schools.

Chapter Four

San Francisco and the Bay Area during the 1930s through the 1960s

COMMUNITIES IN THE URBAN AREA

San Francisco provided a generally supportive environment for the Gladstein firm's activities. This progressive firm probably could not have existed in other American urban areas. The San Francisco Bay Area includes San Francisco, Berkeley, Richmond, and Oakland.

We are all familiar with recent liberal and even radical policies of this region. The Haight-Ashbury district of San Francisco became renowned for systematic tolerance of illegal drug use. The Castro Street area in the city became recognized as a gay community, perhaps the leading such community in the world, and was represented by Harvey Milk on the city's Board of Supervisors in the 1970s. After the turn of the twenty-first century San Francisco's mayor was Gavin Newsom who later became California's Lieutenant Governor. In the new millennium Oakland's liberal mayor was Jerry Brown (later elected for a second time as California's governor) and the city's Oaksterdam University was famous for educating marijuana growers and distributors. Finally there is quintessentially liberal Berkeley. These liberal traditions have existed for some time.

ETHNIC DIVERSITY IN MID-TWENTIETH CENTURY CALIFORNIA

The history of Northern California cannot be understood apart from the experiences of the various ethnic groups that have inhabited this region. Beginning with the Chinese in the mid-nineteenth century Gold Rush Era, Califor-

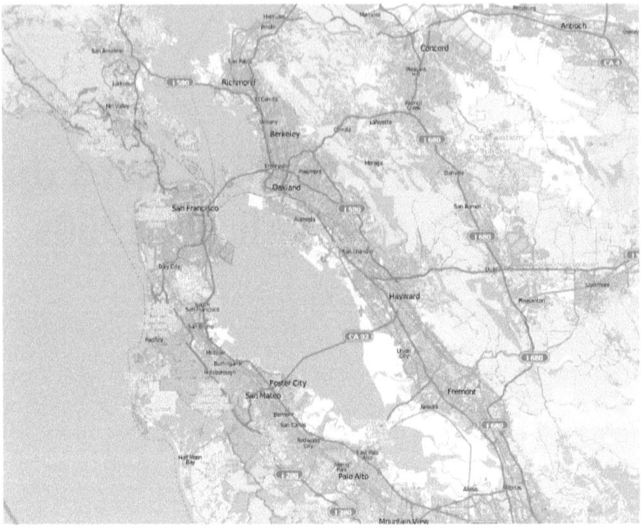

A Bay Area map with San Francisco on the far left and Richmond to the far north. ***Wikimedia Commons.***

nia employers recruited workers from various Asian countries. By the early twentieth century California was producing half of the nation's fruits and vegetables and the immense profits of the agricultural industry depended on the economic exploitation of Asian and Mexican immigrant laborers. Many believed that whites "would be lowered and degraded" by agricultural labor and were not well qualified because they were used to "standing up straight" whereas Asians and Mexicans "were used to stooping, crouching, and bending" (Picture This).

After Chinese immigration was cut off by the U.S. government in 1882 successive waves of immigrants from other Asian countries were hired to work on California's farms (Picture This). When immigration restrictions were placed on one group, employers turned their recruiting efforts to another group. Thus, by the 1930s California's population included immigrants (or the descendants of immigrants) from China, Japan, India, the Philippines, and Korea. In addition to recruiting Asian workers California employers hired Mexicans who were eager to flee the economic and civil unrest in their own country (Picture This). Thus, rural agricultural areas were more ethnically diverse than California's large cities. White laborers believed that these new immigrants threatened their livelihoods and violence often erupted. Not surprisingly, opposition to Asian immigration became "a staple of California politics" (Picture This).

Chinese

San Francisco's longstanding reputation for tolerance includes the peaceful existence of Chinatown (Luedtke 2000). Although the city's Chinese community was relatively "small and isolated" it was by the mid-1930s the largest such community in the United States (Picture This). Because the U.S. government had cut off Chinese immigration more than 50 years earlier most Chinese Americans had little if any contact with friends and relatives in China. In fact many Chinese Americans had been born and raised in the United States and thus knew little about Chinese culture beyond that which they had learned at home. Nevertheless, Chinese Americans in 1930s California most often lived in segregated communities and were generally excluded from attending schools or working in occupations reserved for whites (Picture This). Chinese Americans who wanted to work outside of their own neighborhoods were usually restricted "to grocery, restaurant or laundry businesses, and domestic servant positions" (Picture This).

Japanese

In the 1880s when the United States began passing laws to prohibit Chinese immigration, California employers turned to Japanese laborers for farming, mining, and factory work (Picture This). Many Californians, especially San Franciscans were unhappy that they would have to compete for jobs with yet another group of Asian immigrants. In the early twentieth century the U.S. and Japanese governments reached an informal "Gentleman's Agreement" to slow Japanese immigration. This was justified by Japan's imperialist expansion in Asia.

In the mid-1930s 70 percent of Japanese Americans lived in California. Even though many Californians of Japanese ancestry were well educated and had been born in the United States, anti-Japanese sentiment made it difficult for them to work outside of their own "ethnic economy" which included family farms and stores in Little Tokyo (Picture This). To make matters worse the 1924 National Origins Act cut off Japanese immigration thus devastating commerce in San Francisco's Little Tokyo (Picture This).

Filipinos

Like other Asian immigrants in California Filipinos were primarily employed as itinerant farm workers. Filipinos were California's "last major wave of Asian immigrant labor" prior to WWII (Picture This). Because of American imperialist definitions of the Philippines as a U.S. territory, Filipinos were U.S. nationals. Thus they were able to live and work in the United States at a time when people from other Asian countries were shut out by anti-immigration laws. During the Great Depression of the 1930s the majority of Filipinos in the United States lived in California. Like other non-white immigrant groups Filipinos faced discrimination and violence at the hands of whites. Much of this resentment was rooted in the fact that Filipino immigrants were willing to accept lower wages than white laborers. Additionally many whites were angry that Filipino men were dating white women. Thus, in the early 1930s riots erupted in Northern and Central California wherein Filipinos became the targets of violence and harassment. These factors also influenced the U.S. government's decision to grant the Philippines independence in 1934 thus slowing Filipino immigration, since they were no longer U.S. citizens (Picture This).

Mexicans and Mexican Americans

Many Mexicans and Mexican Americans came to California at the beginning of the twentieth century hoping to work in the state's booming agricultural industry. Because of ongoing civil wars in Mexico, Mexican immigrant farm laborers were able to make much more money in California than they could back home even though they were paid far less than white workers. By the 1920s the majority of California farm laborers were Mexican or Mexican American.

During the Great Depression government officials and white labor union leaders blamed California's high unemployment rate on Mexican immigrants (Picture This) even though the majority of the state's unemployed were white migrants from the Midwest. Moreover Mexican and Mexican American farm workers organized strikes against their employers (often with the help of other minority laborers) to protest low pay and deplorable working conditions. As a result, Mexicans and Mexican Americans endured various types of discrimination including forced removal programs in which even U.S. citizens were deported to Mexico (Picture This).

African Americans

Prior to WWII there were less than 5,000 African Americans in San Francisco and in the 1930s only two African Americans worked for the city. One was a receptionist for the Mayor, the other was a female social worker at San Francisco General Hospital (Fleming 1999). After the war started many African Americans moved to San Francisco according to Thomas Fleming the black former editor (1944–1994) of San Francisco's *Sun-Reporter* newspaper. By 1950 San Francisco had over 43,000 African American residents. Thus there were early efforts to desegregate unions. Nevertheless, as late as the 1960s no blacks were hired by the large San Francisco hotels and thus the NAACP picketed them. In 1964 picketing of the local Sheraton Hotel was prohibited by a local judge. The *San Francisco Examiner* referred to these protestors as un-American and called them Communists.

On the other hand, during the Depression Era Oakland was one of the most well integrated cities in the United States (Picture This). However, even in Oakland, African Americans faced considerable discrimination. Although African Americans were able to find jobs through various New Deal Programs they were typically relegated to low status, low paying positions regardless of their educational background. Typically men were limited to manual labor jobs and women worked as domestic servants in white households (Picture This). Moreover African Americans who worked in the same occupations as whites typically received lower pay and experienced on-the-job segregation, working "only in certain locations or in certain shifts" (Picture This). This was true even for "integrated" work settings (Picture This). Many African American laborers who moved to the Bay Area during WWII settled in Oakland's thriving black community (Picture This). Oakland's black community grew more than 500 percent during the war years.

Native Americans

During the Depression Era many Native Americans lived in areas of the Midwest that were affected by the drought and "dustbowl" conditions and thus they moved to California in search of employment (Picture This). A second influx occurred during the 1950s when Native Americans across the United States moved from the reservations into large cities (Picture This). Native Americans in Los Angeles and the Bay Area greatly outnumbered California's local Native American population (Picture This). For California's urban Native Americans identity was an important issue as can be seen by the formation of the American Indian Movement and the occupation of Alcatraz both of which occurred there in the late 1960s (Picture This).

Identities and Size of San Francisco's Other Demographic and Ethnic Groups

The racial and ethnic diversity in the Bay Area began to pay dividends by helping to nurture a progressive political climate. San Francisco's liberal political culture can be traced back to the mid-1930s when local businesses conceded to striking workers and voters rejected a long time anti-picketing ordinance (Issel 1991). Liberals pursued their goals by placing one of their own in the mayor's office and on the board of supervisors and seeking state and federal funds. There was also religious tolerance in that Roman Catholics and Jews had access to jobs, housing, and even public office.

Roman Catholics and Jews

Roman Catholics comprised 28 percent of San Francisco's population in 1936 and Jews only 6–8 percent, but both groups felt at home in the city and most mayors were either Roman Catholic or Jewish (Issel 1989). In many ways the history of San Francisco is similar to that of the United States and thus we have the growing influence of American Catholics and their influence in labor unions (Issel 2004). The local archbishop supported the 1934 San Francisco longshore maritime strike led by Harry Bridges and this indicates something about Roman Catholic leadership in the city.

One author argues that Bay Area Jews have historically faced little discrimination. Indeed "Being Jewish . . . has proved little hindrance to economic and even social advancement" (Rosenbaum 2009, xv). San Francisco Jews were integrated into the community at a time when anti-Semitism was flourishing in other parts of the United States (Rosenbaum 2009). "In Northern California 'there were no ghettos' (meaning an area of density, isolation, or squalor), according to one observer in the 1920s . . . Indeed, the East European immigrant experience in the Bay Area differed markedly from that in most other big American cities" (Rosenbaum 2009, 197–98). In the years leading up to and during WWII San Francisco's Jewish community remained quiet about the dire predicament of Jews in Europe as they did not want to be viewed as ethnocentric (Rosenbaum 2009).

THE GREAT DEPRESSION

The Great Depression of the 1930s had a profound effect on the United States and Northern California was no exception. The Bay Area, however, was less affected by the Depression than other parts of the country including Southern California (Rosenbaum 2009).

In 1932 about 25 percent of U.S. workers were unemployed (Picture This). In California farm incomes and building permits dropped to a fraction of their previous levels and more than a million state residents found themselves receiving public assistance. Compounding the severe financial crisis, droughts in the Midwest and the resulting "dustbowl" conditions were killing much of the nation's crops and livestock (Picture This). California, however, was relatively unaffected by this phenomenon and some agricultural jobs were available. Multiethnic migrant labor camps appeared throughout the state and by the end of the 1930s over 200,000 people had come to California looking for work. Longtime state residents resented this influx of people and they became particularly concerned when the U.S. government stopped providing these newcomers with financial assistance in 1935 for without federal support they could turn to crime.

Additionally, the lack of employment prospects prompted white labor unions to blame ethnic minority groups for taking jobs that they felt should have been given to other whites (Picture This). As a result African Americans in Oakland were attacked by members of white labor unions. Further, (as we noted earlier) at the request of white labor unions and government officials, many of California's Mexicans and even Mexican Americans were deported to Mexico. Those who stayed in California joined multiracial labor unions so that they would not lose their jobs to unemployed whites from the Midwest who were desperate to find work.

For those who were lucky enough to be employed during the Great Depression working conditions quickly deteriorated as employers took advantage of the competitive labor market by cutting pay, forcing employees to work longer hours, and attempting to destroy labor unions. For California's farm laborers conditions were deplorable. Entire families, from the elderly to small children, worked side by side in the fields. Laborers typically lived in small shacks and under generally miserable conditions:

> Dirt floors were common, as was the lack of functional walls, roofs, and doors. Camps would only rarely have running water. Usually, water had to be carried from a river or ditch, the presence of human or animal waste and farming chemicals in the unfiltered water was a constant danger. (Picture This)

Despite this horrible situation, efforts to organize workers and improve labor conditions were branded "by corporations and their allies as 'Red' or foreign Communist attempts to destroy U.S. industries" (Picture This). For example, during the 1934 Bay Area longshore strike, local newspapers conspired against striking workers by agreeing to support business interests later claiming: "that foreign Communist agitators had seized control of the city" (Picture This).

Despite attempts by the media and others to smear workers rights advocates, California experienced significant labor unrest during the Great Depression. This was largely due to terrible working conditions. Strikes were common as the multiracial and Asian unions, which dominated the state's agricultural sector, confronted their employers.

In 1933 and 1934 Filipino lettuce workers in Salinas formed "one of the first California farm labor unions" and "led the first of several strikes against lettuce growers' in the area" (Picture This). This Filipino labor union soon included Mexican and white workers. These multiracial labor unions helped to define California's labor movement (Picture This).

But perhaps the most well known Depression era strike in California was the San Francisco General Strike in July 1934. The general strike was preceded by the International Longshoreman's Association (ILA) strike which began on May 9th of that year (Calisphere). Bay Area Longshoremen went on strike for nearly three months to protest poor working conditions and obtain union recognition (ACLU of Northern California). The strikers were terrorized by the police and vigilantes and the police shot and killed two strikers near the union hall on July 5th, a date that would later become known as "Bloody Thursday" (ACLU of Northern California). This led to the four day San Francisco General Strike, which shut down the entire city (ACLU of Northern California; Picture This). The general strike was effective because the strikers were from a variety of ethnic backgrounds. Moreover, African American men were told that they would be accepted into the longshore union if they did not cross the picket line. This surely frustrated employers, as they were unable to hire black men to fill in as scabs (Picture This). Also, in 1935 several strikers were shot and killed and many more were arrested in Humboldt County during the Holmes-Eureka lumber strike (ACLU of Northern California; *Humboldt Herald* 2007). And in 1936 another strike of lettuce workers occurred in Salinas (Picture This).

WORLD WAR II

In 1941 soon after WWII began President Franklin Roosevelt outlawed racial discrimination in defense related industries, and consequently, by 1945 the Bay Area saw an influx of more than 46,000 African Americans (Picture This). This time period also saw the mass arrest and internment of Japanese Americans, including many in the Bay Area. In 1942 "Roosevelt signed Executive Order 9066, sending more than 120,000 persons of Japanese descent—men, women and children—to be segregated behind barbed wire in desolate, isolated concentration camps" (National Japanese American Historical Society). The several thousand Japanese Americans in San Francisco were originally modestly successful but as a consequence of the U.S. internment they suffered financially (Taylor 1993). Issel (1991) noted that the Japanese relocation, along with massive black migration helped to develop a concern for human rights during the 1940s and 1950s.

Prior to WWII approximately 5,000 people worked in the Bay Area shipyards (Picture This). During the war, however, Bay Area shipyards employed nearly one-quarter million workers and produced almost 50 percent of "the cargo vessels and warships delivered for the war effort." The City of Richmond was particularly affected by the booming shipbuilding industry. During WWII four new shipyards were created there and these facilities alone employed 90,000 workers including large numbers of women. Also during this time, Richmond's total population increased from 23,000 to over 100,000 (Picture This).

WOMEN DURING WWII

Because of wartime labor shortages many women took manufacturing jobs (Picture This). Thus women became more accepted because they were needed. Women comprised nearly one-third of the 90,000 Richmond shipyard workers and 20 percent of the employees at one shipyard in Oakland. During the war years "no region demonstrated social changes more than the West Coast and the Bay Area. . . . The Bay Area's numerous shipyards hired the greatest number of women defense workers" (Graves n.d.).

HISTORICAL EMERGENCE OF A GAY COMMUNITY

Large numbers of soldiers (both male and female) moved to San Francisco following WWII "to enjoy the newly discovered delight of the same sex" to which the military had introduced them. By the 1950s San Francisco had both gay and lesbian organizations with their own magazines (Warren, n.d.). And San Francisco's gay community gained political clout after 1950 when the state Supreme Court prohibited the closing of a gay bar known as the "Black Cat" ("A Timeline of San Francisco History" n.d.). The court ruled that authorities could not discriminate against bars that serve gays or lesbians ("A Timeline of San Francisco History" n.d.). With this springboard the San Francisco gay community developed early on into a vibrant entity.

In 1961 José Julio Sarria, a popular local singer and gay rights activist, ran for a position on the San Francisco Board of Supervisors thus becoming "the first openly gay candidate in the world to run for public office" ("A Timeline of San Francisco History" n.d.). Although he lost the election, Sarria surprised many by receiving "a hefty 5,600 votes [and] coming in 9th out of a field of 32 candidates" (International Court System n.d.) (Harvey Milk would go on to win this same seat 16 years later). Sarria's relative success demonstrated that San Francisco's gay community had considerable influence in local politics (International Court System n.d.).

Despite the aforementioned 1950 California Supreme Court ruling, San Francisco's gays and lesbians continued to be arrested and harassed by local authorities. In 1963 many of the city's gay bars were forced to close due to police harassment. Thus, in 1965 local bar owners formed the "Tavern Guild of San Francisco" and organized various events to support the gay community including a yearly "drag ball" (International Court System n.d.).

BERKELEY

The anti-communist crusade of the 1950s never caught on in Berkeley primarily because the area had welcomed Communists in the 1930s. Blacklisting hit Hollywood harder than San Francisco though HUAC hearings were nevertheless held in San Francisco. In 1960 University of California-Berkeley students protested the San Francisco hearings after one of their own was subpoenaed to testify (Rorabaugh 1989). And beginning in the 1940s liberal Democrats took control of Berkeley's political establishment, which included the city council and the school board and this paved the way for civil rights activities and the nomination of African Americans for political office (Rorabaugh 1989).

University of California President Clark Kerr was a Quaker and a liberal Democrat. He helped cease a faculty loyalty oath imposed by state legislators during the McCarthy Era and in 1963 he lifted a campus wide ban on communist speakers. During the early 1960s at the University of California-Berkeley Mario Savio and the Free Speech Movement, and later the antiwar movement, were dominant forces and Berkeley's radicals became well known (Rorabaugh 1989, ix). Free Speech leaders proved that they could organize and lead a strike effectively (Burner 1996). Rorabaugh also notes that the Berkeley Free Speech Movement was led primarily by Jews, and that Huey Newton and Bobby Seale founded the Black Panther Party in Berkeley and nearby Oakland. Later we will see that attorney Norman Leonard had a direct hand in this Berkeley activism.

CONCLUSION

Here we have seen the historical diversity and ultimately the tolerance in the Bay Area beginning in the 1930s through the 1960s. The events that occurred during the Great Depression of the 1930s indicate how this economic disaster uniquely influenced the region. The 1934 ILA and general strikes occurred during the height of this depression. The ILA strike involved many ethnic groups and even had the public support of a local Roman Catholic archbishop. In 1937 there was citizen rejection of an anti-picketing ordinance.

In Berkeley during the Red Scare there was public opposition to HUAC hearings in San Francisco. And San Francisco was never hit hard by anticommunist fervor since blacklisting in the state was concentrated in Hollywood, in Southern California. In addition, many Bay Area minority groups had access to jobs, housing, and even public office. This ready acceptance was extended to Roman Catholics, Mexicans, Mexican Americans, African Americans, gays and lesbians, women, Jews, Asians, student radicals at Berkeley, and union members. All ultimately found their place in the Bay Area. We will show that it is in this environment that the Gladstein law firm also found its place in downtown San Francisco, albeit with occasional difficulties.

CHAPTER SUMMARY

The Gladstein law firm flourished in San Francisco's progressive political and social climate. Mid-twentieth century California was ethnically diverse and agribusiness prospered due to the exploitation of Asian and Mexican immigrant laborers. White laborers terrorized Asian residents whom they viewed as a threat to their livelihoods and politicians opposed Asian immigration. Californians of Chinese, Japanese, and Filipino ancestry often lived in segregated communities and worked in segregated occupations. As each group moved to the United States government policies were implemented to restrict immigration from their countries of origin.

By the 1920s most California farm workers were Mexican or Mexican American. Mexican immigrants were unjustly blamed for the state's high unemployment rate and during the Great Depression they organized strikes against their employers. As a result, Mexicans and Mexican Americans faced discrimination and oppressive government policies.

African Americans also faced discrimination, especially in employment. Oakland was well integrated during the Great Depression, but it was not until WWII that significant numbers of African Americans began living and working in San Francisco.

Many Native Americans moved to urban California during the Great Depression and then again in the 1950s in search of employment. For these Californians, identity was an important issue.

San Francisco's progressive political culture has existed since the 1930s. The city's Roman Catholic and Jewish communities have traditionally had access to jobs, housing, and public office. Local Catholics were involved in and supported efforts to improve labor conditions.

Even though California was hurt by the Great Depression the state was not subjected to the drought and dustbowl conditions that plagued the Midwest. Longtime residents resented the ethnically diverse newcomers who worked in the state's agricultural industry and multiracial labor unions were created so that Californians wouldn't lose their jobs to unemployed whites arriving from the Midwest.

Employers capitalized on California's competitive labor market by cutting pay, forcing employees to work longer hours, and allowing inhumane working conditions (Picture This). Corporations and the media labeled organized attempts to improve working conditions as Communist sabotage. Strikes were common, the most famous of which was the 1934 San Francisco General Strike.

During WWII, as African Americans moved to the Bay Area, Japanese Americans were forced into concentration camps. At the same time the Bay Area shipyard workforce increased dramatically as the region produced almost half of the ships delivered for the war effort. Women were integral to this effort.

Following WWII San Francisco's gay community grew significantly. The community had its own advocacy groups and gained political clout after a 1950 California Supreme Court ruling allowed a local gay bar to stay open. Nevertheless, gays and lesbians were harassed by authorities during the McCarthy Era. In 1961 the political power of San Francisco's gay community became evident after José Julio Sarria, an openly gay candidate, ran for public office and received a large number of votes. And in 1965, a group of local bar owners formed the Tavern Guild of San Francisco in order to resist police harassment and support the gay community.

McCarthyism never took hold in Berkeley, a city that had welcomed Communists in the 1930s and whose political apparatus was controlled by liberal Democrats. In 1960 University of California students protested HUAC hearings in San Francisco and later on Berkeley produced progressive social movements including the Free Speech movement, the Black Panther Party, and Vietnam War protests.

Harry Bridges as a young man. *San Francisco History Center, San Francisco Public Library.*

Harry Bridges relaxing in his office. *San Francisco History Center, San Francisco Public Library.*

Chapter Five

Harry Bridges

BRIDGES' CASE KEPT THE FIRM BUSY

Harry Bridges (1901–1990) was the long-term President of the ILWU (Barnes 1990). Bridges immigrated to the United States from Australia in 1921. The photos found just prior to this chapter show Bridges as a young man, through middle age. Unless otherwise cited, all of the materials in this chapter can be found in the Norman Leonard Oral History in the Bancroft Library, Berkeley, California.

The first work Norman Leonard did as an attorney in 1938 was on the Bridges case in Los Angeles for contempt of court. Bridges had sent a telegram to Secretary of Labor Frances Perkins that appeared in the press saying in effect that the courts could not stop the longshoreman's union from joining the CIO. A local judge took offense and cited Bridges for contempt of court. The U.S. Supreme Court ultimately ruled that Bridges had the right to freedom of speech.

Frances Perkins soon selected James M. Landis, a retired Harvard Law School Dean, to preside over an Immigration and Naturalization Service (INS) hearing to determine whether Bridges was a member of the Communist Party and should therefore be deported for belonging to a group which (some believed) "advocated the violent overthrow of the government." There were 45 days of testimony in 1938–1939. An expert witness argued that capitalism and communism were "forms of economic organization" while democracy and dictatorships were forms of government (Ginger 1993, 291). Dean Landis determined that the hearings offered no evidence that Bridges belonged to the Communist Party and thus there was no reason to deport him.

In 1941 the government began a new hearing with New York Appeals Court Judge Charles Sears presiding. After another set of hearings lasting in excess of a month Judge Sears ruled that Bridges could be deported. However, the Board of Immigration Appeals reversed Sears. The deportation hearing before Judge Sears came to an end in June of that year.

Bridges was once again charged with being a Communist and in 1942 U.S. Attorney General Francis Biddle issued a deportation order. The Bridges case was finally heard by the Supreme Court and reversed in 1945, 11 years after the 1934 San Francisco General Strike, 6 years after the hearing before Dean Landis and 4 years after the hearing before Judge Sears. Soon afterwards, Bridges became a naturalized citizen (Ginger 1993).

In 1949 Bridges was indicted for fraud. Judge George Harris presided at the trial and Bridges was convicted in 1950 and had his citizenship voided. So after two attempts to deport Bridges there was another Bridges trial, this time before Judge Harris. The government charged Bridges with making a false statement. Norman Leonard argued in court (since as we will see Richard Gladstein was engaged in other legal matters) that the new charges were prohibited by a 3-year statute of limitations. The atmosphere for Bridges in 1949–1950 was different than it was in 1945. One factor was a 1948 strike and union victory. Then there was a long bitter ILWU strike in Hawaii in 1949. All of this led to the 1949 indictment. The defense goal was to defend Bridges not communism. Norman Leonard, one of Bridges' defense attorneys, recalled the advice he received from his co-counsel, Telford Taylor: "Our job is to vindicate Bridges . . . not to engage in any philosophical discussions . . . about the nature of the Communist Party."

While out of jail on bail pending an appeal Bridges spoke out against the Korean War and Harris sent Bridges to jail. He spent approximately three weeks in jail prior to bail being restored. The U.S. Supreme Court reviewed the Harris decision in 1953 and agreed that the criminal prosecution of Bridges violated the statute of limitations.

Bridges was tried again by the Immigration and Naturalization Service (INS) and in 1955 Judge Louis Goodman ruled in favor of Bridges. The government used new witnesses in each case against Harry—Judge Goodman dismissed the case in 1955 due to an obviously lying government witness who knew nothing about Bridges and who had never been a Communist and, with this, the government gave up after more than 20 years of persecuting him.

Harry Bridges also supported Archie Brown, an ILWU member and avowed Communist Party member who had once run for governor on the Communist ticket. Bridges said that members of the local had the right to elect anyone they "Damn-well pleased" to union office even if the 1947 federal Taft-Hartley Law limiting the power of unions prohibited it. Brown was ultimately convicted under the Taft-Hartley Act for holding union office as a member of the Communist Party and sentenced to six months in jail. His attorney, Richard Gladstein, vowed to appeal the conviction and it was later reversed by the U.S. Court of Appeals for the Ninth Circuit (*San Francisco Examiner* 1962). In 1965 the court of appeals decision was upheld by the U.S. Supreme Court and Brown was vindicated (*United States v. Brown*).

A biography of Bridges by Charles Larrowe (1972) puts many of the details of Bridges' life in proper perspective. Bridges dropped his membership in the IWW because he disagreed with their anarchism. But he also abhorred company unions. Many consequently overestimated his support for and from Communists. Bridges could not be bought and was therefore difficult for employers to deal with. They ultimately decided to use the government to do to Bridges what they could not accomplish themselves. The second Pacific Coast maritime strike of the ILWU in 1936 was even more effective than the strike in 1934 in that it lasted longer and shut down all West Coast ports. Frances Perkins was ambivalent toward Bridges. It was assumed by Bridges' detractors that he was a Communist because he supported Communist causes such as the defense of the Scottsboro Boys and the ILWU always supported racial equality. After being convicted in 1950 by Judge Harris, Bridges asserted that anyone who criticizes government considering the current world situation is liable to be sent to jail.

ADDITIONAL LYING GOVERNMENT WITNESSES AGAINST BRIDGES

One government witness claimed that Harry Bridges was at a meeting of Communists in New York City but in fact ILWU meeting minutes put him at a union meeting in Stockton, California, that same day. Another government witness against Harry claimed to be a "Kentucky colonel" or "Southern gentleman" but in fact was a New York Jew who invented this background to cover his past in the Communist Party. One witness claimed that he had visited Bridges in his office and collected Communist Party dues from him shortly after the Communist Party convention in 1936. However, the office that the witness described was in a building where Bridges did not work until mid-1937 (*Dispatcher* 1955a). Richard Gladstein called this story "a complete fabrication" (*Dispatcher* 1955b).

During the McCarthy era liberals and progressives were blacklisted from waterfront jobs and ships' crews. During hearings the government would say they were security risks. And the defense attorneys would ask "'What evidence?' And they would say 'Oh we can't tell you.'" There was no way to defend against this posture. Gladstein, Andersen, and Leonard belonged to the National Lawyers Guild, an organization which vigorously opposed all government efforts to deport Bridges and continually filed briefs to that effect (Ginger and Tobin 1988).

THE WEAKNESS OF SUCCESS: MODERNIZATION AND MECHANIZATION

Beginning slowly in 1960 the ILWU shrank in size. In San Francisco the ILWU, which had approximately 9,000 to 10,000 members at one time, shrank to 1,500 by the mid-1980s. In 1960 there were 24 million longshore worker hours recorded on the Pacific coast and by 1984 that number was cut to 12 million due to mechanization or containerization. Once men would carry cargo in their hands or on their backs in sacks and walk up the gang-planks. Then slings and ship winches were used that would allow putting 4 or 5 sacks in a sling. Next shore-side cranes were developed allowing bigger and bigger loads. Containers now weigh 20 tons. Harry Bridges finally realized that he could not stop technology the way textile workers tried to do 200 years earlier. Initially the union had no idea that technology would develop in the way that it did. Yet this increased efficiency has allowed union dental, medical, and survivor benefits. There were less than a million tons of containerized cargo in 1960 and by the mid 1980s the figure had risen to 55 million tons. Additionally, the containers can be loaded off sight by non-union workers using large cranes. The images on the following pages show gantry cranes at the Port of Oakland. This should give the reader a sense of the massive scale at which freight is moved in today's longshore environment.

The San Francisco State University Labor Archives has Bridges' 1947 Labor Day Speech at the Civic Center in San Francisco. "The worst Congress in the history of the United States which moved swiftly to comply with the demands of Wall Street . . . and adopted a foreign policy of punishing our allies and rewarding our fascist and Nazi enemies. The Taft-Hartley law was enacted to smash our American unions and to depress American standards. It was also intended to outlaw solidarity between us and the organized labor of other countries. The law must be repealed." Harry Bridges' insistence on speaking his mind tested the limits.

PORTION OF FBI FILE FOR HARRY BRIDGES

Bridges' FBI file consists of approximately 30,000 pages and we received only materials dated March 7, 1950, to April 13, 1953, and February 11, 1958, to November 6, 1959. To receive the entire redacted Bridges FBI file would have involved many years of delay in waiting for the FBI redacting process to protect the identities of all undercover witnesses. Thus, after discussing options with an FBI records analyst, we decided to sample the file from the depths of the McCarthy Era in the 1950s.

Container ship at the Port of Oakland. ***Ingrid Taylar from San Francisco Bay Area - California, USA (Hanjin Container Ship).***

Fear

Bridges characterized un-American activities investigations "as 'a deliberate conspiracy (that) has created the climate in our country under which questions and criticisms of foreign policy become grounds for red-baiting and charges of treason espionage and sabotage'" (7/24/51, Section 1, 62). In the July 7, 1950, issue of the ILWU *Dispatcher* the union Executive Board, which included Bridges, wrote: "As Americans, we are today living in a world dominated by fear. We are afraid that depression is just around the corner and that we'll lose our jobs. We hate the speed-up, but we're afraid to resist it. We are afraid that the cold war will turn into a hot war. We are afraid of the atom bomb, of the H-bomb, of bacterial warfare. We are afraid of Communists, of the FBI, of imprisonment. Fear hangs over us and dominates our lives" (7/24/51, Section 1, 38). A government informant reported that Bridges said during a public speech "that there are 'worse things than going to jail when civil rights are at stake'" (7/24/51, Section 1, 50).

Another government informant noted that Bridges "blamed Vice-President Richard M. Nixon . . . for the . . . 'deaths of Julius and Ethel Rosenberg'" (2/11/58, Section 6, 3). The fear that Bridges attributed to others is not reflected in his own behavior. Bridges was always willing to speak his mind

Container cranes at the Port of Oakland. ***Ingrid Taylar (Flickr: Port of Oakland).***

and this explains why he had an FBI file of approximately 30,000 pages and why the government repeatedly tried to deport him.

Cold War Government Labor Policy

Bridges supported a ceasefire in Korea to avoid an atomic war. The ILWU Executive Board, of which Bridges was a member, was deeply concerned with the Cold War. Although it increased jobs for steel workers it was not good for others because foreign trade was diminished and purchasing power was reduced by high prices and high taxes. The Board said: "We demand the outlawing of . . . atomic weapons as instruments of aggression and mass murder" (7/24/51, Section 1, 41).

In the January 30, 1953, issue of the ILWU *Dispatcher* Bridges noted that "The Eisenhower cabinet of billionaires . . . will bring about a single labor federation that will be permitted to exist, company-union style, so long as it supports Administration policy" (3/25/53, Section 1, 142). In another *Dispatcher* article (January 3, 1958), Bridges noted Lyndon Johnson's warning that the sputnik missile would necessitate American workers giving up the 40-hour-work week, a proposition that Bridges rejected (2/11/58, Section 6, 5).

Peace Making

Bridges said in a speech "'We' should not accept the doctrine of 'Our country right or wrong'" (11/2/51, Section 1, 83). Bridges rejected American involvement in the Korean War and accused the Truman Administration of implementing "'a policy which appears to much of the world as the greatest threat to world peace'" since the Chinese Communist government claimed a "'Chinese Monroe Doctrine'" (7/24/51, Section 1, 15). In the July 6, 1951, issue of the *Dispatcher* Bridges rejected the notion that the United States can act as "the world's cop . . . 'putting out revolutionary fires sweeping . . . [other] parts of the world'" (2/6/52, Section 1, 95). Bridges was something of a prophet for on July 25th, 1958, in the *San Francisco News* he warned "against U.S. intervention in the Middle East [since] 'It looks . . . like we're being forced into this by oil interests'" (8/11/58, Section 6, 20).

The Military Draft

Bridges said that the trade unions must let 18-year-olds know that they do not have to be drafted (7/24/51, Section 1, 49). He stated "'It's pretty easy to send somebody else's kid to die'" (7/24/51, Section 1, 61). In *The Worker* Bridges wrote: "The draft of our 18 year old boys is a crime against America. The whole pro-war policy is a crime against America. The defense of the USA does not require that we arm to destroy the national independence of other people" (7/24/51, Section 1, 69).

U.S. Army Intelligence

Harry Bridges was so infamous that the U.S. Army kept a file on him. On April 26, 2010, the Army released 14 pages of an unknown total (Department of the Army, Intelligence and Security Command, Fort Meade, Maryland) presumably because these details were passed on by confidential informants dealing with military issues. Indeed, all the information came from confidential informants. In 1944 Bridges noted that a Democratic candidate for Congress had been a member of the Ku Klux Klan and Bridges worked for his defeat. Bridges claimed that the judicial bench and the media are permeated by corruption. He stated: "*America will fight the rest of the world by herself in the event of a third world war*" (emphasis added).

On February 12, 1952, Bridges addressed the Filipino Timarau Club of Honolulu. He said that more people are embracing communism "because that form of government offers something better . . . something to eat and more freedom." Bridges spoke of the militarization of the United States stating that the country "is rapidly becoming Fascist" and he said: "Today we are taking orders from the military and we do not dare go against this."

On March 10, 1952, the *Daily Peoples World* newspaper reported that the ILWU Executive Board (which included Bridges) "had unanimously recommended to President Truman and the congress that teams of enlisted men take over the bogged down Korean Peace Talks from the Army brass. A rank and file team will settle the Korean 'police action' in considerably less time without regard to the fortunes or futures of military men or corrupt politicians who hope to profit from the prolongation of the conflict."

Was Harry Bridges a Communist?

Harry Bridges was found guilty of perjury and conspiracy in federal court even though he had freely admitted contacts with Communist Party members in his ILWU union office (7/24/51, Section 1, 70). Bridges consistently denied that he was a member of the Communist Party (7/24/51, Section 1, 69–70; 2/11/58, Section 6, 14–15).

CONCLUSION

The available evidence demonstrates that Harry Bridges was not a Communist although he vocally opposed many U.S. government policies. For this reason the U.S. government spent 20 years trying to deport him. Bridges never attended college. He committed no crimes but nonetheless outraged the FBI simply by speaking his mind during a time when this was not tolerated by U.S. elites. Additionally "Bridges always candidly acknowledged his close ties and cooperation with Communists" (Kutler 1982, 150) and thus was stigmatized by representing party members in the ILWU.

CHAPTER SUMMARY

Harry Bridges was the long-term President of the ILWU and an immigrant from Australia. The U.S. government spent nearly two decades trying to deport Bridges by leveling various criminal charges against him and accusing him of holding Communist Party membership. The government produced a parade of witnesses against Bridges and, with the help of the Gladstein firm, the witnesses and their stories were discredited one-by-one. The authorities were clearly motivated by Bridges' criticism of U.S. government policies and his ability to lead strikes. Bridges publicly supported racial equality and the rights of workers and unions. He criticized Congress and spoke out against the Korean War. Bridges opposed the Taft-Hartley Act and supported free elections for union members. He had a lengthy FBI file as well as a U.S. Army file. Bridges' FBI file noted his belief that un-American activities investigations were merely a means of stifling dissent. It was also noted that

Bridges had supported civil rights, opposed U.S. interventionist policies in Korea and elsewhere, opposed the military draft, and criticized the media, politicians, and judges. Bridges had expressed sympathy for Communists and he had Communist associates but there is no evidence that he was ever a party member.

George Andersen and his client Ida Rothstein. ***San Francisco History Center, San Francisco Public Library.***

Chapter Six

George R. Andersen

The photo found prior to this chapter shows George Andersen as a young attorney in a courtroom. He is standing next to Ida Rothstein an "alleged communist leader" and client. The photo is reproduced with the permission of the San Francisco History Center.

IN HIS OWN WORDS

In the 1930s, during the depths of the Great Depression, the U.S. government was busy imprisoning and deporting alleged Communists. George Andersen represented many of those charged and in one case he stood up in court and insisted that a client who had been jailed for five days be tried immediately (*San Francisco Examiner* 1934). The judge ordered Andersen to sit down but did set an early trial date. In another criminal trial Andersen irritated the judge when he demanded a jury trial for his clients (*San Francisco Examiner* 1933). In yet another case Andersen was threatened with contempt of court charges after he shouted that a trial of labor activists "was a frame-up on the part of shipping interests [that] 'contributed to a fund to capture and prosecute the . . . defendants'" (*San Francisco Examiner* 1936a). During this same trial Andersen accused the District Attorney, Earl Warren, of pressuring potential jurors. This prompted the judge to cite, and then clear, Andersen of contempt charges (*San Francisco Examiner* 1936b).

In 1957 Andersen defended members of the California Labor School who were charged with violating the McCarran Act. The school had set up a branch in Los Angeles called the "School of Jewish Studies" and offered courses on "Negro history" and "Jewish history." Aubrey Grossman, one of Andersen's law partners, was named as affiliated with the school and for some reason it was noted that the school held a Christmas bazaar. The Subversive Activities Control Board decided that the California Labor School must register with the Attorney General as a Communist front organization. [Subversive Activities Control Board, Docket No. 115–55 Report and Order of the Board] [Internal Security Act of 1950 (McCarran Act)]. The government claimed that the California Labor School taught the Marxist-Leninist position that "no changes of society of an important kind take place except by revolution." Andersen argued that the McCarran Act violated the First Amendment to the Constitution in that it interfered with "free education, speech, press and public dissemination of ideas."

In 1956 as Andersen defended the California Labor School before a U.S. Subversive Activities Control Board a government witness said she believed that "she had seen him at [Communist] meetings, but she was not positive." "She's a liar," Andersen told reporters (*San Francisco Chronicle* 1956a).

In hearings before the House of Representatives Committee on Un-American Activities (86th Congress, Second Session 1960) Andersen answered why his client, Archie Brown, was not present to testify. "If you recall, he was ejected from the meeting yesterday morning. I don't believe he was allowed in this morning, either. He has twice tried to get into this room and each time he has been refused. I am going to tell the committee this: Unless they let him in that door, the next time he comes there with me, I am going to tell him to go home." To say the least, George Andersen was an assertive and fearless representative for his clients.

Andersen ran for public office on several occasions. On November 5, 1935, he appeared on the ballot for a San Francisco municipal judge position. Andersen stated that he was well qualified for the post because "as a believer in labor's cause and constitutional rights I have been for a number of years a defender of labor and political prisoners in court" (Declarations of Candidacy 1935). Also, on November 2, 1937, Andersen stood for election to the San Francisco Board of Supervisors. If elected, he pledged to work for "labor's constitutional rights; including the right to organize, strike and picket; a square deal for the unemployed; better and cheaper housing for all working people and opportunities in our schools where all children shall study the Constitution and the Declaration of Independence." The sponsors for his candidacy included men and women; homemakers, a nurse, a stevedore, a firefighter, a seaman, and three longshoremen (Declarations of Candidacy 1937). In 1943 a judge to whom Andersen had lost an election denied Andersen's request for confirmation of his U.S. citizenship (*San Francisco Examiner* 1943).

As early as 1934 Andersen said that he had been receiving threatening phone calls. He asked the police department to provide him with a guard or else let him carry a gun. Both requests were denied (*San Francisco Chronicle* 1934).

In 1949 Andersen represented alleged Communists at their deportation hearing. He said to the Chief Inspector at the hearing "I object to your interpreting anything in this hearing. You are incapable of fairly determining conclusions of fact and law in this case. You are biased against Communist Party Members." The Chief Inspector threw out the objections and would not let Andersen "question him about his personal views" (*San Francisco Chronicle* 1949). For his part, Andersen testified in a court hearing that he had not been a member of the Communist Party for "ten years" (*San Francisco Chronicle* 1956b). This admission of past Communist Party membership was undoubtedly red meat for his opponents.

IN THE WORDS OF OTHERS

George Andersen was born in Denmark in 1900 and died in San Francisco in 1965 (*San Francisco Examiner* 1965). He dropped out of school in the sixth grade and worked for a time as a laborer to help support his mother. During WWI Andersen worked as a journeyman boilermaker and had a reputation as "a damn good trade unionist" (*Dispatcher* 1966). In 1924 he served in the Air Force Reserve (California Historical Society n.d.). This, according to one of Andersen's sons, was to satisfy his interest in flying biplanes without personal cost (E-mail to John Galliher, August 30, 2010).

One of Andersen's sons noted that his father was not religious and seldom went to church. Even with his lack of formal education Andersen convinced the law school at the University of San Francisco, a night law school, to admit him. In 1927 he graduated alongside the late former governor Pat Brown and was admitted to the California Bar (State Bar of California). After getting his law license Andersen immediately took cases that were so unpopular he had trouble renting office space in San Francisco (E-mail to John Galliher, March 23, 2009).

In the aftermath of the 1934 San Francisco general strike "thanks to the daily dose of anti-Red poison administered to the public by the press, groups of business men . . . thugs, and super-patriots did exactly what the Reds had been accused of doing: they took the law into their own hands and indulged in violence" (Seldes 1937, 285). The mob broke into private homes and offices, confiscated and destroyed property ignoring all constitutional rights. The San Francisco police assisted the criminals by entering the damaged buildings, ". . . destroy[ing] . . . what was left undestroyed, and arrest[ing] . . . the victims, not the aggressors" (Seldes 1937, 286). In fact 400 "Reds" were imprisoned "but not one thug was touched." Even though he had been threatened by the vigilantes Andersen defended the accused Communists "demand[ing] jury trials." And "For this invocation of constitutional rights [the judge] . . . threatened him with contempt action" (Seldes 1937, 286). At about the same time Andersen appeared before another judge and again requested jury trials for his clients who, in this instance, were police raid victims. This second judge called Andersen's request "ridiculous." Andersen argued that his clients were arrested while engaging in "peaceable pursuits" and that "a mass trial would be illegal unless all had been arrested at the same time." The judge opined "these men are enemies of the state." Turning to Andersen he said "and if you talk too much, you will be held in contempt of court" (Virtual Museum of San Francisco n.d.; see also Selvin 1996, 217).

Also in 1934 while Andersen was entering a plea of innocence on behalf of a striking seaman the judge was so annoyed that he ordered the man returned to his cell. The irritated judge then pointed out that Andersen was "foreign born." In yet another early case Andersen represented 400 peach workers who were on strike and picketing. As a consequence of his efforts the relevant law "became the first local anti-picketing ordinance to be declared unconstitutional in the middle '30s" (*Dispatcher* 1966).

Andersen was frequently not paid for his efforts. "He didn't get his just due since it was a labor of love for him" (Raineri 1991, 91). In 1935 Andersen paid his own way to Hawaii to defend striking longshoremen protesting intolerable working conditions.

In January 1948 George Andersen survived being shot after two unknown men who barged into his office to threaten him with pistols. The *San Francisco Examiner*'s (1948a) inflammatory headline read "Gunman Shoots George Andersen, Lawyer for Reds." The police reported that ". . . it was the first known law firm holdup in San Francisco" (*San Francisco Chronicle* 1948). However, Andersen's law partner Richard Gladstein was sure that the motive was not robbery but intimidation since they had been threatened often for defending union members. After shooting Andersen in the shoulder and hitting him on the head with a gun the gunmen left without stealing anything. The gunmen were neither caught nor identified by law enforcement despite the offer of a cash reward from the Gladstein firm for information leading to their arrest and conviction (SFSU Labor Archives; Andersen FBI file 11/3/48, Section 3: 53; *San Francisco Examiner* 1948b).

In the year following Andersen's death his law partners held a memorial service for him in the Longshore Hall in San Francisco ("Memorial Meeting in Tribute to George Andersen" 1966; SFSU Archives). The opening tribute was given by Louis Goldblatt, Secretary-Treasurer of the ILWU. Goldblatt mentioned that George was born into poverty and did not want a funeral service since "he believed a man's life spoke for itself and no one could add to or detract from it. He had no use for the funeral service itself, considering it a contrived combination of custom and commercialism." Aubrey Grossman, Andersen's one-time law partner and fellow National Lawyers Guild member spoke next about Andersen's original law office. "He had no secretary. It wasn't really a lawyer's office. . . . One of these little compartments

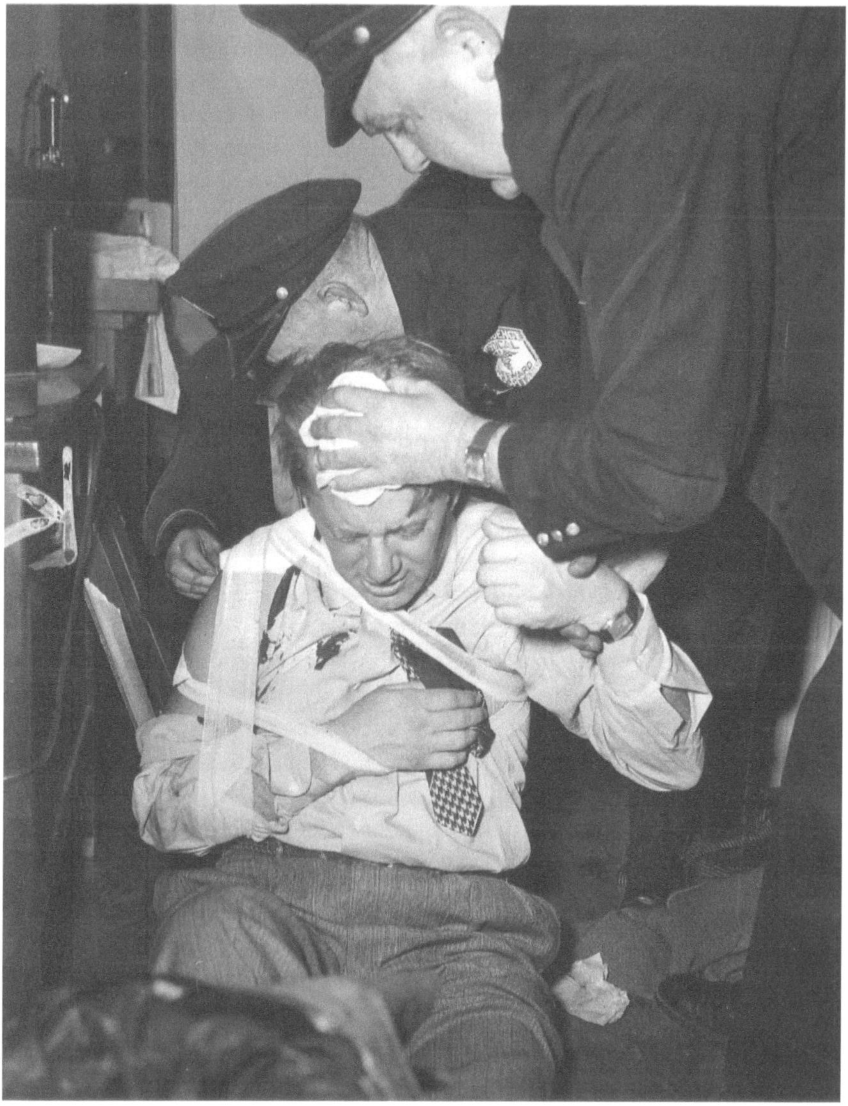

George Andersen shortly after he was attacked in his office. *San Francisco History Center, San Francisco Public Library.*

along a hallway. . . . He had . . . represent[ed] unpopular causes . . . [and his] law firm . . . had thrown him out." Next the head of the NAACP noted that Andersen was a partner in a firm that hired the first black lawyer. Then Harry Bridges spoke. He remembered that in 1935 his union sought to organize workers in Hawaii but they could not find a lawyer in the territory willing to represent the union workers so Andersen traveled there to provide representation. Finally Gladstein spoke. "Though George and I by temperament and background were different, and though each of us had created his own separate law firm, we traversed paths that were more or less parallel. So it would be no surprise that we should decide in the year 1945 to combine our forces." Andersen's obituary was prominently published in the ILWU *Dispatcher* (1966) and appropriately titled "George R. Andersen Dies; Devoted Legal Career to Rights of Workers."

FBI FILE FOR GEORGE ANDERSEN

Andersen's FBI file includes 669 pages (1940–1965). The FBI had recommended Andersen "for custodial detention pending investigation in the event of a national emergency" (5/17/41, HQ 100-2865, Section 1, 4). The Bureau referred to Andersen as "a 'bad egg' as far as communist agitation is concerned" (8/8/40, HQ 100-2865, Section 1, 1) and it considered its case against him to be "important to the Internal Security of the country" (07/6/50, HQ 100-2865, Section 1, 6). In a memo to the United States Attorney General (1/22/42, HQ 100-2865, Section 1, 44), FBI Director J. Edgar Hoover stated that Andersen's "connection with Communist Party activities in the San Francisco area makes him a most likely source of information on general Party affairs." The Bureau also noted that Andersen had served in the military (Air Reserve) from 1923 to 1926 and had been honorably discharged (2/4/43, HQ 100-2865, Section 1, 64). The FBI stated that Andersen "is not known to have served in World War II" and that he had not been asked to serve "due to his age, marital status and dependents" (5/1/64, HQ 100-2865, Section 6, 44). It was noted that his wife the physician Dr. Francis Foster was a "well known radical" (5/17/41, HQ 100-2865, Section 1, 5). Most of the FBI file, however, focuses on Andersen's legal practice.

Andersen's Legal Practice

In 1936 an FBI informant noted that Andersen is "Very active as an attorney for various communist leaders and reported to be the 'brains' behind Harry Bridges" (HQ 100-2865, Section 1, 2). A later file entry noted that Andersen had assisted other defense attorneys with the trial of Harry Bridges (7/25/50, 100-HQ-2865-June, Section 1, 3). In 1936 Andersen "[r]eceived 37,673 votes for Judge of the Municipal Court on the Labor Party ticket" and represented people in prison who were "visited by Communists regularly" (5/17/41, HQ 100-2865, Section 1, 8). In 1938 Andersen again ran for a Judge position this time at the Superior Court level (5/17/41, HQ 100-2865, Section 1, 8).

Andersen told an FBI Special Agent that he would not allow the Bureau to interview one of his clients unless the interview took place in his (Andersen's) office (1/28/53, HQ 100-2865, Section 3, 111). The file also indicated that Andersen represented William Schneiderman, the California State Secretary of the Communist Party when the government attempted to revoke Schneiderman's citizenship in the early 1940s (7/14/43, HQ 100-2865, Section 1, 71, 75). Andersen also represented Elmer Hanoff and Pete Bonilla, both of whom the government had tried to deport (2/4/43, HQ 100-2865, Section 1, 61; 3/23/53, HQ 100-2865, Section 3, 111). Other clients included California Communist Party officials Louise Todd, Anita Whitney, and Elsie Crane (08/26/41, HQ 100-2865, Section 1, 22 7/14/43, HQ 100-2865, Section 1, 76).

Opposition to Racism

An informant stated that Andersen wanted to help African Americans "in Welders Union, local 81" and it was noted that "thirty-five to forty-five per cent" of the Bethlehem shipyard welders were African American (8/12/43, HQ 100-2865, Section 1, 89). An informant also advised that Andersen's law firm represented African American boilermakers who had been "discharged from the Marinship Yards for failure to pay dues to an auxiliary union" (12/9/43, HQ 100-2865, Section 2, 29). The California courts ruled that the union must offer full membership to African Americans rather than relegating them to an auxiliary union (3/11/44, HQ 100-2865, Section 2, 34).[1] In this case the defendants were represented by Andersen, Herbert Resner, and Thurgood Marshall. Andersen and Resner eventually obtained "a California Supreme Court . . . ruling that any union which does not admit Negro workers to full union membership cannot enforce a closed shop contract" (6/13/46, HQ 100-2865, Section 3, 26).[2]

As an attorney for the International Labor Defense (ILD) Andersen handled the appeal of Festus Coleman, an African American man "convicted of rape and robbery in San Francisco" (7/14/43, HQ 100-2865, Section 1, 73). An April 8, 1942, *People's World* newspaper article noted that the San Francisco NAACP sponsored a "mass meeting" in support of Coleman, and Andersen was scheduled to speak at the meeting as a representative from the ILD (7/14/43, HQ 100-2865, Section 1, 73). Later that year another *People's World* article stated that Andersen supported a conference held by the "Coleman Defense Committee" with the aim of having Coleman pardoned. A third article stated that Andersen was on a "Delegation Committee" that was assembling "a petition to the California State Advisory Board" in support of Coleman (7/14/43, HQ 100-2865, Section 1, 73). FBI informants claimed "that the Coleman Defense Committee was organized and . . . controlled by the Communist Party" (7/14/43, HQ 100-2865, Section 1, 73).

Andersen was also involved with the Civil Rights Congress (CRC) an organization which appeared on the Attorney General's List of Subversive Organizations (AGLOSO) [7/15/52, HQ 100-2865, Section 3,102]. Andersen served on the CRC's Bail Bond Committee (7/15/52, HQ 100-2865, Section 3,100) and donated money to this organization (10/12/53, HQ 100-2865, Section 3, 116).

Was George Andersen a Communist?

J. Edgar Hoover noted that Andersen ". . . is undoubtedly one of the outstanding Communists on the West Coast and the fact that he is generally consulted with reference to important Party matters indicates that a technical surveillance on Andersen is likely to be particularly productive in keeping us informed on policies of the Party" (2/17/42, HQ 100-2865, Section 1, 44). It was claimed that Andersen is "consulted on legal and financial matters for the [Communist] Party" and that he had represented the Party "since 1935 or 1936" (7/25/50, 100-HQ 100-2865, June, Section 1, 2). The FBI would later state that they were reluctant to interview Andersen as doing so "would embarrass the Bureau in view of his hostility" (2/26/65, HQ 100-2865, Section 6, 47).

The file noted that Andersen was a member of the "Communist Party in San Francisco" as well as the "Hay Market Branch of the Party" for which he was the Financial Director and "People's World Drive Director" (1/2/48, HQ 100-2865, Section 3, 47). It was also mentioned that the Communist Party had paid for Andersen to attend law school (7/25/50, 100-HQ 100-2865, June, Section 1, 2). The FBI stated that Andersen appeared as a sponsor on letterhead supporting Walter Lambert, a Communist Party candidate for Congress (7/14/43, HQ100-2865, Section 1, 71). On June 10, 1953, a confidential informant stated that a meeting of the "Bay Area Committee to Save the Rosenbergs" was to be held at Andersen's home (10/12/53, HQ 100-2865, Section 3, 119). Another informant stated that this organization was supported by the Communist Party (10/12/53, HQ 100-2865, Section 3, 118). It was later noted that Julius and Ethel Rosenberg were "legally executed" on June 19, 1953 (6/24/58, HQ 100-2865, Section 5, 61).

The FBI also noted that Andersen was involved with the Northern California Committee for the Protection of Foreign Born (NCCPFB) and that he was scheduled to be the master of ceremonies for an event sponsored by this organization on November 16, 1963 (3/6/64, HQ 100-2865, Section 6, 24–25). The NCCPFB was linked to the American Committee for the Protection of Foreign Born (ACPFB), which was on the AGLOSO (8/16/63, HQ 100-2865, Section 6, 13). The FBI also mentioned that in September 1963 Andersen was listed as a "sponsor" on ACPFB stationery (3/6/64, HQ 100-2865, Section 6, 24). Andersen was also involved with the Russian American

Society (RAS), another organization which appeared on the AGLOSO (10/12/53, HQ-100-2865, Section 3, 116, 117). Andersen attended a banquet held by this organization and gave a speech "in which he praised the Russian people for their cultural contributions to the world and stated that whenever he encounters a reactionary who hates Russia and Russians he advises them to read Russian books or get acquainted with Russian culture" (10/12/53, HQ-100-2865, Section 3, 117-118).

Andersen was also accused of trying to help the Communist Party legally acquire arms (5/17/41, HQ 100-2865, Section 1, 4). In a 1939 *Peoples World* article Andersen was asked if he was a member of the Communist Party. He indicated that he was not but stated that Communist Party membership should not ". . . prevent a man from exercising his right of free speech" (1/3/47, HQ 100-2865, Section 3, 38). In truth, as we have seen earlier, Andersen's own words indicate that he had been a member of the Party earlier in the decade.

Victim of Threats and Violence

In 1934 while representing accused Communists before a Municipal Court Judge Andersen asked to be relieved of his duties and requested assistance from the police. "'My life has been threatened' he said in a low shaken voice. 'I have been threatened by vigilantes'" (2/4/43, HQ 100-2865, Section 1, 62–63). A *San Francisco Examiner* article dated July 20, 1934, indicated that Andersen had approached the San Francisco Police Department on July 19 to ask for protection. Andersen told the police that vigilantes "said they were going to wreck my offices . . . and were going to take me for a ride from which I won't be able to walk back" (HQ 100-2865, Section 1: 61). A February 8, 1946, *Dispatcher* article noted that Andersen's representation of clients arrested during the 1934 West Coast Maritime Strike resulted in threats of "'hanging,' and additional promises to blow his office to smithereens" (6/13/46, HQ 100-2865, Section 3, 26). Theory became a reality on January 10, 1948. The San Francisco Police Department Records indicate that two armed men entered Andersen's law firm offices where Andersen struggled with one of the men trying to grab the man's gun. In the melee Anderson was shot allowing the men to escape (1/10/48, HQ 100-2865, Section 3, 53).

Claims of Sexual Indiscretions

A confidential informant noted that Andersen "has possibly engaged in illicit relations" with a woman living in Berkeley (2/4/43, HQ 100-2865, Section 1, 65). Andersen was also "[r]eported to be of low moral character and to have had illicit relations with different women" (2/4/43, HQ 100-2865, Section 1,

61). An informant later advised that Andersen was involved in an extramarital affair (7/24/44, HQ 100-2865, Section 2, 48).

DEATH

Andersen died in December, 1965. His obituary noted that since 1945 he had been associated with the firm of Gladstein, Andersen, and Leonard (*People's World* 1966).

CONCLUSION

There is no evidence that Andersen was required to keep in touch with a draft board during WWII. This is not surprising given his age and marital status at the outbreak of the war. Additionally, he had previously served in the military. Andersen was the poorest of all the partners during his youth, as well as in his early career prior to joining the Gladstein firm. He endured threats and assaults and until joining the Gladstein firm he had difficulty finding office space. On at least two occasions, Andersen was threatened with contempt of court by judges after requesting jury trials for his clients. His FBI file was shorter than that of Gladstein but twice the size of Leonard's. Two of Andersen's children became practicing attorneys. In a telephone conversation with John Galliher on July 18, 2012, one of Anderson's sons recalled that his father always "felt that the FBI was behind his assault in his office and that a rookie officer panicked when his father tried to fight back." George Andersen "was a guy who came up through labor and felt that labor was getting the short end of the stick. As soon as he graduated from law school he sued the metal workers union to which he belonged."

CHAPTER SUMMARY

George Andersen was born in Denmark in 1900 and he grew up poor. As a young man he worked as a laborer, a journeyman boilermaker, and served in the Air Force Reserve. While working as a boilermaker Andersen acquired a reputation as "a damn good trade unionist." In 1927 he became a lawyer after graduating from night law school at the University of San Francisco. Andersen began his career by taking unpopular cases and, as a result, was fired from a law firm and had difficulty finding office space. Andersen was an assertive and fearless advocate for his clients. He represented labor activists and accused Communists and was threatened with violence on numerous occasions. His clients included striking agricultural and longshore workers, Communist Party officials, African American boilermakers, police raid victims, the California Labor School, Harry Bridges, Archie Brown, Elmer Hanoff, Pete Bonilla, and William Schneiderman. In 1948 Andersen was assaulted and shot in his office by two unknown intruders who were never caught nor identified by law enforcement. Andersen spoke out against the McCarran Act and was threatened with contempt of court charges on several occasions including two instances in which he had demanded jury trials for his clients. In one landmark case Andersen's efforts resulted in "the first local anti-picketing ordinance to be declared unconstitutional during the middle '30s." Andersen believed in helping laborers and often received little compensation for his efforts. In at least one instance Andersen was accused of attending Communist Party meetings. He denied this but admitted that he had been a Communist Party member during the 1930s. Andersen ran for public office several times with the promise to help laborers. He stood up for the rights of workers and opposed racism. Thus he had a 669-page FBI file in which the Bureau relayed accusations of sexual indiscretions and accused him of being involved with various Communist organizations and organizations supported by Communists such as the Bay Area Committee to Save the Rosenbergs.

NOTES

1. See also *James v. Marinship Corp.*, 25 Cal. 2d 721 (1944).
2. Ibid.

Norman Leonard being escorted out of a hearing room. *San Francisco History Center, San Francisco Public Library.*

Norman Leonard relaxing in his office. *San Francisco State University Labor Archives and Research Center.*

Chapter Seven

Norman Leonard

The first photo found just prior to this chapter shows Norman Leonard being escorted out of a Congressional hearing by an aged federal employee. Leonard's FBI file contains a cropped version of this photo, which was published in *The Worker*. The caption reads: "Attorney Norman Leonard . . . counsel for the Intl. Longshoremen's and Warehousemen's Union (CIO), was forcibly ejected as he sought to advise client testifying at House labor subcommittee hearings in San Francisco" (12/7/48, 7). The second photo shows Leonard relaxing in his office. The first photo is reproduced courtesy of the San Francisco History Center at the San Francisco Public Library. The second photo can be found in the San Francisco State University archives.

EARLY LIFE

Norman Leonard was born in 1914 and died in 2006 (Costantinou 2006). He became the firm's writer and researcher. Leonard's parents were Eastern European Jews who immigrated to the United States and originally lived in the Bronx where Norman was born. Neither had much formal education and Leonard's father worked in the New York garment industry as a cutter. A Garment Workers' Union strike left the family without financial support and they all moved to Los Angeles just before Norman graduated from high school.

Leonard finished high school in Los Angeles and went to UCLA in 1930 majoring in political science. After UCLA Leonard went to Columbia University where he earned an MA in international relations and international law and then a law degree in 1938, receiving a scholarship and meeting his wife Marjorie there. She, too, was an attorney. As a law student Leonard was an editor of the *Columbia Law Review* (SFSU Labor Archives, Personal

Biography). Leonard was a life-long registered Democrat (SFSU Labor Archives). Unless otherwise cited, all the materials in this chapter can be found in the Norman Leonard oral history in the Bancroft Library, Berkeley, California.

JOINING THE GLADSTEIN LAW FIRM

Just as Norman was set to graduate from Columbia Law School his New York City lawyer friend Carol King told him about the Gladstein law firm in San Francisco. "I'd never heard of it." He made this contact and took the position in 1938. Carol King worked with Gladstein and others but was never a member of the firm.

LEONARD'S ROLE IN THE GLADSTEIN LAW FIRM

Leonard became the Gladstein firm's brief writer and Richard Gladstein was the courtroom litigator. As we noted in chapter 5, Leonard's first assignment with the firm was to defend Harry Bridges for contempt of court. With Leonard's help, Bridges was ultimately exonerated by the U.S. Supreme Court. In addition to his writing and research duties Leonard did a lot of industrial accident work since longshore and warehouse work was dangerous. Leonard was in awe of Richard Gladstein. "Richard was a brilliant cross-examiner, probably the best lawyer that I ever had the fortune to work with." Gladstein, Andersen, and Leonard "stayed that way for quite a while." By 1965 Leonard "was pretty much the chief counsel for the union" and he eventually referred to other union members as "brothers." In an April 28, 1987, address to the AFL-CIO lawyers in San Francisco Leonard reminisced about his career noting that he had primarily represented trade unions (SFSU Labor Archives).

DEFENDING PICKETERS

Early in his career Leonard convinced "the Appellate Department of the Alameda County Superior Court" to overturn an anti-picketing ordinance because it violated free speech rights. In 1939 the United Rubber Workers had gone on strike and were picketing in Emeryville, California. The president of the union was arrested for violating a local law prohibiting picketing. Leonard argued in the union official's defense that this ordinance was unconstitutional and on appeal the courts ultimately agreed.

By the time Leonard returned from WWII "the labor movement was chomping at the bit to get out from under wartime labor restrictions." In the late 1940s a group of telephone operators went on strike in San Francisco and

Leonard acted as their legal adviser. There was a massive picket line of women that the police could not handle and they turned to the union president to ask the crowd to disperse.

CLIENTS IN CALIFORNIA, NEVADA, HAWAII, AND ELSEWHERE

Leonard fought against deportation and supported naturalization for numerous people who had been in the United States for years but discovered that their countries of origin would not take them back. Leonard and Marge went to LA for several months to defend the leading Communists in California.

MILITARY SERVICE

Leonard enlisted in the Navy in 1942 and after 60 days of very basic training in such things as naval procedures and navigation he was commissioned an Ensign. Leonard recalled: "it . . . was very obvious then—we were fighting against Fascism, against dictatorships. We were fighting for what I believed to be—and still believe [to be]—a democratic form of government; I felt I ought to be supporting such a fight." This experience and explanation says a lot about this man. By April 1943 he was sent to Guadalcanal. When Mrs. Roosevelt made an official visit there in 1944 Leonard was assigned the duty of selecting an honor guard to escort her. He selected two black men from the steward's department (the only assignment available for African Americans at the time). Mrs. Roosevelt expressed her appreciation for having black men in the honor guard. Leonard was discharged in December 1945.

LEONARD'S ANALYSIS OF THE MCCARRAN ACT

Leonard's brainpower is clearly reflected in his "Analysis of the Internal Security Act of [November] 1950 (McCarran Act)" [Box 5, Folder 11 Southern California Archives]. He explains that a Communist front organization is one that uses its resources and personnel

> to further or promote the objectives of any Communist action organization, or the world Communist movement. The quoted phrase is ambiguous. An organization which uses its resources to advocate higher wages or the abolition of racial discrimination is clearly using its resources to further the objectives of the world Communist movement.

Officers of such organizations who failed to register were subjected to a fine of $10,000, 5 years in prison, or both. Moreover "Each day of failure constitutes a separate offense." Functionaries of law enforcement such as judges, jurors, or witnesses were protected from pickets by a fine of $5000 or a year in prison or both.

> The indictment claims that by agreeing to teach and advocate the principles of Marxism-Leninism, and by organizing the Communist Party for the purpose of teaching and advocating Marxism-Leninism, the defendants thereby agreed to teach and advocate force and violence to overthrow our government. But the law itself does not say that the Communist Party is illegal.

DEFENDING AUBREY GROSSMAN

Leonard also defended Aubrey Grossman, a law partner of his who vigorously represented his clients and thus ran afoul of some judges. Leonard became involved in a case where Grossman had been representing a group of Indians (Native Americans) who were arrested for trespassing on land allegedly owned by a power company that the Indians claimed had been stolen from them. Grossman was cited by the California State Bar Association for conduct unbecoming a lawyer after coming into conflict with the judge in the case. Leonard cross-examined the judge. Grossman refused to apologize. At the hearing Grossman brought in 100 Indians for the audience and probably as a consequence got just a "slap . . . on the wrist." With Leonard serving as Grossman's attorney the U.S. Supreme Court ultimately saved Grossman from disbarment in California (*San Francisco Examiner* 1974).

OTHER PROGRESSIVE CAUSES

Leonard strongly opposed various forms of bigotry. He noted the thinly veiled anti-Semitism of a Ninth Circuit Court of Appeals judge and opposed discrimination against gay people by Immigration and Naturalization and Alcohol Control laws. The Free Speech Movement at Berkeley involved 800 students, including Leonard's son Steve, and Leonard got involved in this way. Leonard "lashed out" at tape recordings made of hundreds of protesters on the Berkeley campus and the behavior of the police (*San Francisco Examiner* 1965).

San Francisco attracted Vietnam era selective service violators, and Leonard defended some of them in federal court. In 1969 Leonard published a column in the *San Francisco Chronicle* (May 29) titled "Answer to General Hershey" who had been quoted in the newspaper the previous day. As the director of the Selective Service System, General Hershey seemed upset by the fact that over 100 Bay Area attorneys were offering legal counsel to those charged with draft violations. The General suspiciously asked where all the fees were coming from and Leonard noted that most of the money came from the defendants themselves as well as from their friends and lawyers.

FBI FILE FOR NORMAN LEONARD

Leonard's Legal Practice

Leonard's FBI file (1947–1973) includes 378 pages and focuses on his legal practice. The file noted that Leonard "is a member of the Hay-Market Branch of the Communist Party in San Francisco and in 1946, pledged $50.00 per month as a sustainer to the Party through this Club. . . . [His] law firm is composed almost entirely of members of the Communist Party and specializes in labor law. They also handle all of the legal work of the Communist Party" (12/16/47, 4, 5). Similar to George Andersen, Leonard was designated "for apprehension by [the FBI] . . . in the event of a national emergency" (11/20/50, 16). The FBI believed that if such an event were to occur, Leonard ". . . would [not] be sympathetic with the aims of the U.S. Government" (10/25/57, 96). Also similar to Andersen, the FBI noted that an interview with Leonard "might prove embarrassing to the Bureau" (10/8/58, 116).

The file confirmed that on October 22, 1948, while defending the ILWU during a Congressional hearing led by Representative Charles Kersten, Leonard "was removed from the court room by the United States Marshal" after "loudly and angrily" protesting that a client's "constitutional rights were being violated" (6/10/49, 10; 6/2/54, 50, 51). Leonard gave a speech to the California Labor School on October 17, 1950, in which he stated that the California Loyalty Oath "was unconstitutional and violated one's civil rights" (5/14/51, 20). And in 1951 Leonard was scheduled to lead a California Labor School workshop to "*help progressive people meet the attacks of employer-dominated courts and Un-American committees*" (12/14/60, 151, italics in original). The California Labor School had been classified by the Attorney General as a "subversive organization" (5/14/51, 20).

In 1950 Leonard gave a speech to the Northern California Committee for the Protection of Foreign Born (NCCPFB) in which he noted that the McCarran Act was unconstitutional (6/2/54, 52). He also provided the NCCPFB with legal assistance (11/18/66, 326) and was honored at dinners sponsored by this organization in 1954 (6/2/54, 52) and 1962 (10/22/62, 250). An FBI informant noted that the NCCPFB was involved in "defending the foreign born in deportation proceedings and in securing support for the repeal of the Walter-McCarran Law" (10/22/62, 251). The NCCPFB was also affiliated with the American Committee for the Protection of Foreign Born, which, like the California Labor School, was classified by the Attorney General as a "subversive organization" (6/2/54, 51). Other "subversive organizations" with which Leonard was involved include the Civil Rights Congress (6/10/

49, 9; 5/14/51, 20) and the Joint Anti-Fascist Refugee Committee (6/2/54, 49–50). Leonard additionally held a leadership role in the Citizens Committee to Preserve American Freedoms (CCPAF), which the HUAC had labeled as a Communist front organization (4/20/62, 239; 12/3/63, 271). The FBI stated that the CCPAF ". . . specializes in propaganda aimed at abolishing the Committee on Un-American Activities and discrediting the Federal Bureau of Investigation" (12/3/63, 271). Leonard was also involved with the Committee to Secure Justice for the Rosenbergs, which an FBI informant claimed was supported by the Communist Party (6/2/54, 38; 6/2/54, 47).

Leonard "was sworn in as a defense attorney at the [Los Angeles] bail hearing [for] . . . the Smith Act defendants" (11/13/51, 32) and he handled the appeal when the ILWU was ordered to pay $750,000 in damages (6/2/54, 51). An entry in Leonard's file noted: "Subject has furnished valuable assistance to the . . . [Communist Party] by defending, in court, Harry Bridges . . . [as well as] the ILWU in a damage suit in 1951 . . . [and] the Smith Act defendants in Los Angeles" (5/31/55, 64). Additionally, Leonard represented seamen in a successful challenge to ". . . the U.S. Coast Guard's 'screening program'" (10/25/57, 96), as well as an individual accused of violating the Taft Hartley Act (5/31/55, 66). Leonard also represented the National Union of Marine Cooks and Stewards (12/14/60, 151) and he helped to free on bail a person "convicted . . . of harboring a communist fugitive" (10/3/56, 86).

In 1956 and 1957 Leonard attended House Committee on Un-American Activities (HUAC) meetings in San Francisco where he represented witnesses who had invoked the Fifth Amendment and refused to testify. Also, in 1957 he served as counsel in a deportation case based on '"past Communist Party membership'" (10/25/57, 95).

Testimonials

On March 23, 1958, Leonard gave a talk at a reception honoring Oleta Yates "for the stand she took when tried under the Smith Act in refusing to identify other members of the Communist Party" (10/8/58, 108). Leonard's FBI file included a copy of a letter that he wrote praising the 400 people who attempted to persuade Congress to abolish the HUAC. This effort, Leonard felt, was at least partially due to the "magnificent" advertisement in the January 2, 1961, *Washington Post* which included the name of Eleanor Roosevelt among other dignitaries (5/4/61, 211). Leonard also attended a reception honoring Frank Wilkinson who served 9 months in prison for opposing the HUAC (4/20/62, 240). Leonard was "master of ceremonies" at a January 30, 1965, event sponsored by the *People's World* newspaper, which the FBI labeled "a west coast communist dominated and controlled weekly publication" (12/8/65, 304, 306). During the event Leonard introduced, among others, Bettina Aptheker, a Berkeley student and leader of the campus Free Speech Movement that began in the fall of 1964 (12/8/65, 305, 307).

Leonard was also involved in Vietnam Summer to oppose the military draft law and on August 22, 1967, he attended a meeting where he explained the law, discussed how it works, and noted "exemptions, amendments . . . and changes" (11/21/67, 354). That same year Leonard was scheduled to discuss "Judicial Review of Selective Service Orders" at a conference on Selective Service Laws sponsored by the National Lawyers Guild (11/21/67, 353). And Leonard helped to file motions in federal court challenging the constitutionality of the draft law (11/15/68, 365). An FBI informant claimed that Leonard "was active in youth groups of the Communist Party and was forming academic freedom groups in the various law schools in the San Francisco Bay area [sic]" (5/14/51, 18).

Leonard's file included a copy of a December 9, 1961, *People's World* article titled "High Court Edict to be Dramatized." The article announced an upcoming reenactment of the U.S. Supreme Court's 5–4 decision to ban the Communist Party under the McCarran Act. The reenactment was to take place in San Francisco on December 15 and Leonard would portray Justice Hugo Black (12/7/61, 231).

Military Service

On December 1, 1942, Leonard "was commissioned as an Ensign in the U.S. Naval Reserve" (12/16/47, 5) and on November 24, 1945, "[h]e was detached from active duty as a Lieutenant" (12/16/47, 5). While in the Navy, Leonard worked as a Legal Officer handling court martials. Leonard's efficiency reports noted his "outstanding record as a defense attorney" (8/29/47, 2). On February 2, 1953, the *Daily People's World* indicated that Leonard requested an injunction from the Federal District Court in San Francisco to stop "the Navy from conducting a 'loyalty hearing' against him . . . [since] witnesses against him . . . would not be testifying under oath, and he would be unable to cross-examine them." An unfavorable verdict could have led to the loss of his reserve commission and veteran's rights even after having served "18 months on active duty at Guadalcanal." Leonard resigned from the Navy "under honorable conditions . . . on September 30, 1953" (6/2/54, 44).

U.S. NAVY FILE FOR NORMAN LEONARD

The U.S. Navy also kept a file on Norman Leonard and 25 pages of it were released. One page duly noted his legal practice with the Gladstein firm whose members were all "well known Northern California Communists." Another entry noted that a neighborhood investigation was conducted and it was determined that Leonard had campaigned for a Communist nominee in an election and one neighbor believed that Leonard had a "definite Communist outlook." A third entry observed that the partners in the Gladstein firm subscribed to the *People's World*, a Communist newspaper and that they were members of the National Lawyers' Guild.

CONCLUSION

By all accounts Leonard was the most mild-mannered of the three law partners. The records indicate that he was neither threatened with disbarment nor by thugs, nor was he shot or imprisoned. He was the only partner who served in the military during WWII. He was a Naval officer stationed primarily in Guadalcanal. Yet Leonard did not flinch from defending Harry Bridges and other labor union members accused of being Communists. Leonard defended those accused of violating the 1940 Smith Act as well as the 1950 McCarran Act. At least early in his career he was primarily a brief writer and legal researcher. In a 2012 e-mail to John Galliher Leonard's last law partner recalled their first meeting in 1980 noting that Leonard was a quiet and reserved man in his late 60s. He was tall and erect and had "longish" white hair and a white beard. While Leonard was a person of few words he had enormous personal dignity and in working with him his law partner learned that he was a brilliant legal theorist who had several U.S. Supreme Court victories to his credit.

CHAPTER SUMMARY

Norman Leonard was born in 1914 to working class Eastern European Jewish immigrant parents. Leonard grew up in New York and moved to Los Angeles during high school. He attended college at UCLA and later graduate and law school at Columbia University where he edited the law review and met his wife Marjorie. After graduating from law school in 1938 Leonard joined the Gladstein firm and worked primarily as a writer and researcher. Leonard defended Harry Bridges and other foreign nationals whom the U.S. government had tried to deport. He also did industrial accident work eventually becoming "pretty much" the chief counsel for the ILWU. In one early case, Leonard helped to overturn an anti-picketing ordinance. He also defended accused Communists and workers who were picketing their employers including rubber workers and telephone operators. Leonard enlisted in the U.S. Navy in 1942 and was discharged in 1945. He felt that he was "fighting against Fascism" and supporting democracy. Leonard criticized the McCarran Act and defended his law partner Aubrey Grossman ultimately helping to save Grossman from disbarment. Leonard opposed anti-Semitism and discrimination against gay people and he supported the rights of student protestors at Berkeley. Leonard also defended Vietnam era selective service violators.

Leonard's 376-page FBI file focuses on his legal practice. It was noted that Leonard and most of his law partners are Communist Party members and that their firm specializes in labor law and provides the Party with legal assistance. The FBI wanted to arrest Leonard "in the event of a national emergency" but they were afraid that interviewing him may embarrass the Bureau.

Leonard was ejected from a 1948 Congressional hearing and he openly criticized the California Loyalty Oath and the McCarran Act. Additionally, he was involved with various organizations that the government had labeled "subversive" or "Communist." Leonard represented clients charged with Smith Act and Taft Hartley Act violations, as well as Harry Bridges, seamen screened by the Coast Guard, HUAC witnesses, and a former Communist whom the U.S. government had tried to deport. Leonard also represented the ILWU and the National Union of Marine Cooks and Stewards and he helped to free on bail a person "convicted of harboring a communist fugitive."

Leonard spoke at a reception for a Communist Party member, wrote a letter supporting HUAC protestors, and attended a reception honoring Frank Wilkinson who was imprisoned for opposing the HUAC. Additionally, Leonard was "master of ceremonies" at a *People's World* event during which he introduced the Berkeley Free Speech activist Bettina Aptheker. Leonard also opposed the Vietnam draft, explained the draft law at a meeting, and challenged the law in court. An informant claimed that Leonard was involved in Communist Party youth groups and helped to set up "academic freedom groups" at local law schools. The file also contains an article noting that Leonard was scheduled to participate in a reenactment of the U.S. Supreme Court's decision to ban the Communist Party under the McCarran Act.

Leonard's FBI file noted that he was affiliated with the Northern California Committee for the Protection of Foreign Born, the Civil Rights Congress, the Joint Anti-Fascist Refugee Committee, the Citizens Committee to Preserve American Freedoms, and the Committee to Secure Justice for the Rosenbergs.

Leonard was a Legal Officer in the U.S. Navy from 1942 to 1945. Even though his performance was "outstanding" and he had served at Guadalcanal the Navy tried to subject him to a "loyalty hearing" which would have threatened his reserve commission and veteran's rights.

Leonard's Navy file stated that his law partners were Communists, he had campaigned for a Communist politician, and one of his neighbor's believed that he had a "communist outlook." The file also noted that the Gladstein law partners subscribed to the *People's World* and were members of the National Lawyers Guild.

Richard Gladstein looking out of his apartment window *Southern California Library*

A young Richard Gladstein ***Southern California Library***

A young Richard Gladstein ***San Francisco History Center, San Francisco Public Library***

Chapter Eight

Richard Gladstein

The first three photos found just prior to this chapter show 1) Richard Gladstein from his apartment window, probably in the late 1930s, 2) a commercial photo of Gladstein, and 3) another photo of him in formal courtroom attire. Unless otherwise cited, all of the information in this chapter can be found in the Southern California Library Archives.

Richard Gladstein lived from 1908 to 1981 (*Dispatcher* 1981). He was born in Connecticut and his mother and father began as factory workers. Gladstein attended high school in Oakland and later worked his way through college at the University of California (Box A, Folder 4). In 1931 he graduated with top honors from Boalt Hall Law School at the University of California and passed the California Bar exam. Gladstein initially sought employment at the Alameda County District Attorney's office but their quota for Jews had already been met (Stein 1975). So he practiced law in a firm until late 1935 or early 1936 when the firm's partners told him that he would have to give up defending labor unions or find employment elsewhere (Stein 1975). So in the fall of 1936 Gladstein started his own firm with Aubrey Grossman (Kutler 1978) and later acquired additional partners including George Andersen and Norman Leonard. Gladstein became "one of the first labor lawyers in San Francisco" (*Dispatcher* 1974). During his career he was arrested for picketing and (as we will discuss later) sentenced by Federal Judge Harold Medina to 6 months in federal prison for contempt of court. Like George Andersen and Norman Leonard, Gladstein was a member of the Progressive National Lawyers Guild.

MAJOR CASES

Gladstein defended Harry Bridges three times from 1938–1955 (1938–1939, 1941–1945, and 1955) and was Bridges' Chief defense counsel in 1939. In 1936 Gladstein successfully defended picketers in Oakland, California, and in 1937 he obtained a federal court injunction prohibiting employers' use of a blacklist against protesting lettuce pickers in the Salinas Valley. In 1938 Gladstein secured NLRB certification of the ILWU as a legal representative for all west coast longshore workers and in 1940 he won a U.S. Supreme Court decision protecting the right to peaceful picketing. In 1946 Gladstein won $1.5 million in back pay for plantation workers in Hawaii and he successfully defended the California CIO against a $3 million libel suit. In 1948 Gladstein successfully defended John Caughlan, a Seattle labor lawyer accused of perjury for denying his membership in the Communist Party (Box A, Folder 4). Also in 1948 Gladstein handled the Reinecke hearing in Hawaii, a case involving two schoolteachers, one of whom was indicted under the Smith Act, and both of whom lost their jobs after being accused of holding Communist Party membership. And in 1949 Gladstein was a defense counsel for 11 Communist Party leaders tried under the Smith Act in New York before Federal Judge Harold Medina. This is when Medina cited Gladstein for contempt and sentenced him to six months in federal prison. The contempt conviction forced Gladstein to withdraw from defending Bridges against another government deportation attempt. Gladstein defended Bridges one last time in 1955.

WORLD WAR II

The May 11, 1941, edition of the *San Francisco Chronicle* noted that Gladstein "Is Almost in the Army." The San Francisco State University Labor Archives and Research Center includes a December 30, 1941, letter from Gladstein to his San Francisco Draft Board indicating his presence in San Francisco and his registration number. On August 29, 1943, Gladstein's Draft Board classified him as 3A due to his four children, and he was reclassified as 2A on April 27, 1945, but reclassified again to 4A on September 15, 1945.

BEGINNING DEFENSE WORK

Gladstein's correspondence tells us something about his personality and his skill as an attorney. Gladstein wrote to Judge Leon Gray (12/22/36): "It is clear from case law that an employer will not be granted an injunction against peaceful picketing conducted in connection with a strike. Such ordinances are only adopted through requests or pressure of employer's organizations." The judge agreed (*San Francisco Chronicle* 1937).

Gladstein wrote to a San Francisco union official:

> Here is my position. While I am very glad to have the cases against six of our union people dismissed, I feel that the two others likewise should be dismissed. Refusal to dismiss these two cases is nothing short of discrimination against the C.I.O., since it places the District Attorney on record as dismissing all cases for which the A.F. of L. is responsible, but makes a distinction against the C.I.O. (11/3/38)

Gladstein continued: "Please see what you can do to pull the District Attorney into line. Frankly, if I am compelled to go to trial in the two remaining cases, I will . . . point out to the jury that A.F. of L. people receive favors from the Police Department and the District Attorney, whereas C.I.O. people are made the goats" (11/30/38).

A letter to colleague Carol King on 10/21/43 shows Gladstein's playful side:

> I earnestly hope your health permits you to keep up on the Bridges brief. Sulfa is a wonderful drug, except that you have to drink an enormous amount of liquid, none of which may contain spirits. It seems a terrible waste to use so much of one's capacity to consume liquid without being allowed to have liquor. (Bridges folder 10, box 8)

The following year Gladstein wrote to King: "If Harry should seek successfully to enlist in the U.S. Army what do you think the chances would be of obtaining citizenship?" (March 28, 1944 Bridges file 11, box 8).

Gladstein had a friend in high places and received a personal letter from San Francisco District Attorney Pat Brown thanking him for his support during Brown's successful run for California Attorney General (9/10/46). In 1958 Gladstein received two letters from the Pat Brown for Governor campaign thanking him for his endorsement and financial support (March 17, April 16, unfiled papers).

NERVES OF STEEL

In 1941 at a deportation hearing for Harry Bridges Gladstein laughed at a government lawyer's claim that he was a member of the Communist Party. Gladstein said "I certainly deny it and you are a fool" (*San Francisco Examiner* 1941). Gladstein wrote a Supplement to Memorandum of Respondent (California District Court):

> peaceful picketing was conducted by two labor unions to induce the operators of a grocery store not to remain open for business on Sundays. History teaches us that when those rights are suspended, the right to possess and enjoy private property rapidly vanishes. Peaceful picketing is a fundamental right protected by the federal and the state constitutions.

This was in response to the government's assertion that picketing was not a constitutional right since it was not explicitly mentioned in the federal or state constitution. Gladstein had warned the picketers as follows:

> Dear Sirs and Brothers:
> Almost 50 warehousemen and students were arrested for picketing the Berkeley Woolworth store in connection with a strike in September, 1936. We want to remind you that only the peaceful picketing portions of the ordinance were involved in this case. Police officers can still interfere with picketing by falsely charging intimidation, threats, or coercion.

Gladstein's early prominence is reflected in the fact that he was asked to speak at the 1943 National Lawyers Guild Convention in Chicago (2/20/43). Gladstein noted (Bridges folder 9 box 8):

> There are workers in war industries chafing against enforced idle time, seeing machines go unused, having their skill wasted; having one's sex or the color of one's skin remaining a bar to participation in the country's production fight. The singling out of this man Harry Bridges for hounding and persecution over a long period is a great problem. We are at war with fascism and all that it means in the way of shackling the human brain. The decision against Bridges is a blow to free thought. The longshoremen have stopped work 35 times in protest against the shipment of war supplies to Japan.

On October 28, 1955, the National Lawyers Guild asked the U.S. Supreme Court to prohibit the U.S. Attorney General from placing it on the list of subversive organizations (Southern California Library Archives).

LITIGATORS ARE MORE AT RISK

Strident words were sometimes spoken in court by Gladstein. Though they could have been written by George Andersen or Norman Leonard Gladstein's passion always shows through. Gladstein went to Hawaii to defend those in a Smith Act prosecution that involved the "development of the ILWU and the smashing of feudalism in Hawaii" (Leonard 1986). Husband and wife schoolteachers John and Aiko Reinecke had been fired after their school district accused them of holding membership in "a secret society called the Communist Party . . . and [claiming that] there is reasonable doubt as to their loyalty to the United States" (*Honolulu Star Bulletin* 1999). John

Reinecke and six others were soon indicted by the HUAC under the Smith Act which banned "advocate[ing] and teach[ing] the necessity of overthrowing the government of the United States by force and violence" (*Honolulu Star Bulletin* 1999). The defendants were arrested by the FBI in August 1951 and following a nearly two-year trial, all were convicted. (This verdict was later overturned by the U.S. Supreme Court.) In a radio address Gladstein linked the case to attempts by "powerful forces in this country to destroy democracy" (*Dispatcher* 1948).

Gladstein made an opening statement in Hawaii on the nature of the American Communist Party (Box 1, Folder 2). The Communist Party desires

> the establishment of Socialism by the free choice of the majority of the American people. Reactionaries blame war on the Soviet Union. But it is absurd to assert that this Socialist, war-ravaged country wants war. The American people are already paying through the nose for Wall Street's insane imperialistic adventures. [Gladstein stated that the United States should] Withdraw American troops from Korea and break diplomatic and economic ties with Franco's Spain and abandon economic, political and military pressures on the countries of Latin America. The Communist Party demands a capital levy on big fortunes and corporations to finance essential social legislation. The destruction of the rights of Communists is the classical first step down the road to fascism. The Communist Party demands that the Ku Klux Klan be outlawed and defends the right of the Negro people to full representation in government. Here in Hawaii, this local witch hunt is being organized by powerful economic interests.

These words reflect both the courage and character of Richard Gladstein.

Gladstein's brief for the Hawaii case reads in part: "That the Communist Party of the United States seeks the establishment of Socialism in this country does not in any way render its existence as a political party illegal." Article I, Section 2 of the U.S. Constitution provides that citizens "have the right to alter or reform the same [government] whenever the public good may require it. Without constitutional merit, let alone factual merit, therefore, would be the argument that the Communist Party of the United States is a conspiracy simply because its aims coincide closely with that of Communist Parties of other nations" (Memorandum of Law in Support of Proposition that Engaging in Activities in or Being a Member of the Communist Party of the United States is Protected by Labor Code, Box 1 Folder 15).

Then there is Gladstein's cross-examination of Louis Francis Budenz, a former Communist Party member and government witness in Hawaii (Southern California Archives, 8/7/48):

Gladstein laid a trap for Budenz.

Q. "You wouldn't think it was any evidence of Communism if a public school teacher in Hawaii, in a matter of social studies simply sets forth the contents of the law, by way of analysis without expressing his own views one way or the other, correct?"

A. "Correct."

Q. "But would you agree that the American people have the right to create, form or support whatever political party they see fit to support?"

A. "Yes, except that they certainly have no right to support a party which is nothing but an appendage to a foreign dictatorship."

Q. "Isn't it true that the Communist Party teaches that when the majority of the people want to change from capitalism to socialism, that it can be done peacefully, that would be preferable and desirable?"

A. "They teach that it is inevitable that there will be a shattering of the government by violence."

Q. "Isn't it a fact that when you were in the Communist Party you were taught that according to Lenin there could only be a revolution that the people of that particular country would make and carry through?"

A. "That phraseology was used at one time but, it has now been amended."

Q. "Isn't it true that there are lots of people in the Communist Party who are perfectly good loyal Americans?"

A. "A Communist cannot be a loyal American."

Q. "Do you agree that the American people have a right to revolutionize our society, that is, to change it from capitalism to socialism?"

A. "They have that right."

Q. "As long as the American people have freedom, liberty, democratic rights, they certainly would be opposed to any idea of revolution. Correct?"

A. "They would indeed."

Gladstein set up a situation where the government witness was forced to agree that revolution would never occur in a just society.

Richard Gladstein Goes to Prison

In 1949 Gladstein defended the leaders of the New York Communist Party who were prosecuted under the Smith Act for advocating the violent overthrow of the U.S. government. Since this trial overlapped with the third Bridges deportation trial he could not assist with Bridges' defense (*San Francisco Chronicle* 1949c; Kennedy 1981).

The New York trial was very combative on both sides. A government prosecutor cross-examined one defendant on the theory of Marxism and Leninism but got nowhere with this line of attack. The trial ended on October 14, 1949.

As noted earlier, following the trial, Federal Judge Harold Medina cited Gladstein for contempt of court and sentenced him to six months in prison beginning on November 15, 1949. A divided Supreme Court affirmed the conviction. Three Supreme Court Justices agreed with the defense that the conviction was a violation of freedom of speech (Civil Rights Congress 1952). Gladstein stated that the conviction was a product of "the political nature of the case" rather than actual contempt in the courtroom (*Dispatcher* 1949). He argued that "By attacking the freedom of those who defend the civil rights of others, there is created a sinister intimidation against free thinking and plain speaking" (*Dispatcher* 1949).

Following his contempt conviction but before going to prison Gladstein spoke at a public school in Berkeley. A member of the local Republican women's club tried unsuccessfully to prevent Gladstein from speaking since schools should "be used to keep the highest loyalty to our country" (*San Francisco Chronicle* 1949b).

Gladstein began serving his contempt sentence on April 24, 1952, ultimately spending 6 months in federal prison (*San Francisco Chronicle* 1952; 1955b).[1] He was transported to prison in leg irons and held incommunicado as might be appropriate for a convicted mass murderer. ILWU local 3 protested this "humiliating treatment" of a man of "calm logic and peaceful nature" (*Dispatcher* 1952). Gladstein's imprisonment was publicly opposed by several hundred attorneys (*Recorder* 1950; Folder 9 Box 5).

When Gladstein was released from prison he was welcomed back to his law practice by leaders of the ILWU referring to him as "Brother Gladstein" (9/29/52). However, during the first year after he was released from prison he could not assist with Bridges' defense because of the stigma associated with the contempt conviction. Gladstein remarked that he had to forego working on Bridges' criminal case "because it would obviously be to . . . [Bridges'] detriment to have Richard Gladstein, who had just been convicted of contempt in a case involving communists come and defend Harry whose defense was that he was not a communist" (Kutler 1978, 30).

Richard Gladstein's argument to the jury in the New York Communist trial was prophetic:

> They are on trial for conspiring to raise against our government, not their arms, but their voices to criticism. If these men can be imprisoned for conspiring to speak what some people regard as dangerous thoughts, then you and I and most Americans will no longer be secure. Because, who is to say that what you express will not by someone be thought to be dangerous or improper or unlawful. It is altogether unique in American history to place on trial in a courtroom a body of thoughts upon which an entire political party is founded. It has been the American tradition always to place political parties and their program on trial, but not in a court; they go on trial in the public arena of political debate to be accepted or rejected by the free choice of the American people expressed at

> the ballot box. Discrimination means men being burned because, when they worship their God, they read from the Talmud or the Old Testament; or being lynched because their skin pigmentation is dark.

Gladstein thus raised the specter of racism.

During the New York trial Richard Gladstein wrote about his reasons for defending the accused Communist leaders: "I regard this case and the consequent attack on the Bill of Rights as the most important civil liberties issue in America today. If the liberties of my clients are taken away, the liberties of all Americans are in jeopardy. In Germany the process began with the destruction of the rights of Communists; it ended with the Holocaust" (SFSU Labor Archives Richard Gladstein Member of Defense Counsel to 11 Communist Leaders 10/10/49). Gladstein further stated that he had represented the Communists because "the defense of every group and minority is my bounden duty as a lawyer" (*Dispatcher* 1949). In 1951, Gladstein became involved in another Smith Act case when he assisted with the defense of 12 California Communist leaders who had been indicted by a federal grand jury (*San Francisco Chronicle* 1951).

In 1952 a federal judge in Hawaii sought to have Gladstein disbarred due to his New York conviction but the judge was disqualified on grounds of prejudice (*San Francisco Chronicle* 1955a). As a result of the Hawaii action the State of California also attempted to have Gladstein disbarred (Kutler 1978). Both attempts were unsuccessful (Wiecek 2006).

During the 1955 trial of Harry Bridges Gladstein had the following exchange with the federal prosecutor, Mr. Gillard (Southern California Archives, Bridges Folder 20, Box 17):

> Mr. Gladstein: "Is it not true that you at no time said that you had told the government agent that you were collecting money from Bridges as Communist Party dues?"
>
> Mr. Gillard: "I object to the question as calling for an opinion and conclusion of the witness."
>
> Mr. Gladstein: "I am seeking to establish as fact that he did not say these things in the deposition."
>
> The Court: "I will sustain the objection."

Even without the support of the judge in this case, Gladstein prevailed.

In 1956 an American Bar Association representative wrote to Gladstein asking him to join the ABA (June 6, 1956). Gladstein declined the offer for two reasons. He mentioned in passing the history of racism at the ABA but saved his most biting criticism for its current practices. To be qualified to join the ABA it was necessary to answer if the "applicant had ever been disbarred or whether or not he had ever been affiliated with the Communist Party or any other subversive organization." Gladstein wrote: "If your organization should decide to abandon these inquiries that I regard as inappropriate, I will be most happy to complete the application" (June 11, 1956). The ABA didn't budge nor did Gladstein.

Gladstein's closing argument in the defense of Seattle, Washington attorney, John Caughlan on September 23, 1948 (Box 4 Folder 5), is worth considering.

> Here we have a charge against a man in the legal profession that he, when he took an oath to tell the truth, he didn't tell the truth. That makes it a very serious charge. A man can represent an association professionally and that doesn't make him a member of that organization. I don't care about any other relationship. I am talking about membership. One witness sees people in a Communist meeting, therefore they are members of the Communist Party. John Caughlan already had been for a year or so the attorney for the Communist Party and there was no secret about it. He was at the Moose Hall with a thousand to twelve hundred others. I went to High Mass some years ago. That didn't make me a Roman Catholic. It was also claimed that he was a fellow traveler with Communists. His law office door was always open to everybody. And so he represented certain elements in this city and in this state which some of you may dislike. But they have a right to legal representation. They have a right to have John Caughlan as their confidential adviser. And John has a right to practice law for organizations which the government's Canwell Committee calls Communist dominated or Communist front. John's fight against the Canwell Committee is because that committee follows an un-American practice. It is unfair.

Gladstein could have been talking about his own career.

In 1959 (February 16) the House Committee on Un-American Activities published a report on "Communist Legal Subversion: The Role of the Communist Lawyer." A special section was devoted to Richard Gladstein. The committee heard sworn testimony indicating that much of Gladstein's time was spent defending "Communist causes" (U.S. Congress. House: 41). The report also noted that following the conviction of the defendants in the New York Communist trial Gladstein toured the West Coast speaking to lawyers and reading aloud portions of the trial transcripts. The lawyers were "astound[ed] . . . at the lack of justice and fair play" (U.S. Congress. House: 43).

WOMEN AND THE GLADSTEIN FIRM

Richard's wife, Caroline Decker Gladstein (Gladstein 1978) was born in Macon, Georgia, in 1912, and was the daughter of Eastern European Jewish immigrants. In her early teens she became involved in radical politics and trade union organizing due to the influence of her older brother and sister. Her brother was blacklisted and could not find employment. In the early

1930s she moved to California and began working with the Cannery and Agricultural Workers Industrial Union organizing migrant workers in camps throughout California. According to a granddaughter (E-mail to John Gallih-er, July 4, 2012) as a labor organizer and still a very young girl in 1933 she successfully led a strike by the Cotton Workers Union. For her efforts on behalf of workers she was sentenced to three years in prison under the California Criminal Syndicalism Act. Soon after arriving in California in 1932 she had married Jack Warnick an agricultural labor organizer. The marriage did not survive her imprisonment. After her release she became a legal secretary, married Richard Gladstein and reared four children. For a time she worked for the Gladstein firm but this involved working seven days a week and it was just too much along with her family. She regretted not having gone to college and becoming a lawyer.

The Gladstein firm represented Doris Brin Walker when Cutter Laboratories in Berkeley, California, fired her after three years of employment (Labor Arbitration Board 1950; Brotsky 2005). She began work there in 1946 and was discharged from her clerk typist position in 1949. Company records indicated that she had never been arrested for a crime and that her performance was consistently satisfactory. (This is where the Gladstein law firm becomes relevant.) The company argued that Walker had concealed the facts that she was a member of the California Bar Association, had been employed by the Gladstein firm, and had been a member of the Communist Party. Apparently the company equated employment with the Gladstein firm as another sign of subversion. (The company neglected to say that she also concealed from them the fact that she was a member of Phi Beta Kappa and had served on the editorial board of the *California Law Review* as a law student.) Walker's answer to these charges was that she left the law firm because of boredom and that the charges of communism were "an absolutely unwarranted invasion into [her] . . . private beliefs." The majority of the Labor Arbitration Board agreed.

HATE MAIL TO AND HARASSMENT OF RICHARD GLADSTEIN

Richard Gladstein received several pieces of hate mail during the 1950s. A July 22, 1955, note reads: "I know damn well Harry [Bridges] and the rest of the rats have been Reds for years. You and your client and witnesses are God-damn liars. (signed) Mike the stevadore [sic]." Another note from the same era says: "The U.S.A. doesn't want that skunk Bridges and we are fed up with Red bastards including yourself" (signed) "Connie" (Bridges Folder 1, Box 17). Finally there is an undated and unsigned letter "You God-damn Kike Jew son of a bitch, you are a stinking Red Commie, its too God-Damn Bad Hitler didn't get you and your family, and that goes for Harry Bridges"

(Unfiled papers 1959). Even in the courtroom Gladstein faced harassment. While defending ILWU official Chris Mensalvas during the government's attempts to deport him, Frank Montoya, a government witness "snarl[ed] the word 'Jew' at Gladstein and asked: 'Do I have to answer these questions for this Jew?'" (*Dispatcher* 1951). Additionally, on June 28, 1949, Gladstein reported in a *San Francisco Chronicle* (1949a) article that his life had been threatened by an anonymous telephone call. Richard Gladstein's FBI file indicates that J. Edgar Hoover likely agreed with much of what was said in these letters and phone call.

FBI FILE FOR RICHARD GLADSTEIN: 858 PAGES

Gladstein's Legal Practice

Gladstein's file noted: "Subject is a Key Figure. He is an attorney who is known to furnish important assistance to the Communist movement" (3/19/58, HQ 100-8174, Section 3, 12). A similar entry referred to Gladstein as "a leading Communist Party (CP) attorney" (4/5/61, HQ 100-8174, Section 3, 55). The FBI also noted that Gladstein was a member of the National Lawyers Guild in 1962 and 1964–1968 and that the Guild was categorized as a "Communist front" organization (10/1/62, HQ 100-8174, Section 3, 73, 75; 9/25/64, HQ 100-8174, Section 3, 132; 9/30/65, HQ 100-8174, Section 3, 147; 9/29/66, HQ 100-8174, Section 3, 162; 4/25/72, HQ 100-8174, Section 3, 173).

On April 22, 1960, the Northern California Committee for the Protection of Foreign Born sponsored a dinner honoring Gladstein for 25 years of service on "behalf of Labor and Civil Liberties" (9/27/60, HQ 100-8174, Section 3, 50). And on June 5, 1964, Gladstein spoke at a testimonial dinner of this organization (9/25/64, HQ 100-8174, Section 3, 132) where he was quoted as saying "even the communists are getting their [constitutional] rights restored. They can talk on campuses and travel" (9/25/64, HQ 100-8174, Section 3, 134).

In the late 1950s Gladstein represented a group of seamen who had previously been designated as "waterfront security risks" and were suing the U.S. government for lost wages (3/19/58, HQ 100-8174, Section 3, 9). Gladstein also represented Archie Brown, a "publicly-known CP [Communist Party] member" (10/11/62, HQ 100-8174, Section 3, 78). Brown was tried and convicted under the 1959 Landrum-Griffin Act, which made it illegal for Communist Party members to hold union office.[2]

An FBI file entry on 10/1/62 (HQ 100-8174, Section 3, 80) reported that Gladstein: "tries to convey the impression that he is only trying to do the best for his clients and that he really is not a Communist." The FBI wanted to interview Gladstein but was afraid that doing so may give him the impression that they "consider his past to amount to a good deal more than a 'pinkish attitude.'" As with Gladstein's law partners the FBI was concerned that an interview with him may cause "embarrassment to the Bureau" (10/1/62, HQ 100-8174, Section 3, 80). Thus it was noted that he should be interviewed away from his office or home. The FBI believed that Gladstein's cooperation "could furnish valuable information concerning CP [Communist Party] finances and membership" (10/1/62, HQ 100-8174, Section 3, 80).

Gladstein's file also noted that he was found in contempt of court by New York federal judge Harold R. Medina on 10/14/49 (11/9/49, HQ 69-604, Section 1, 1). The file included the contempt certificate filed against Gladstein and his co-counsel for their conduct in the case of *United States of America v. Foster, et. al.* (11/9/49, HQ 69-604, Section 1, 3). For his part Gladstein received 6 months in prison for 18 specific contempts (11/9/49, HQ 69-604, Section 1, 49). Among other accusations, the certificate noted that during the trial the lawyers: "Suggested that various findings by the Court were made for the purpose of newspaper headlines; [and] insinuated that there was connivance between the Court and the United States Attorney; [and] repeatedly made charges against the Court of bias, prejudice, corruption, and partiality" (10/3/49, HQ 69-604, Section 1, 5).

The contempt certificate also includes examples of Gladstein in action and in conflict with Judge Medina during the trial (11/9/49, HQ 69-604, Section 1):

Mr. Gladstein: ". . . your Honor . . . you are preventing me from showing . . . proof of the corruption of the system here . . . " (14).

The Court: "I consider your language offensive and not fitting for an officer of this court" (14).

Mr. Gladstein: "It gets so that even before I ask a question it is sustained, the objection to it" (23).

The Court: "Now that I consider a distinct impertinence" (23).

Mr. Gladstein: "And that includes the badgering tone and the bullying and blustering tone towards the witness" (38).

Mr. Gladstein: "I submit that the Court is now making it plain that it no longer wishes to hear evidence from the defendants" (29).

Mr. Gladstein: "May I object to the Court's . . . inference?" (33).

The Court: "Your objection is noted. It is overruled" (33).

The Court: "I will hear no argument" (33).

Mr. Gladstein: "I want to note my objection on the record" (33).

The Court: "You have noted it. Sit down" (33).

Mr. Gladstein: "I object to that" (33).

The Court: "Will you sit down or must I call an officer to put you down?....Your field day is over" (33).

Mr. Gladstein: "I resent your Honor's remarks" (33).

Mr. Gladstein: "I want to object to the court making a direction to this witness and pointing his finger at the witness in an intimidating way. I assign that as misconduct, your Honor" (40).

A report written by the Detroit Chapter of the National Lawyers Guild and the Wolverine Bar Association noted that on the first day of the New York Communist trial (*United States of America v. Foster, et. al.*) and several thereafter over 400 police officers guarded the courtroom and its corridors. This led prospective jurors to view the defendants as dangerous criminals. The Court refused to stop this in spite of defense counsel protests (6/15/50, HQ 69-604, Section 2, 187).

Gladstein's FBI file also included an amicus curiae brief filed by the National Lawyers Guild in support of Gladstein and his co-defendants (3/8/50, HQ 69-604, Section 2, 3). A similar amici curiae brief filed on behalf of approximately 500 petitioners reads in part:

> By their oaths as lawyers, defense counsel were obliged to try the case according to their own lights, with zeal and the exertion of their utmost learning and ability, without regard to whether this met with the approval or the sharpest disapproval of the judge or public press. The Canons of Professional Ethics prescribe no less (3/8/50, HQ 69-604, Section 2: 45).

Additionally, Gladstein received verbal support from federal judge Michael J. Roche in whose courtroom he was trying another case:

> In all the years that I have known you, Mr. Gladstein, and in all of the occasions when you have appeared before me, you have always been of extreme help to the court, courteous, dignified and demeaning yourself in accordance with the highest traditions of the Bar. It comes to me as a shock that this misfortune in New York should have occurred. I do not understand how any judge could possibly reach the conclusion that you should be sent to jail. (3/20/50, HQ 69-604, Section 2, 58)

The Second Circuit Court of Appeals denied Gladstein and his co-defendants a rehearing by a split vote and a U.S. Supreme Court majority affirmed the convictions and sentences (3/10/52, HQ 69-604, Section 53). In the dissenting opinion Justices Douglas and Frankfurter argued that both the lawyers and Judge Medina were at fault with each side having participated in "an unseemly demonstration of garrulous discussion and of ill will and hot tempers" (3/10/52, HQ 69-604, Section 53, 92). Additionally, Justices Black, Douglas, and Frankfurter noted that it was an error for the judge to hear his own charges and Justices Black and Douglas argued that the defendants were not granted their constitutional right to a jury trial (3/10/52, HQ 69-604, Section 53, 92).

Was Richard Gladstein a Communist?

An unknown informant claimed that Gladstein held membership in "the Lawyers Group of the Communist Party in San Francisco from approximately 1936 to 1950" (9/17/57, HQ 100-8174, Section 3, 3). Another informant said that he and Gladstein had attended Communist Party meetings together (1/9/58, HQ 100-8174, Section 3, 7; 3/19/58, HQ 100-8174, Section 3, 9). On August 6, 1958, yet another informant said he had been told by a third person "that one of the two people who recruited him into the CP [Communist Party] was Richard Gladstein" (9/17/58, HQ 100-8174, Section 3, 15–16). However, Gladstein made the following statement to FBI officials on August 27, 1957: "I am sure you fellows have a dossier on me higher than I could see over, but if you will review your file carefully you will discover that I have never endorsed the Communist party line" (9/17/57, HQ 100-8174, Section 1, 3). The FBI never followed his advice.

Gladstein's Family

An FBI memo from J. Edgar Hoover to a State Department official noted that Richard and Caroline Gladstein were scheduled to travel to France, Austria, and Italy and legal attaches were notified so that they could contact "appropriate security services in order that they may be advised of any pertinent information developed" (10/26/62, HQ 100-8174, Section 3, 81). Hoover noted that Gladstein was traveling with his wife who "in addition to her reputation as a communist, was also known as a woman of very loose morals" (11/26/62, HQ 100-8174, Section 3, 82). And for some reason another file entry noted that Richard Gladstein's father, Joseph Gladstein, had been accused of adultery (4/18/63, HQ 100-8174, Section 3, 112). Such salacious comments in an FBI file could not be contested.

CONCLUSION

Among the law partners Gladstein had the longest FBI file. This surely was due to his role as the litigator or public face of the firm, but also because he was good at what he did in the courtroom. Much of Gladstein's FBI file is composed of his cross-examinations of government witnesses and challenges to judges. Like his partners Gladstein did not have a privileged social class background, having worked his way through college. He was praised by Harry Bridges and became an "honorary member" of ILWU Local 10 (*Dispatcher* 1976). A 1974 *Dispatcher* article noted Gladstein's "long record of defense of the rights of working people, the foreign born and others who came under government attack, particularly during the 1950s" (*Dispatcher*

1974). Thus it is not surprising that Gladstein was threatened through the mail, imprisoned for contempt of court, and threatened with disbarment.

An early 1940s partner in the firm was Herbert Resner. His son was named Thomas after Tom Mooney who was a famous San Francisco labor leader of the early twentieth century (E-mail to John Galliher, June 28, 2012). One of Gladstein's sons who became a practicing attorney wrote that he was appalled by the FBI claims of infidelity directed toward his grandfather and his mother. These charges simply demonstrate the unbridled power of the Bureau (E-mail to John Galliher, June 27, 2012). "My father believed that power of concentrated labor was a necessary counter-weight to the power of concentrated capital. Many idealists, liberals, anarchists, progressives, socialists, and communists moved into the labor movement. I do not believe my father was a communist, but obviously defended some of them." Unlike many of his associates "he believed in the U.S. Constitution and Bill of Rights. Throughout his career he couldn't be bought and he wouldn't be bullied." Richard Gladstein's son also commented on the intruders who assaulted George Andersen in his office. "If they had wanted to kill George, they could have and would have. If they [merely] wanted to intimidate George, why not waylay him privately? George wasn't the head of the firm, and wasn't the lead counsel in the Bridges case [or any other significant cases]" (E-mail to Colin Wark, June 28, 2013). The intruders actually wanted to kill my father but did not know what he looked like and thus they asked George Andersen for his wallet to find out if he was in fact Richard Gladstein (E-mail to Colin Wark, June 28, 2013). My father was not yet in the office since he was delayed at home by caring for a sick child (E-mail to Colin Wark, August 16, 2010). "It was George's refusal to cooperate that led to his getting shot that day according to everything I was told" (E-mail to Colin Wark, June 28, 2013).

CHAPTER SUMMARY

Richard Gladstein was born in Connecticut in 1908 and moved to California where he attended high school, college, and law school. After becoming an attorney Gladstein worked in a firm for several years before starting his own firm and becoming "one of the first labor lawyers in San Francisco" (*Dispatcher* 1974). During his career Gladstein was arrested for picketing and served a prison sentence for contempt of court. He was also a member of the National Lawyers Guild.

Gladstein's early clients included Harry Bridges, picketers, agricultural workers in California and Hawaii, the CIO, and the ILWU. Gladstein also represented a fellow labor lawyer charged with perjury and a schoolteacher charged under the Smith Act. In 1949 Gladstein defended Communist Party leaders in New York and was cited for contempt of court and sentenced to prison.

During World War II Gladstein received various draft classifications but never enlisted in the military. Gladstein's correspondence illustrates his skill as a defense attorney. Gladstein wrote to a judge to stop a picketing injunction and he wrote to a union official stating that the police and District Attorney were favoring the AF of L over the CIO. Gladstein also wrote letters to his colleague Carol King joking about her consumption of the drug Sulfa and inquiring about the possibility of Harry Bridges obtaining citizenship. Gladstein received letters from Pat Brown in which Brown thanked Gladstein for supporting him in his campaigns to become Attorney General and later the Governor of California.

Gladstein scoffed at a government lawyer's claim that he was a communist and wrote a memo supporting the right of labor unions to picket a grocery store. He nevertheless reminded the picketers that the police could bring false charges against them.

In a speech to the 1943 National Lawyers Guild Convention Gladstein stated that employment discrimination and the inefficient utilization of resources was crippling the war effort. He also criticized the government's persecution of Harry Bridges and mentioned that the longshoremen had protested the shipment of supplies to Japan. Ten years later the National Lawyers Guild was struggling to avoid the Attorney General's blacklist.

Gladstein was a powerful orator and an assertive advocate for his clients. He traveled to Hawaii to defend clients charged under the Smith Act. During the trial Gladstein stated that the Soviet Union has no reason to go to war with the United States and he criticized U.S. economic and military imperialism. He noted that the Communist Party supports progressive social and economic legislation and he argued that the persecution of Communists moves the country toward fascism. Gladstein also refuted the government's argument that the U.S. Communist Party is a conspiracy simply because its goals parallel those of Communist Parties in other nations.

During a cross-examination Gladstein compelled a government witness to agree that revolution would never occur in a just society. And in 1949 Gladstein defended New York Communist Party leaders charged under the Smith Act. Following the trial Gladstein was cited for contempt of court and sentenced to six months in prison. He said that his conviction was politically motivated and that these types of actions suppress free speech.

After being convicted Gladstein spoke at a public school in Berkeley before serving his prison sentence in 1952. Many people opposed his imprisonment and harsh treatment by the authorities. After his release Gladstein had to briefly forego working as Bridges' attorney.

During the New York trial Gladstein had argued that the defendants were on trial merely for dissent and that their prosecution threatened the freedom of expression. He linked the case to racial and religious intolerance. In justifying his representation of the New York Communists Gladstein noted that civil liberties are at stake and he felt that it was his duty as a lawyer to help "every group and minority." In 1951 Gladstein assisted with another Smith Act case in California.

In 1952 there were attempts to disbar Gladstein in both Hawaii and California and in 1955 he successfully defended Harry Bridges. In 1956 Gladstein wrote a letter declining to join the American Bar Association noting the organization's racist past and inappropriate questions on the application. While defending fellow lawyer John Caughlan, Gladstein noted that Caughlan's representation of Communists and attendance at one of their meetings did not imply that Caughlan was himself a Communist Party member. Gladstein noted that Caughlan has a right to represent whomever he pleases and everyone has a right to legal representation. A 1959 HUAC report stated that Gladstein had defended "Communist causes" and had toured the west coast speaking to lawyers about the New York Communist trial.

Richard Gladstein's wife Caroline became involved in labor organizing at a young age and moved to California where she successfully led a cotton workers strike and was imprisoned for her efforts. After her release she became a legal secretary and married Richard Gladstein. She briefly worked for the firm and went on to raise four children.

The Gladstein firm successfully represented Doris Brin Walker in a labor dispute with Cutter Laboratories. The company had fired her claiming she had not disclosed the fact that she was a lawyer who had worked for the Gladstein firm and was a member of the Communist Party.

During the 1950s Gladstein received several pieces of hate mail and faced anti-Semitic harassment in the courtroom. And in the late 1940s he received a threatening phone call.

Gladstein's nearly 900-page FBI file noted that he was a "key figure" and "leading Communist Party . . . attorney" (4/5/61, HQ 100-8174, Section 3, 55) as well as a member of the National Lawyers Guild, which was a Communist front organization. In 1960 the Northern California Committee for the Protection of Foreign Born honored Gladstein at a dinner and in 1964 he spoke at an NCCPFB testimonial dinner. In the 1950s Gladstein represented formerly blacklisted seamen suing the government for lost wages and in the 1960s he represented Archie Brown who had been tried under the Landrum-Griffin Act.

The FBI wanted to interview Gladstein but was afraid to do so for various reasons. Gladstein's file also mentioned his contempt of court conviction and included the contempt certificate which listed the charges against Gladstein, his sentence, some of the conduct in which he and his co-counsel had allegedly engaged, as well as a verbal exchange between Gladstein and Judge Medina. It was also noted that Gladstein and his co-counsel protested the heavy police presence at the New York Communist trial. The file also included an amicus curiae brief filed by the National Lawyers Guild in support of Gladstein and his co-defendants along with a similar brief filed by approximately 500 petitioners. Gladstein received additional support from a federal judge.

The Court of Appeals refused to hear the case against Gladstein and his co-defendants and the convictions and sentences were affirmed by a divided U.S. Supreme Court. The dissenting justices argued that both sides were at fault, that it was an error for the judge to hear his own charges, and that the defendants were denied their right to a jury trial.

Gladstein stated that he had never endorsed the Communist party line, though FBI informants claimed that he had been an active member of the Communist Party. The FBI noted that Gladstein and his wife were planning to visit Europe and that legal attaches had been notified. J. Edgar Hoover alleged that Caroline Gladstein had been known as a "communist" with "loose morals" and the FBI noted that Gladstein's father was an accused adulterer.

NOTES

1. Stein (1975) claims that Gladstein spent five months in prison and that his sentence was reduced by one month for good behavior.

2. The U.S. Court of Appeals later reversed Brown's conviction and in 1965 the reversal was upheld by the U.S. Supreme Court (*U.S. v. Brown* 1965).

Chapter Nine

Conclusion

The Creation of Legal Culture

THE INTERNAL ENVIRONMENT CREATED BY THE GLADSTEIN FIRM

When environments are discussed one typically focuses on details external to groups and organizations. There are also internal environments. The concept of internal environment originated in biology and "suggests that the body fluids . . . in higher animals form an internal environment which provides the conditions of existence for their cells" (Robin 1979, 257). The internal environment of the Gladstein firm can consist of current employees—we know most about Andersen and Leonard, management—we know most about Gladstein, corporate culture, the philosophy of leadership, and leadership styles. It also includes current customers and services offered—the most important customer was Harry Bridges and the firm specialized in labor law. In addition, the values of the organization and its social networks are involved (CliffsNotes.com) such as the values reflected in the National Lawyers Guild and the Northern California Committee for the Protection of Foreign Born.

The most important aspect of the Gladstein firm's internal environment was its long-time client Harry Bridges. What really exasperated the bankers and industrial leaders was that as Harry Bridges moved up in the union he did not become more moderate and protective of his position but rather became more defiant ("Harry Bridges"). This attitude may have resulted from his tough, lonely six years at sea. Additionally, as a young teenager, Bridges became keenly aware of class differences when he was made to collect rents from poor people in Melbourne, Australia, by his father, a politically conservative real estate agent (Fortune 1977; "Harry Bridges"). Many of the tenants did not have the money to pay and Bridges resented being put in this position ("Harry Bridges"). Bridges was also influenced by his uncles who supported the Australian Labor Party ("Harry Bridges"). Bridges was popular among longshoremen because he always listened to their complaints. "He would nod his narrow head, a smile curving his thin lips [saying] of course." He enjoyed hanging around waterfront saloons with the union members. Bridges found that the most militant waterfront workers were members of the Communist Party (CP). The employers called him "Red Harry" and the press referred to him as an alien.

Of course, what drove all of this was the vast and monstrous FBI led by the savage J. Edgar Hoover. George Andersen's career was followed closely by the FBI, he was threatened, physically attacked in his office, and opposed by judges at every turn. The Hearst press did not treat him fairly as he represented union members and members of the Communist Party. Norman Leonard was also followed by the FBI, and the U.S. Navy attempted to deprive him of benefits despite the fact that he had served in a combat zone during WWII. Leonard defended picketers and CP members, criticized anti-Semites, and opposed the military draft during the Vietnam war. Richard Gladstein was followed by the FBI, he defended Harry Bridges, picketers, CP members, and CIO members. Additionally, he was sent to jail after defending CP members and received considerable hate mail.

In a July 21, 2012, e-mail to John Galliher a former partner in the firm from 1968 to 1980 explained both the internal and external environments of the firm. He explained that prior to joining the firm he had attended law school at UC Berkeley and after graduating in 1960, he worked for the government of California. Then, in 1966 he joined a San Francisco law firm offering services to business. A year spent representing corporate America was as much as he could endure and he took a position with the Gladstein firm even though the business firm warned him and his wife that he was ruining his legal career by deciding to practice law "with a group of known communists." This hostility describes a significant part of the external environment of the Gladstein firm.

Now we address the internal environment provided by the partners of the firm. The aforementioned former partner joined the Gladstein law firm in 1967 after Gladstein and Leonard made him an offer. Although he had met George Andersen prior to that time he did not know him personally since Andersen died in 1965. However, he opined that: "everything I have read or heard about George satisfies me that he, like Richie and Norman, was a fine lawyer and a principled liberal thinker" (E-mail to John Galliher, July 21, 2012). He noted:

> We at the Gladstein law firm . . . were sustained by generous retainers from Harry Bridges and the ILWU along with other progressive unions. . . . In my time at the firm, I represented, without fee, the Black Panthers, student protestors at UC Berkeley (Mario Savio's group), minority students at San Francisco State College, the Communist Party, conscientious objectors to the Vietnam war and the United Farm Workers. These *pro bono* efforts took an enormous amount of time. Never did Richie or Norman question whether I should spend my time on those efforts. They sacrificed a fair portion of our income in favor of representation on behalf of progressive causes.

He also described the environment provided by the law firm in the person of Norman Leonard:

> Norman Leonard is the best lawyer and finest man I have ever met. When I was appointed to the bench in 1980 (and leaving the firm), a question arose as to my capital share in the firm. Norman and I had a ferocious argument. His view was that I should receive more than the accountants had calculated. I said I should not receive more. We duked it out to a resolution, but how many lawyers can say that their partner was holding out for them to receive a bigger share of the pie?

Aubrey Grossman was an undergraduate friend of Leonard's at UCLA and later a partner in the Gladstein law firm before leaving for Los Angeles. At UCLA Grossman played football and later nearly failed to attract his wife while a student at Berkeley because she thought that all football players were "stupid" (*San Francisco Chronicle* 1999). As an attorney Grossman's activities reflect something of the culture of the firm. Like his law partners Grossman represented his clients vigorously and thus ran afoul of some judges. As we noted in chapter 7 Grossman was cited for conduct unbecoming a lawyer while defending Native Americans charged with trespassing. Norman Leonard represented Grossman in the case and helped to save Grossman from disbarment.

As an early partner in the Gladstein law firm it is predictable that Grossman's early career paralleled that of Richard Gladstein: 1) like Gladstein he received his legal training at UC Berkeley, 2) like Gladstein he was a member of the Law Review there, and 3) like Gladstein, Harry Bridges was among his first clients (*San Francisco Chronicle* 1999). In addition to defending Native Americans Grossman assisted civil rights activists during the 1950s and 60s and defended Vietnam draft resisters during the 1960s and 70s. In 1950, after demanding a stay of execution for a black man accused of rape in Mississippi, Grossman was beaten by men he thought were off-duty police officers (Aubrey Grossman; *San Francisco Chronicle* 1999).

Allan Brotsky was a member of the firm from 1948 to 1957 (Brotsky 2005). His involvement, too, shows a good bit about this organization. Brotsky was born in Detroit in 1920 and his parents were poor European Jewish immigrants. He moved to LA when he was 16 and entered UCLA in 1937. At UCLA Brotsky was involved in the Young Communist League. In 1939 he enrolled at Columbia University law school where as a top student he was an editor for the *Columbia Law Review*. After graduating from law school in 1942 Brotsky was drafted. The Army invited him to join the Provost Marshal's Office but he refused saying "I don't want to become a policeman" (Brotsky 2005, 24). He later stated: "the objective became to defeat Hitler and the Nazis, I wanted to go overseas and help" (Brotsky 2005, 24). He was an officer, a second lieutenant, but he never got outside of the United States and was discharged in 1946.

Soon after leaving the Army Brotsky joined the Gladstein firm. Like his law partners Brotsky was a member of the National Lawyers Guild. He stayed on with the firm until 1957 when he and some of the other younger lawyers left because they felt that the partners were neglecting the needs of their clients in favor of making money. Brotsky had nevertheless admired the Gladstein firm's accomplishments: "They not only were the leading labor law firm on the progressive side, but they also were the leading civil liberties and civil rights firm" (Brotsky 2005, 34). Brotsky continued to practice until 1979 when he became a law professor.

While working for the Gladstein firm Brotsky assisted Norman Leonard with the 1948 West Coast Maritime Strike. And in the 1950s Brotsky assisted Leonard with the "Senate Internal Security Subcommittee Hearings in San Francisco." During these hearings, where labor leaders were subpoenaed, Brotsky and Leonard were removed from the hearing room for insisting on the right of witnesses to counsel. The next day there were headlines: "'Lawyers Thrown Out of Hearing Room' which made them look like damn fools" (Brotsky 2005, 63).

In 1949 the Gladstein firm assisted the Richmond, California, chapter of the NAACP and Brotsky was assigned the case (Brotsky 2005). Richmond Lucky stores did not employ African Americans and the NAACP and Progressive Citizens of America (PCA) requested that the grocery store chain hire African Americans in proportion to African American patronage. When the request was denied these groups picketed one of Lucky's stores and Lucky obtained an injunction against the picketing in Contra Costa County Superior Court. Soon thereafter two NAACP members defied the injunction and were cited for contempt of court. When the picketers challenged the injunction in court Lucky's attorneys successfully argued that a requirement to hire a proportionate number of African Americans would constitute a "quota." Thus the picketers demands were unlawful and so was their picket. The California Supreme Court and later the U.S. Supreme Court upheld this ruling (Brilliant 2010).

STUDYING LAW FIRMS

Elizabeth Chambliss (2010) wrote an essay outlining how scholars should analyze environments in law firms. Chambliss thus provides a template for our study of the Gladstein firm as an organization. Chambliss distinguishes between the influence of the firm and the impact of the broader society of which the members are a part. With the Gladstein example, the impact of the society and the firm appeared to be identical. The problem is that in the modern United States the culture of the firm becomes more diluted as the firm grows and becomes more dispersed. In the Gladstein case we have no evidence that the impact of the firm and its three partners was diluted. They all lived the same culture that the firm supported.

Chambliss notes that the days have passed when law firms existed only in one office and where members stayed with the firm for their entire careers. This stability was largely reflected in the Gladstein example. Norman Leonard spent his entire career with the firm while Richard Gladstein and George Andersen spent the majority of their careers with the firm.

When the law firm is studied it is often referred to as an unhappy place where there is a "Soul for Sale" (Chambliss 2010, 3). This was not at all true of the Gladstein partners from the 1930s through the 1960s who lived their personal lives and practiced law on the basis of principle. Yet law firms have escaped the attention of those studying organizations. This makes our study of the Gladstein law firm all the more significant.

CONCLUSION

In the United States of the 1950s peace and prosperity seemed to camouflage a troubled political climate. Many in the United States felt that their way of life was being threatened by communism. There were clearly grounds for this concern since after WWII the Soviets had annexed most of Eastern Europe, China had fallen to the Communists in 1949, and in 1950 the United States sent troops into Korea to contain the Communists (Layman 1994). There were both internal and international threats. Racism played a significant role in the internal threats. In 1955, fourteen-year-old African American Emmet Till was murdered in Mississippi by whites for allegedly merely flirting with a white woman. Also that year Rosa Parks began the Montgomery, Alabama, bus boycott that was later joined by Dr. Martin Luther King. And in 1957 Little Rock Central High School required the presence of federal troops due to threats of racial violence by whites angered by modest integration. Along with racism, sex was an important worry. Professor Alfred Kinsey established his sex clinic at Indiana University that thrived until his death in 1957. Also in 1957 Beat poet Allen Ginsberg's San Francisco obscenity trial created a scandal and the anti-materialism of Jack Kerouac's book *On The Road* alarmed many citizens.

On the international scene in 1951 General Douglas MacArthur warned of Chinese aggression after being fired by President Truman for leading U.S. troops in Korea. In 1959 Fidel Castro brought communism to Cuba. The Soviets made their first atomic bomb in 1949 thereby catching up with United States and they put Sputnik into orbit in 1957 bypassing the U.S. science program. The situation was made all the worse by the belligerent Soviet leader Nikita Khrushchev. Nazi scientist Wernher von Braun became a U.S. citizen in 1955 showing that turning a blind eye to Nazi transgressors was not enough to protect the American scientific advantage over the Soviets (Halberstam 1993). In this environment fears of Jews, Communists, immigrants, and labor unions ran rampant. Such were the litany of issues that provided the environment for the harassment and indeed the existence of the Gladstein firm.

The Gladstein, Andersen, and Leonard firm existed from 1945 when Andersen joined the firm until he died in 1965—20 years. (Leonard had joined the firm in 1938 after graduating from law school.) As the firm's litigator, Gladstein collected his partners as the senior partner and researcher/brief writer. As the most visible senior partner Gladstein endured racial harassment, was threatened with physical abuse, sent to prison, and threatened with disbarment. Like other marginalized individuals and organizations this law firm was "hidden from history."

Summary of Differences

The Bridges FBI file is approximately 30,000 pages in length, Gladstein's file is 858 pages, Andersen's is 669 pages, and Leonard's is 376 pages. Bridges and Andersen were gentiles and Gladstein and Leonard were Jewish. Gladstein and Leonard were native-born Americans while Andersen and Bridges were immigrants. Additionally, Gladstein and Leonard graduated from elite law schools while Andersen graduated from a night law school far outside the elite circle and Bridges did not go to college. Thus, religion, ethnicity, and educational pedigree were not litmus tests for participation in this firm.

Of the four only Leonard served in the military during WWII, as a Naval officer. While working as lawyers Gladstein and Andersen were threatened, Leonard was not. Gladstein was imprisoned for defending eleven Communists in New York. Andersen was shot by thugs apparently trying to intimidate him. Leonard was never threatened, shot, nor imprisoned although the Navy attempted to strip his reserve commission in 1953.

Summary of Similarities

All four (Gladstein, Andersen, Leonard, and Bridges) were alleged by the FBI to be Communists. Although none were party members Andersen admitted that he was once a member. All of the law partners clearly had working class origins. And we know that Gladstein worked his way through college. All of the law partners defended those accused of violating the 1940 Smith Act for advocating Marxist thought and principles. All of the law partners worked for the ILWU and one of its renowned officers, Archie Brown, a well-known member of the Communist Party, as well as the union's longtime president Harry Bridges. All of the law partners were members of the left-leaning National Lawyers' Guild and were involved with the Northern California Committee for the Protection of Foreign Born. Bridges, Andersen, and Leonard were involved in the unsuccessful efforts to Save Julius and Ethel Rosenberg from execution. This is noted in their files. All three lawyers had FBI files, as did Harry Bridges. Indeed his file was many times larger than those of the attorneys. The Bridges cases were the primary driving force behind the "courtesy stigma" (Goffman 1963) imposed upon the law firm.

Those who supported Julius and Ethel Rosenberg were also suspect. Yet it is well to remember that the Rosenbergs did not confess to being "atomic spies" (Schrecker 1994, 139). As noted, the attorneys were members of the National Lawyers Guild which was founded in 1937 and was the first racially integrated bar association. The Guild's memorandum stated: "We must conclude that the trial judge's assertion that the Rosenbergs put into the hands of the Russians the atomic bomb, is entirely unfounded" (Ginger and Tobin 1988, 97) and that prejudice, passion, and propaganda triumphed over facts in this case. Guild attorneys defended Julius and Ethel Rosenberg and, as we mentioned earlier, the Guild defended the rights of free speech and picketing for workers, and opposed the 1947 federal Taft-Hartley Act (Auerbach 1976; Bailey 1982). As noted above the Gladstein partners were also members of the Northern California Committee for the Protection of Foreign Born. This organization was affiliated with the American Committee for the Protection of Foreign Born, which was founded in 1923 to protect the rights of immigrant workers to organize and strike even though a Republican Congress and White House rejected such rights. Not surprisingly, this organization and the Citizens Committee for Harry Bridges were included in the Attorney General's list of subversive organizations.

The Gladstein, Andersen, and Leonard law firm existed during the dark days of the McCarthy Era, but the firm was based in the generally supportive San Francisco Bay Area. The treatment of these attorneys demonstrates the political excesses of this period and also shows how important the firm was in providing an environment where law could be practiced in a humane and progressive fashion. In conclusion, we have powerful albeit indirect evidence on the environment created in the Gladstein law firm. Clearly it was the firm against the world. The FBI hounded their every move. One can only imagine how the partners would have condemned J. Edgar Hoover. Democratic as well as Republican presidents and their Attorneys General were equally seen as foes. It is not difficult to guess what the partners must have said to one another about Presidents Truman, Eisenhower, or Nixon. On the other hand they all appeared to feel that they were "brothers" to the ILWU members and to their old friend Harry Bridges. Most of the American Bar Association and U.S. society in general wanted nothing to do with the members of this law firm. This widespread opposition obviously pressured the partners to stick together. It is easy to speculate that they would be deeply concerned with the problems of the foreign born in the United States today as well as the slumping labor union movement. Yet in today's more complicated world the Gladstein partners would have been called on to decide whose interests to defend, undocumented immigrants, or union members.

In a July 10, 2012, e-mail to John Galliher an attorney practicing since the 1940s who knew all three of the partners explained the subtleties and unclear distinctions of legal practice from the 1930s to the 1950s:

> Progressive lawyers represented many Communists in many jurisdictions. Many clients were members of the Communist Party [CP]; many were CP leaders; some were sympathizers. They were called to testify before Congressional and State legislative committees; to respond to Immigration Service deportation arrests; and to defend themselves against criminal charges for activities during strikes. The lawyers were all members of the National Lawyers Guild. Some were dues-paying members of the CP and attended meetings where CP lawyers spoke. But many had no official connection with the CP. Before each national convention of the National Lawyers Guild, there would usually be a meeting of CP lawyers to decide what position they should take on important NLG issues. No one ever questioned anyone's attendance or asked for proof of CP membership. It was hoped that no one was a stool pigeon.
>
> Richard Gladstein was one of the official CP lawyers. Obviously, the most famous lawyers were the ones who tried cases and represented witnesses before Congressional committees. [But] Gladstein was not a loner. He had law partners. He knew other lawyers all over the country with whom he met and discussed strategies and tactics. [While] he did not think he had all the answers he certainly thought well of himself—which was a necessary quality in someone seeking to convince a judge and 12 jurors to follow his recommendations about the proper outcome of each [important and high visibility] trial.

As noted earlier, the current incarnation of the firm is Leonard Carder (E-mail to John Galliher, August 13, 2012). It has grown and by 2012 it had 20 associates and partners working in two offices, one in San Francisco, the other in Oakland. Norman Leonard's last law partner learned that Leonard was generous with his junior colleagues in financial matters but also in assigning them the more interesting and significant cases and eschewing the practice of having associates write a brief and then having a senior partner insert their own name. The firm continues to represent militant unions including the ILWU and thus "is still perceived by many as a 'left wing' firm." "We don't mind that a bit" (E-mail to John Galliher, August 13, 2012), especially since the attorneys are apparently no longer shot, imprisoned, nor threatened with disbarment for merely representing their clients.

Epilogue

The FBI had unlimited funds that allowed them to harass and humiliate many diverse and loyal Americans. Future research should focus on other activities of the FBI during the period in question. Other progressives including military and government officials, university administrators, professors, students, scientists, writers, entertainers, and racial and religious minorities likely found themselves targets of the FBI. The experiences and treatment of women can also be studied to see obvious signs of sexism. They were likely suspicious to the FBI merely because of their sex. This is particularly true for women who were politically active or members of the workforce. This book shows what can happen in a society when too much money and power is secured by one law enforcement agency.

Future research could also provide an internal audit of the FBI using interviews with retired agents, fired former agents, and present agents as well as internal reports of agency records. Such an investigation could also look into the life and career of Senator Joseph McCarthy and his supporters and colleagues, including Roy Cohn. Others who worked closely with and for the FBI could also be studied. For example, Whittaker Chambers who attacked alleged Communist Alger Hiss could be analyzed. One could also look at federal records and Wisconsin state records to see what materials Senator McCarthy left. And not only could one study what impact McCarthyism had on Wisconsin politics but one could study the impact the era had on other states both liberal and conservative, northern and southern. What impact did McCarthyism have on Mississippi politics and also on New York politics? On the other hand one could study what life was like for those individuals or groups identified as Communist.

One could focus on individuals or groups and one could study the oppressors or the oppressed. For example, one could conduct research on groups of

FBI agents or individual agents. One could also conduct research on groups of FBI victims (as we did here) or individual victims. In at least one instance more than one group acted as an oppressor. The FBI and the Federal Bureau of Narcotics presumably worked in tandem. Alternative research methods might be used, including content analysis. It might also be interesting to speculate on a theoretical understanding of these events. One could use a critical or Marxist interpretation of the relevant events or analytical induction using Grounded Theory or move all the way to a social psychological rendering of these activities.

Appendix A

Chronology of the Gladstein, Andersen, and Leonard Law Firm

1936	Richard Gladstein and Aubrey Grossman start the law firm that would later become Gladstein, Andersen, and Leonard.
1936	Richard Gladstein successfully defends picketers in Oakland, California.
1937	Richard Gladstein obtains a federal court injunction prohibiting employers' use of a blacklist against protesting lettuce pickers in the Salinas Valley.
1938	Norman Leonard moves from New York to San Francisco and joins the Gladstein law firm.
1938	Richard Gladstein obtains NLRB certification of the ILWU as a legal representative for all west coast longshore workers.
1938	Norman Leonard defends Harry Bridges for contempt of court.
1938–1939, 1941–1945, 1949, and 1955	The Gladstein law partners defend Harry Bridges during the U.S. government's attempts to deport him.
1939	Richard Gladstein becomes Harry Bridges' chief defense counsel.

1940	Richard Gladstein wins a U.S. Supreme Court decision protecting the right to peaceful picketing.
1942	Norman Leonard enlists in the U.S. Navy.
1945	George Andersen joins the Gladstein law firm.
1945	Norman Leonard is discharged from the U.S. Navy and rejoins the Gladstein law firm.
1946	Richard Gladstein wins $1.5 million in back pay for plantation workers in Hawaii.
1946	Richard Gladstein successfully defends the California CIO against a $3 million libel suit.
1948 (January 10)	George Andersen is shot in his law office by two unknown men who are never caught nor identified by law enforcement.
1948	Richard Gladstein defends John Reinecke in Hawaii after Reinecke is accused of holding membership in the Communist Party, fired from his teaching position, and arrested for violating the 1940 Smith Act.
1948	Richard Gladstein defends John Caughlan a Seattle labor lawyer accused of perjury for denying his alleged membership in the Communist Party.
1948 (October 22)	While defending the ILWU during a Congressional hearing Norman Leonard is removed from the courtroom after advocating for his client's constitutional rights.
1949 (October 14)	While representing Smith Act defendants in New York Richard Gladstein is cited for contempt of court and sentenced to six months in federal prison by Judge Harold Medina.
1951	Richard Gladstein assists in the defense of 12 California Communist leaders indicted by a Federal Grand Jury for violating the Smith Act.
1952	Richard Gladstein serves time in federal prison as a result of his 1949 contempt conviction.
1957	George Andersen defends members of the California Labor School who are charged with violating the 1950 McCarran Act.
1960	Richard Gladstein is honored at a dinner for 25 years of service to the Northern California Committee for the Protection of Foreign Born.

1961–1962	Richard Gladstein defends Archie Brown who is indicted under the Landrum-Griffin Act for holding union office as a member of the Communist Party.
1965 (December 29)	George Andersen dies in San Francisco.

Appendix B

George Andersen FBI File: 100-HQ-2865 June Section 1

Page 1:

SAC, San Francisco — July 25, 1950

Director, FBI — CONFIDENTIAL – JUNE

GEORGE RICHARD ANDERSEN, was.
INTERNAL SECURITY – C
(Your file 61-146)
(Bureau file 100-2865)

Reference is made to your form FD-142 dated July 6, 1950, at San Francisco, submitted under the caption "Gladstein, Andersen, Resner and Leonard, Internal Security – C." This form is being placed in the file of the captioned individual in view of the similar recommendation for a technical surveillance on this law firm received in the Andersen case by your form FD-142 dated September 14, 1949.

Your recommendation at this time for a technical surveillance on the law firm of Gladstein, Andersen, Resner and Leonard is not approved because of the active participation of this law firm in the appeals of Bridges, et al, and because of the pending appeal in the contempt citation of Israel Richard Gladstein.

PLC: mac

Page 2:

Office Memorandum UNITED STATES GOVERNMENT

TO: D.M. Ladd Date: July 25, 1950

FROM: A.H. Belmont JUNE

SUBJECT: GEORGE RICHARD ANDERSEN, WAS.

INTERNAL SECURITY - C

PURPOSE

To advise you of a recommendation from San Francisco for installation of a technical surveillance on the law firm of Gladstein, Andersen, Resner and Leonard, 240 Montgomery Street, San Francisco, California, telephone Douglas 2-4821.

DETAILS

Form FD-142 dated July 6, 1050, at San Francisco recommending this technical surveillance is attached.

BACKGROUND INFORMATION

This law firm has seven active partners, Israel Richard Gladstein, George Richard Andersen, Herbert Resner, Norman Leonard, Allen Brotsky, Lloyd McMurray and Ewing Sibbett. A former partner, Harold M. Sawyer, acts "of counsel" retaining office space at the same location. Gladstein, Andersen, Resner and Sawyer are in the Security Index and have been designated key figures by San Francisco. Leonard and [redacted] are in the Security Index. Sibbett has been investigated but is not in the Security Index. No investigation has ever been conducted on [redacted] has been investigated and in April 1949 was reported to be a member of the Dewey Davis Club of the Communist Party in San Francisco.

This law firm has represented high officials of the Communist Party in various litigations and its members are in regular contact with Communist Party leaders. George Andersen is known to have been an attorney for the Communist Party since 1935 or 1936, his legal education having been financed by the Party. Andersen is consulted on legal and financial matters for the party and it is believed that Andersen acts as the financial agent for the

Communist Party in the transmission of funds from the Communist Party National Headquarters in New York City to California.

Enclosure
PLC: mac

Page 3:

This law firm originally represented the defendants in the prosecution of Harry Renton Bridges, Henry Schmidt and James Riley Robertson but it withdrew from the case after Gladstein was cited for contempt in New York because of his actions as a defense attorney in the trial of the eleven Communist Party National Board members. Andersen is reported to have assisted the defense attorneys during the trial and conviction of Bridges, et al. Gladstein was later sentenced on the contempt citation and his case is presently on appeal. San Francisco has advised that this law firm and Vincent Hallinan are now attorneys of record in the appeal on file in the Bridges case. This law firm represents many known Communist Party members in various litigations as well as many aliens under deportation proceedings.

On September 14, 1949, San Francisco submitted form FD-142 recommending a technical surveillance on the office of George Richard Andersen, the law firm being identified at that time as Gladstein, Andersen, Resner and Sawyer. At that time San Francisco furnished information that this law office was serviced by five trunk telephone lines which entered through a switchboard. San Francisco's recommendation was declined by the Bureau because of the then pending Bridges trial.

OBSERVATIONS

In view of the number of individuals known to be active Communists who are associated with this law firm it would appear that this surveillance should prove productive if installation were approved by the Bureau. It is recommended, however, that this request be denied at this time for the following reasons which, it is believed, outweigh the benefits which might be gained:

1. Because the law firm is presently representing Bridges on his appeals from conviction and from cancellation of his citizenship. It is also to be noted that the Senate Judiciary Committee has recently requested the Department to determine if Bridges' present activities warrant cancellation of his bail bond.
2. Because of Gladstein's contempt sentence in New York City which is on appeal.
3. Because of the law firm's activities in defending Communist Party members and deportation cases.

If the existence of the proposed technical surveillance became known to Bridges or this law firm it would provide propaganda material for the Communist Party, civil rights front groups and the National Lawyers Guild in their continuing attacks on the Bureau and it might materially affect the Bridges case. The policy has been followed in the past that the Bureau should not become involved in the Bridges trial in any way. It is believed that this policy should continue to be followed during the appeal in that case.

It is to be noted that during the time this law firm represented Bridges, prior to the court trial, they tried to draw the Bureau into the Bridges case on a motion to dismiss by alleging that the Bureau had used illegal wire tapping on Bridges in 1941 at the Hotel Edison in New York City and that as a result evidence against Bridges had been illegally obtained. Although this motion was denied, it does show that the members of this law firm are "wire tapping conscious."

ACTION

If you approve there is attached a memorandum to San Francisco declining the recommendation in this matter.

Page 6:

6. Type of case involved:

INTERNAL SECURITY - C

7. Connection or status of subject in the case:

This law firm has represented high officials of the Communist Party in various litigations and members of the firm are in constant contact with these leaders. The firm is composed of seven active partners and a former name partner who is semi-retired but retains office space and acts "of counsel." The active partners are as follows: ISRAEL RICHARD GLADSTEIN, GEORGE R. ANDERSEN, HERBERT RESNER, NORMAN LEONARD, ALLEN BROTSKY, LLOYD McMURRAY, AND EWING SIBBETT. The former partner who acts "of counsel" is HAROLD M. SAWYER. All have been identified as CP members. Records of the Clerk of the U.S. Circuit Court for the Ninth (see attached)

8. Specific information being sought:

Information relative to Communist Party policies on national, state, and local levels. Information as to the financial transactions of the Communist Party and the identity of persons furnishing financial support. Membership of the Haymarket Club, the lawyers' branch of the Professional Section, Communist Party of San Francisco County.

9. Reasons for believing the specific information will be obtained by the technical surveillance:

The senior partner, GLADSTEIN, was one of the defense attorneys in the recent trial of the eleven Communist Party leaders in New York City, and in such capacity is in close touch with CP leadership on a national level. GEORGE R. ANDERSEN is deeply involved in the financial affairs of the Communist Party and in such capacity is in close touch with WILLIAM SCHNEIDERMAN, State Chairman, and other ranking functionaries. NORMAN LEONARD has been identified as organizer of the Haymarket Club. HAROLD M. SAWYER acted as counsel for WILLIAM SCHNEIDERMAN before the California Senate Committee in April, 1950.

10. Importance of case and subject:

This case is important to the Internal Security of the country.

Page 7:

7. (Con't)

Circuit reflect that this law firm, together with VINCENT HALLINAN, are the attorneys of record in the appeal of HARRY BRIDGES, et al. from the recent conviction.

Page 8:

11. Possibilities of obtaining desired information by other means (Explain in detail):

No live informant is available and no other source can supply this information.

12. Risks of detection involved:

None

13. Probable length of technical surveillance:

Ninety days

14. Request made for technical surveillance by any outside agency (name specific official, title and agency):

No

Page 9:

15. Remarks:

The members of this law firm, as previously pointed out, are all members of the Communist Party, and through their constant contacts with leading Party functionaries, are in position to greatly influence policies and activities of the Party on local, state and national levels. It is their activities as Communists which is of primary interest; the fact that they are attorneys is secondary.

It is to be noted that one technical installation would yield coverage on at least seven persons prominent in the machinations of the Communist Party in San Francisco where no coverage now exists.

16. Recommendation of Assistant Director:

17. Recommendation of Assistants to the Director:

George Andersen FBI File: HQ 100-2865 Section 1

Page 1:

ANDERSEN, GEORGE R. COMMUNIST

544 Market Street (Business)

69 Piedmont Street (Residence)

San Francisco, California 8-8-40

Official attorney for the Communist Party. Member of the Executive Committee, Emergency Defense Committee and Executive member of the San Francisco District Communist Party. Member National Committee for Defense of Political Prisoners, Northern California Branch. (1934). Elected Vice-Director, National Committee for Defense of Political Prisoners. Member of Downtown Section of the Communist Party. Recently joined the American League against War & Fascism but due to his connection with the International Labor Defense as defense attorney, his name does not appear in any of the group bulletins. Considered a "bad egg" as far as communist agitation is concerned. In a legal capacity, attends all secret meetings to give legal advice to the movement. Spoke at a meeting of the United Labor Party in San Francisco on 9-22-35. Listed on convention program as "Militant Labor Attorney." Reported one of the "brains" behind Harry Bridges. Member No. 2, Inner Circle of Ten, Communist Party. The expense of his office rental is purportedly borne by the local Communist Party District. (1935). Director, Committee for Defense of Political Prisoners. Member of International Workers Order who pay his traveling expenses in connection therewith. Member San Francisco Inner Council, Communist Party. Member No. 6 Executive Committee, Communist Party. Contributor in 8-31-36 issue of Pacific Weekly, a Communist publication. (1936) Candidate for San Francisco Supervisor on Communist Party ticket. (1937) Candidate for Judge [continued on page 2]

Page 2:

GEORGE R. ANDERSEN

[continued from page 1] of Superior Court with Herbert Resner, another well known Communist attorney acting as his campaign manager. (1938) (Conf. Inf. [redacted] 100-2-45)

Contained in a list of known Communist furnished the San Francisco office by Conf. Inf. [redacted] on 10-4-39. (100-2-45)

Is an official of every known Communist Branch in San Francisco and is the authorized attorney for the International Labor Defense. (Conf. Inf. [redacted] Nov. 1939, 100-2-45) Member of the Educational Membership Committee composed of Communist Party members "either with or without membership cards" and who will have charge of the Communist Education Program in 1940 (Conf. Inf. [redacted] Nov. 1939, 61-7590-503 p 18; 100-2-45)

One George Anderson apparently identical with above, is a defendant in the complaint filed in the case entitled Ivan Francis Cox vs. the 13th District of the Communist Party et al., before the State Superior Court in San Francisco, Calif. on 12-9-37. He is described therein as being a member of the Communist Party and the legal adviser of the "inner-group" or executive committee of the 13th District of the Communist Party, and is also the legal adviser of the defendants Harry Bridges, Wm. Schniederman [sic] (State Sec. of the Communist Party) et al. (Copy of complaint in file 61-7559-2128; 100-2-45)

"Attorney for the International Labor Defense (People's World, 4-3-39, 61-7591-141X)

"Very active as an attorney for various communist leaders and reported to be the 'brains' behind Harry Bridges. (Conf. Inf. [redacted] 1936, 100-2-45).

Page 4:

FEDERAL BUREAU OF INVESTIGATION

THIS CASE ORIGINATED AT SAN FRANCISCO, CALIFORNIA	FILE NO. 61-146

REPORT MADE AT	DATE WHEN MADE	PERIOD FOR WHICH MADE

SAN FRANCISCO	5/17/41	11/15; 12/5/40; 1/30; 2/17, 24-27; 3/4; 4/26; 5/12/41

TITLE	CHARACTER OF CASE
GEORGE R. ANDERSEN alias George Anderson	INTERNAL SECURITY (C)

SYNOPSIS OF FACTS:
This individual is recommended for custodial detention pending investigation in the event of a national emergency and the Bureau has been supplied with a custodial detention memorandum. Subject born Copenhagen, Denmark, 9/19/00 of American parents, resides 69 Piedmont Ave., San Francisco, maintains law offices at 544 Market St., San Francisco. Graduated from law course, San Francisco College 1927. Admitted practice of law California 1927. Member of California State and San Francisco County Bar Associations. During practice in association with HERBERT RESNER has been candidate for Municipal Court Judge, United Labor Party ticket, candidate for San Francisco City Supervisor, Communist Party ticket, and candidate Superior Court Judge, San Francisco County. Has been reported legal counsel for Communist Party, International Labor Defense, Communist Party front, Alaska Cannery Workers and CIO. Reported member of Communist Party, National Committee for Defense of Political Prisoners and Friends of Abraham Lincoln Brigade, Communist Party front. During practice has defended several known Communists and fellow travelers on various charges. Has stated that he is a defender of political prisoners and that he is not a member of the Communist Party. In 1938 was mortgagee of premises at 121 Haight St., San Francisco, State and County headquarters, Communist Party. Reported as having at one time attempted to devise legal means for Communist Party to obtain arms. Presently in practice of law, defending WILLIAM SCHNEIDERMAN, California Secretary, Communist Party, an action for revocation [continued on page 5]

Page 5:

of his citizenship. Subject's brief in this case approved by EARL BROWDER, National Secretary, Communist Party. Maintains six bank accounts in San Francisco, probably using some of funds to assist in work of People's World newspaper and Communist Party and to furnish bail bond to SAM DARCY, prominent Communist, now on trial for perjury. Maintains almost daily contact with officials of People's World newspaper and Communist

Party, who make requests of him for money. Has stated to one Communist Party worker that he, subject, is his banker. Co-signers on one bank account are well known Communists. Signator on another is his secretary and wife of registered Communist and militant labor worker. Subject married to DR. FRANCES FOSTER, well known radical, has three children. Sister married to ALEX NORAL, prominent Communist and Workers' Alliance official.

Details:

This investigation is predicated upon information received from Confidential Informant [redacted] There is set out below in brief summary from the information required by the Bureau in Internal Security cases, together with that required by the Bureau in teletypes dated March 3 and March 6, 1941:

Name:	GEORGE R. ANDERSEN alias GEORGE ANDERSON
ADDRESS	Residence – 69 Piedmont Ave., San Francisco; Business – 544 Market Street,San Francisco
OCCUPATION	Attorney
NATIONALISTIC TENDENCIES	Communist
RELATIVES	DR. FRANCES FOSTER, wife; three small children

Page 6:

ORGANIZATIONS:	San Francisco County Bar Association; California State Bar Association
CITIZENSHIP:	United States, born Copenhagen, Denmark of American parents
NATIONALITY:	Scandinavian

DESCRIPTION:	(see below)	
	Age	41 (born Copenhagen, Denmark 9/19/00)
	Height	5'9"
	Weight	140
	Hair	Reddish brown
	Eyes	Gray
	Complexion	Medium
	Build	Medium
	Glasses	Wears glasses

There are contained in the San Francisco file two copies of the photograph of subject.

There is set out below a chronological summary of the information received at this office from Confidential Informant [redacted]

1934 – Reported to be official attorney for the Communist Party at $150 per month, plus court fees. Reported to be member of the National Committee for Defense of Political Prisoners.

1935 – Reported to be brother-in-law of ALEX NORAL and to be Labor Party candidate for Municipal Judge. During campaign was described as militant labor attorney. Reported to be attorney for International Labor Defense, Communist Party front group. His declaration of candidacy in connection with his campaign for Municipal Judge is quoted below:

"That I shall have been a resident of the City and County of San Francisco for a period of at least five years and an elector thereof for a period of at least one year immediately prior to the time for taking such office; that my name is GEORGE R. ANDERSEN; that my residence address is 61 Divisadero Street, San [continued on page 8]

Page 7: [continued from page 9]

and wife of KARL YONEDA, Communist longshoreman worker for Alaska Cannery Workers and militant CIO Union member. A few days after the writing of this check the International Labor Defense posted $5000 cash bond for SAM DARCY, former State Secretary of the Communist Party and presently defendant in the Government suit for perjury in connection with voter's registration.

A monitor of Accounts #3, 4, 5 and 6, all at the American Trust Company, Palace Hotel Branch, reveals that these accounts are all used for small items for the firm of ANDERSEN-RESNER, attorneys, 544 Market Street, and for ANDERSEN's personal use and for the household use of ANDERSEN and his wife, DR. FRANCES FOSTER.

Signature on Account #2 are any two of the following: GEORGE R. ANDERSEN, Trustee, HELEN K. PELL, MINI CARSON and ELEANOR FAUROT.

HELEN PELL was Executive Secretary of the Inter-Professional Association, Communist front group, and has been reported to now be Organizational Director of the American Peace Mobilization, also a Communist front group.

MINI CARSON is a registered Communist Party voter for the election year 1940, a member of the Communist Party State Central Committee in 1938, and is actively engaged in the support of the defense of SAM DARCY.

ELEANOR FAUROT is connected with the International Labor Defense in Oakland, California.

Signators on Accounts #3 and 4 are GEORGE R. ANDERSEN, HERBERT RESNER, his law partner, and ESTHER BROWN, his secretary. She is the wife of ARCHIE BROWN, registered Communist Party voter for the election year 1940 and members of the Communist Party State Central Committee for that year and candidate on the Communist Party ticket for State Treasurer, State Assemblyman and U.S. Congressman for the election years 1934, 1936 and 1940, respectively.

The subject is the only signator on Account #1 and is signator alternately with his wife, FRANCES FOSTER, on Account #6.

The only information given regarding himself to the banks when the above accounts were opened was that he was born in Denmark; that his father's name is JOHN and that his mother's name was LYDIA. He also stated that he was engaged in the practice of law with HERBERT RESNER, 544 Market Street, San Francisco.

Page 8:

[continued from page 6] Francisco; that my business or occupation is attorney at law. My qualifications for said office are as follows: I am the son of a pioneer California family, my grand-parents having settled in Santa Cruz in 1850. I have lived 32 years in San Francisco and was educated in this city's public school, admitted to the Bar in this city in 1927. I am a member of both the San Francisco and California State Bar Associations. As a believer in Labor's cause and Constitutional rights, I have been for a number of years a defender of Labor and political prisoners in court. My belief is justice for all the people fits me to serve the city as Judge of the Municipal Court."

1936 – Received 37,673 votes for Judge of the Municipal Court on the Labor Party ticket. Defended ANITA WHITNEY, well known Communist and subject of a San Francisco Internal security case, on a perjury charge. Attorney for EARL KING and FRANK CONNER, of the well known, KING-CONNER-RAMSAY case. Defendants now in San Quentin Penitentiary and visited by Communists regularly. The case if championed by Communists and People's World newspaper, official Communist Party organ on the West Coast.

1937 – LOUISE TODD LAMBERT, as LOUISE TODD, paroled to him. This woman is the wife of RUDY LAMBERT, prominent Communist worker at Party headquarters, 121 Haight St., San Francisco. LOUISE TODD was subsequently employed by him. Attorney for Alaska Cannery Workers. California State Chairman and sponsor of Abraham Lincoln Brigade, Communist Party front, made up of American volunteers fighting for the Communists in the recent Spanish civil war. Candidate for San Francisco City Supervisor on the Communist Party ticket.

1938 – Candidate for Judge of the Superior Court with HERBERT RESNER, law partner, campaign manager. Reported to be member of the Communist Party.

1939 – Reported to be attorney for International Labor Defense. Stated at Sacramento, Calif., 4/6/39, when asked if he were a member of the Communist Party, "No, but if I chose to be a member, I would be and I don't think that membership in the Communist Party should prevent a man from exercising his right of free speech." Appeared befor [sic] the California State Assembly 4/24/39 to voice his [continued on page 9]

Page 9:

[continued from page 8] disapproval of the Criminal Syndicalism Act. Reported to be attorney for the CIO. Defended LUCIEN GEORGE as attorney. GEORGE arrested for distributing Communist campaign handbills. Attorney for WILLIAM SCHNEIDERMAN, California State Secretary, Communist Party in Government suit for revocation of SCHNEIDERMAN's citizenship.

Investigation by Special Agent (A) E.F MINOUX reveals that subject maintains in San Francisco six separate bank accounts, which are as follows:

1. GEORGE R. ANDERSEN, Special account

   Savings account #17435

   Wells Fargo Bank and Union Trust Company, Main Office

2. GEORGE R. ANDERSEN, Trustee
   Checking account
   Bank of America Day and Night Branch

3. ANDERSEN and RESNER, Special Account
   Checking account
   American Trust Company, Palace Hotel Branch

4. ANDERSEN and RESNER, general account
   Checking account
   American Trust Company, Palace Hotel Branch

5. GEORGE R. ANDERSEN, special account
   Checking account
   American Trust Company, Palace Hotel Branch

6. GEORGE R. ANDERSEN or FRANCES FOSTER
   Checking account
   American Trust Company, Palace Hotel Branch

Monitoring of Account #1. GEORGE R. ANDERSEN, Special Account, beginning May 9, 1939, shows three large deposits in the amounts of $1000, $3000, and $5000 and various smaller ones. One withdrawal was made on January 12, 1940, in the amount of $1000. This balance has steadily increased from $247.00 to $4,834.14. The authorized signator is GEORGE R. ANDERSEN.

Monitoring of Account #2 from November 2, 1940, shows a check dated November 9, 1940, in the amount of $4000 to ELAINE BLACK, well known Communist and active worker for the International Labor Defense

[continued on page 7].[1]

Page 10:

Confidential Informant [redacted] advised that subject is in almost daily contact with the offices of the People's World newspaper and the Communist Party headquarters and that most of these contacts are made for the purpose of obtaining money by those organizations from subject. During those contacts he has made arrangements to supply them with money, and at one time stated to a prominent worker at Communist Party headquarters that he, subject, is that individual's banker.

S.F. file #100-659-3 contains a report from the San Francisco Police Department to the effect that subject has been seen in the company of DR. FRANCES FOSTER and that she and subject resided together at the same address and are either married or living together as man and wife.

S.F. file #97-4-136 contains information to the effect that ANDERSEN and RESNER were reported in May 1940 to be working to determine whether or not there was any legal method by which the Communist Party could obtain arms. This information came from a confidential source, the reliability of which is not known. The information in full as received from this informant is contained in letter directed to the Bureau from this office May 11, 1940.

In file 61-322-290 is a letter undated received at this office June 17, 1940, from [redacted] wherein it is stated that subject is the Communist Party attorney and that his legal education was financed by that Party. The reliability of that information is not known to this office.

[redacted] advised that on October 31, 1938, a trust deed to 121 Haight Street, Communist Party headquarters, was executed to secure payment of $8,125.00 to GEORGE R. ANDERSEN. This informant also advised that subject is the brother-in-law of ALEX NORAL, local Workers' Alliance Chairman and registered Communist, and that because of this relationship ANDERSEN obtains the law business from the Communist Party. Informant also stated that subject has stated at different times that he was born in the United States and in Denmark.

Agent R.C. TAYLOR examined the records of the California State Bar Association, which revealed that ANDERSEN was admitted to the practice of law in California October 7, 1927. It also shows that he is a graduate of the San Francisco College in night law school. No information regarding his personal history was shown.

The records of the District Court of Appeals for the First District, 438 State Building, Civic Center, San Francisco, revealed

Page 13:

A search of the records of the Motor Vehicle Department was made, with negative results.

At the San Francisco Police Department Agent was advised that the International Labor Defense pays subject's fees for the defense of Communists; that he, subject, was supposed to have been born in San Francisco and that he has three brothers (?) ALEX NORAL, NORMA PERRY and ELVIA NORAL. That Department was unable to give the source of this information.

The purpose of the above background and investigation was to obtain sufficient information regarding subject and his father to determine whether or not the subject is presently a citizen of the United States. It was not possible without spending and unreasonable amount of time on this case to determine the exact parentage of subject for the purpose of examining the naturalization papers of his father, with the furtherpurpose [sic] of determining subject's exact citizenship status. However, at the Bureau of Immigration and Naturalization in the Post Office Building at San Francisco, the naturalization records were examined on one JOHN C. ANDERSEN, who is probably subject's father. These records indicated that this person became a citizen at the age of 18 in 1884 and that he was a native of Sweden.

In the absence of Bureau instructions to the contrary, no further investigation will be made to establish subject's citizenship.

For administrative purposes, this case is being closed at this time, subject to being reopened upon receipt of further information regarding this individual.

Page 17:

CUSTODIAL DETENTION MEMORANDUM

GEORGE R. ANDERSEN, alias	COMMUNIST
George Anderson	San Francisco
	File 61-146

Residence: 69 Piedmont Street, San Francisco
Business address: 544 Market Street, San Francisco

The name of the above individual is submitted to the Bureau for consideration for custodial detention in the event of a national emergency. The following information is summarized from the San Francisco File.

1. GEORGE R. ANDERSEN, alias GEORGE ANDERSON
2. Residence: 69 Piedmont Street, San Francisco; Business Address: 544 Market Street, San Francisco; Source: City and Telephone Directories.
3. Nationalistic tendency: Communist. Source: [redacted]
4. Citizenship Status: U.S. citizen, born in Denmark of U.S. citizens. Source: records of San Francisco Law School, and interview with CARL H. KRESS, 1595 43rd Avenue, San Francisco.

5. Subject has for past several years been prominently associated with the Communist Party as attorney (Source: [redacted]. Supplies them with funds and acts as their banker. (Source: [redacted] and bank account monitor, see report of Special Agent R.E. MAYER, San Francisco, 5-17-41, case entitled GEORGE R. ANDERSEN, wa; INTERNAL SECURITY, San Francisco File 61-146). Has been associated with the International Labor Defense and has been United Labor Party and Communist Party candidate for Municipal Judge and City Supervisor. (Source: [redacted] Is legal counsel for the International Labor Defense and presently defending State Secretary of the Communist Party on action for revocation of his citizenship. (Source SFPD and [redacted]. Reported to be member of Communist Party (Source: [redacted]. His practice is exclusively with Communists (Source: [redacted] and Alfred D. Martin, San Francisco Bar Association). Holds mortgage on Communist Party Headquarters premises, 121 Haight Street, San Francisco (Source: [redacted].

100-2865-4 [Italics denote handwritten text.]

Page 19:

August 26, 1941

MEMORANDUM FOR MR. L.M.C. SMITH
CHIEF, SPECIAL DEFENSE UNIT

There is transmitted herewith a dossier showing the information presently available in the files of this Bureau with respect to George R. Andersen, with aliases whose address is 69 Piedmont Avenue, San Francisco, California.

It is recommended that this individual be considered for custodial detention in the event of a national emergency. The information contained on the attached dossier constitutes the basis for appropriate consideration in this regard.

It should be understood, of course, that additional information may be received from time to time supplementing that already available in the Bureau's files, and as such data are received they will be made available to you so that the dossier in your possession may be supplemented thereby.

It will be greatly appreciated if you will advise this Bureau at your earliest convenience as to the decision reached in this case.

Very truly yours,
[signed] *J.E. Hoover*
John Edgar Hoover

Director

Page 22:

ANDERSEN, GEORGE R.

Very active as an attorney for various Communist leaders and reported to be the "brains" behind Harry Bridges. (Conf. Inf. [redacted] 1936, 100-2-45)

Resided in San Francisco for 32 years. Admitted to California State Bar in 1927. (Admitted in campaign statements in 1935, Conf. Inf. [redacted] 100-2-45)

One George E. Anderson, a Communist Attorney in San Francisco, probably identical with subject, was working at the Bethlehem Shipyards, at San Francisco when the Communists "found him and sent him to school"; the Communist Party at San Francisco financed Anderson's law course at some school in the East. [redacted] 9-17-40, 39, 915-558, p. 790)

In 1935 subject and Leo Gallagher carried on the negotiations for the purchase of the land and building at 121 Haight St., San Francisco, which since then has been used as C.P. headquarters. (Lloyd W. Dinkelspiel, Nevada Bank Bldg., San Francisco, October, 1940. 39-915-558, p. 94)

He was attorney representing Louise Todd, who on February 7, 1935 was sentenced to serve [continued on page 23]

Page 23:

ANDERSEN, GEORGE R.

[continued from page 22] 1 to 14 years for perjury. (Chet Flint, investigator for District Attorney, Oakland, California, 39-915-618, p.161) in connection with the falsifying of signatures on a petition to place the Communist Party on ballot in 1934. She served time in Tehachapi Prison, California from 11-18-35 to 12-19-36, when she was paroled to subject, for whom she was working, on July 9, 1937. (Patrick Farrelly, U.S. Immigration and Naturalization Service, San Francisco, 39-915-618, p. 158-161). Louise Todd handled the Lawyers' Professional Unit by Communist Party directly from subject's office. [redacted]

In 1936 and 1937 subject was a member of the Professional Section of the Communist Party, which [redacted] informant. [redacted] in sworn statement dated [redacted] to Beverly Hills, Cal., P.D., statement now in files of U.S. Immigration and Naturalization Service, San Francisco, 39-915-619, p. 100)

In connection with the "Point Lobas" murder case, in which one Cherbourg was found drowned; informant [redacted] Sept. 1940, 39-915-619, p.140)

Page 24:

ANDERSEN, GEORGE R.

On or about January 5, 1938, at subject's request, one [redacted] went to subject's office and subject there requested him to [redacted] Informant refused to sign. (39-915-618, p. 177)

His name appeared upon the letterhead of the International Labor Defense, as one of its Legal Advisory Committee. (Copy of letter in file, 3-16-38, 61-7559-2520)

Subject is a member of Communist Party. (Testimony of John E. Ferguson, 1424 Southwest Montgomery St., Portland, Oregon, before Dies Committee, 12-7-38, 39-915-287)

He is State Chairman and Legal adviser of the Schneiderman-Darcy Defense Committee, which on 4-17-40 mailed a letter to U.S. Attorney Frank J. Hennessy, San Francisco, protesting his prosecution of an action to cancel American citizenship of William Schneiderman, State Secretary of the Communist Party. (U.S. Attorney Frank J. Hennessy, San Francisco, 61-7618-47)

Page 25:

ANDERSEN, GEORGE R.

One Ray Hepler, head of the Communist Unit in the Polk-Marina district, California, stated in informant's presence, that subject and Herbert Resner, Attorneys for the Communist Party in San Francisco, were working to determine if there was any legal method by which the Communist Party could obtain firearms. [redacted] 5-11-40, 39-915-618, p.178)

Informant, who was a member of the Communist Party, stated that C.P. officials had instructed her if she were ever arrested while on strike or other picket duties, that she was to contact immediately the I.L.D. (International Labor Defense), and that Mr. Anderson, [sic] possibly identical with subject, was the attorney for this organization. [redacted] 9-14-40, 39-915, p. 83)

On 12-10-40, one Isaac Folkoff, who is active in the financial affairs of the C.P. in San Francisco contacted subject and requested that he be given $150.00 (S.A.R.E Mayer, FBI, San Francisco, 100-19248-1)

His wife, is Dr. Frances Foster. (Confidential Informant [redacted] San Francisco, 12-19-40, 100-10940-2) who has been active in C.P. activities. (Record of San Francisco, P.D., 12-11-40, 100-10940-2)

Page 26:

ANDERSEN, GEORGE R.

He is representing William Schneiderman in the taking of an appeal from an order of Federal Court, San Francisco, revoking the citizenship of Schneiderman for membership in the Communist Party. (People's World, 4-8-41, 39-915-1017; People's World, 4-2-41, [illegible] 915-990)

[illegible] in arguing an appeal in the Schneiderman case before the Ninth U.S. Circuit [illegible] of Appeals, 4-11-41 at San Francisco, stated the case shouldn't be tried before [illegible] but rather before a political forum of the American people,' and alleged it [illegible] attempt to silence the Communist Party. The Schneiderman-Darcy, Committee called [illegible] to the Attorney General in Washington, D.C., (People's World, 4-12-41, 39-915 [illegible]

Page 32:

JOHN EDGAR HOOVER
Director

Federal Bureau of Investigation
United States Department of Justice
Washington, D.C.

January 22, 1942

LW: ELC

MEMORANDUM FOR MR. KRAMER

RE: GEORGE ANDERSEN
INTERNAL SECURITY, C

Confidential Informant [redacted] stated that it is the intention of the Communist Party in California to take advantage of the times and attempt to have its name placed on the ballot in the 1942 elections. The Communist Party attorney in San Francisco, George Andersen, has taken the matter up with Charles Johnson, of the State Attorney's Office, and has urged that since the Russians are now at war, it would be to the best interests of the national defense to allow the Communist Party to take part in elections. William Schneiderman, State Secretary of the Communist Party, is considering the advisability of continuing the pressure on the Attorney General and the State Legislature or of instituting a law suit "which would prevent the passage of such laws in the future."
George R. Andersen [Italics denote handwritten text.]

Respectfully,
Lish Whitson [signed]
Lish Whitson

Page 44:

Memorandum for the
Attorney General

George R. Andersen
544 Market Street
San Francisco, California

Authorization for this technical surveillance which was requested in my memorandum of November 10, 1941, was disapproved by you on November 19, 1941. However, I wish to emphasize at this time that the position of George R. Andersen in connection with Communist Party activities in the San Francisco area makes him a most likely source of information on general Party affairs. The records of the Federal Bureau of Investigation reflect that George R. Andersen has long been identified with the Communist Party movement as has his law partner, Herbert Resner. These attorneys have represented the Communist Party and its leaders on several occasions and were in the background during the recent Bridges and O'Neill cases. Andersen is the official attorney for the Communist Party in the San Francisco district and is a member of the Executive Committee of the Party.

An examination of the account carried as "George R. Andersen, Special," at the Wells Fargo Union Bank of San Francisco has revealed an interesting picture of Andersen's Party ties. For example, it was ascertained that on December 5, 1941 a check was drawn on the account payable to "cash" in the amount of $6,000, this being on the same date that $6,000 in $20.00 bills was deposited to the account of Harry Kramer of the Peoples World. A further check on these transactions revealed that on December 3, 1941 Harry Kramer had drawn a check to the account maintained by him for the operation of the Peoples World, this check being No. 4255 in the amount of $6,000, to the order of "National Committee, Communist Party, U.S.A." Obviously Andersen's withdrawal of December 5, 1941 was intended to cover the Peoples World's contribution to the Party.

George R. Andersen is undoubtedly one of the outstanding Communists on the West Coast and the fact that he is generally consulted with reference to important party matters indicates that a technical surveillance on Andersen is likely to be particularly productive in keeping us informed on policies of the Party.

Page 54:

Federal Bureau of Investigation
United States Department of Justice
Washington, D.C.

March 12, 1942

EGF: MLC
61-10170

MEMORANDUM FOR MR. D.M. LADD

Call: 12:40 p.m.
Dictated: 10:50 a.m., 3-14-42

SAC Pieper of the San Francisco Office was notified at this time that authority has been obtained from the Attorney General for the establishment of technical surveillance on the following individuals and organizations:

Steve Nelson
Oleta O'Connor Yates
International Labor Defense
Communist Party Headquarters, Oakland, California.

On that occasion, Mr. Pieper made inquiry as to the status of his requests for technical surveillances on the Peoples World (West Coast Communist Daily Publication) and George R. Andersen, Communist Attorney, which he had forwarded to the Bureau in a confidential letter of January 2, 1942. Mr. Pieper was advised that both the latter surveillances had been disapproved by the Attorney General.

Respectfully
[signed] *E.G.F*
E.G. Fitch

Page 55:

Federal Bureau of Investigation
United States Department of Justice
San Francisco, California
March 27, 1942

Director
Federal Bureau of Investigation
Washington, D.C.

Re: GEORGE R. ANDERSEN, with aliases;
Internal Security (C).

Dear Sir:

Reference is made to the Bureau letter dated March 10, 1942, Bureau file 100-2865, referring to a statement contained in the January General Intelligence Monthly Summary from the San Francisco office on the part of

George R. Andersen, Communist Party attorney, to the effect that "for all we know, six months from now the situation may be back where it was".

This statement on the part of ANDERSEN was made during a telephone conversation between him and Special Agent R.L. King, of this office. This conversation was occasioned by reason of the fact that just prior thereto an attempt had been made to have JOHN BROMAN, a member of the editorial staff of the People's World, Communist newspaper, come to the San Francisco Field Division for the purpose of discussing his status under the Selective Training and Service Act, it having been determined that some discrepancies appeared in the questionnaire filed by this individual. BROMAN was telephonically requested to appear at the San Francisco office but had refused to do so and approximately five minutes after the conversation with BROMAN, GEORGE R. ANDERSEN called and desired to know why this office was desirous of talking with JOHN BROMAN, ANDERSEN stating that he represented the members of the staff of the People's World and that these individuals were reluctant to call at the San Francisco Bureau office on any matter.

It was explained to ANDERSEN that the desire to talk with BROMAN was based upon the official duties of this Bureau and that it was a matter which was preferred to be handled personally with MR. BROMAN. ANDERSEN thereupon stated that, unfortunately, he would not permit BROMAN to come to the San Francisco Field Division and that if Agents of this office desired to interview BROMAN they would have to see him in his, ANDERSEN'S presence and in the office of ANDERSEN.

During this conversation GEORGE R. ANDERSEN stated that in the past year or two the People's World had printed several things of an uncomplimentary nature concerning the Federal Bureau of Investigation and, as stated above, the members of the staff had a reluctance to come to a Bureau office. ANDERSEN then stated that, however, at the present time and in view of the present war situation "things were different" and it [continued on page 56]

Page 56:

Director – Page 2 March 27, 1942

[continued from page 55] was the desire of the People's World staff members to do everything in their power to cooperate with the FBI in its present program. Agent KING thereupon asked MR. ANDERSEN if the latter did not think that perhaps the People's World had been under a misapprehension in the past when it had engaged in attacks upon the Bureau and to this ANDERSEN replied that that possibly could be and he then added the statement in question, namely, "For all we know, six months from now the situation may be where it was." This statement by ANDERSEN, of course, had reference to the possibility that six months from now the Communists may be again attacking the Bureau, such an eventuality probably occurring only as a result of a changed international situation which might find Russia either passively or actively allied again with Germany, and it was with this thought in mind that the statement by ANDERSEN was considered significant and so reported in the San Francisco General Intelligence Summary dated January 19, 1942, Bureau File 66-7777-47. No additional report of this matter has been made in any other file.

It might be explained that GEORGE R. ANDERSEN did pay an official visit to the San Francisco Bureau office, at which time he desired to report the activities of various German and Fascist organizations in the San Francisco area, which information had been secured by him from HARRISON GEORGE, Editor at the People's World. Nothing with reference to Communist matters was discussed at the time of this visit and the information was accepted from ANDERSEN on the basis of any other volunteer informant or complainant and, for the Bureau's information, the matter was followed up and a discussion subsequently had on this material between Agents of this office and ANDERSEN and HARRISON GEORGE in ANDERSEN's office.

In the General Intelligence Summary it was not thought necessary or advisable to set out the facts which occasioned the telephone call on the part of ANDERSEN to the San Francisco office.

Very truly yours,
[signed] *N.J.L. Pieper*
N.J.L. PIEPER
Special Agent in Charge.

Page 58:

May 12, 1942

Dear Sir:

There is set forth below a name and address which has been furnished to the American Censorship authorities with the request that all communications coming into or leaving the United States bearing this address, be copied.

George R. Andersen
69 Piedmont Street
San Francisco, California

If this address has been recently changed or is incorrectly reflected by the Bureau files, this matter should be called to the Bureau's attention.

If there are any other names or addresses or variations of spelling of a subject's name which should be placed on the Censorship Watch Lists, this matter also should be brought to the Bureau's attention.

Very truly yours,

[signed] *John Edgar Hoover*
Director

Page 61:

FEDERAL BUREAU OF INVESTIGATION

Case originated at	SAN FRANCISCO, CALIFORNIA	File No. 61-146

Report made at	Date Made	Period	Report Made by:
SAN FRANCISCO, CALIFORNIA	2/4/43	12/10,11,26,30/42	JAMES L. HAY

Title:		Character:
		CHANGED
GEORGE RICHARD ANDERSEN, with		INTERNAL SECURITY - C
alias:	George Anderson	Custodial Detention

SYNOPSIS
OF FACTS:

Confidential informant [redacted] advises that INTERNATIONAL LABOR DEFENSE interested in defense of ELMER HANOFF, deportation subject, and that ANDERSEN is apparently handling the case. Subject in 1934 asked for police protection from Vigilante Committee that had threatened his life. Subject registered for Selective Service and classified 3A. Reported to be of low moral character and to have had illicit relations with different women. Subject cashed check for $6,000 two days after the People's World sent check for $6,000 to the National Committee, Communist Party. On same date, $6,000 was credited to account of HARRY KRAMER, Business Manager of People's World, local Communist paper. Custodial Detention Card issued and subject's dangerousness classification is A-1. Subject placed on Censorship Watch List. Information from general files of San Francisco Office set forth. Mail cover placed.

Page 62:

REFERENCE: Bureau File 100-2865. Report of Special Agent R.E. MAYER, dated May 17, 1941, at San Francisco.

DETAILS: The title of this case is being changed to reflect subject's true name as GEORGE RICHARD ANDERSEN, as it is shown on his Selective Service Registration Card, and to delete the name of GEORGE R. ANDERSEN.

On May 20, 1941, Confidential Informant [redacted] advised that the INTERNATIONAL LABOR DEFENSE is interested in the defense of ELMER HANOFF in his deportation case, and that they expect the bail to be around $3,000. The informant also advised that GEORGE R. ANDERSEN took HANOFF to the Office of the Immigration and Naturalization Service, 801 Silver Avenue, on the afternoon of May 20, and surrendered him for arrest on an eleven-year old warrant in connection with deportation. It was his intention to get out a writ of Habeas Corpus in the event the Immigration authorities held him on the warrant. Inspector W.E. Walsh advised that ANDERSEN and HANOFF did come to his office that afternoon.

The San Francisco Examiner on July 20, 1934, carried an article advising that the subject [Andersen] appealed to the San Francisco Police Department for protection on July 19, 1934, stating, "I had threats from some of these Vigilantes. They said they were going to wreck my offices just like they wrecked those other places, and were going to take me or a ride from which I won't be able to walk back." The article stated that Captain J. J. O'Meara assigned two men to escort Anderson [sic] to his office and said he would provide a police escort when the lawyer comes to the Hall of Justice to defend Communists on July 20. An appeal by Andersen for permission to carry a gun was taken under advisement.

The San Francisco Chronicle newspaper for July 20, 1934, carried a similar article, which advised that ANDERSEN had appealed to the police for protection, stating that he was going to be "taken for a ride," and his downtown offices wrecked. ANDERSEN stated that the threatening telephone call came from a party representing himself as the spokesman for a mysterious Vigilante Committee of twenty-five.

The San Francisco Call Bulletin of July 21, 1934, stated that a "majority of the three hundred and fifty alleged radicals in jail here today received a blow when they learned that they had been deprived of the services of Attorney GEORGE ANDERSEN who has defended many Communists [continued on page 63].

Page 63:

[continued from page 62] "in court as representative of the INTERNATIONAL LABOR DEFENSE, a Communist organization. ANDERSEN, appearing before Municipal Judge GEORGE J. STEIGER, asked to be excused from defending the asserted Communists awaiting trial and at the same time sought aid of the police that Communists had so often defied in the past. 'My life has been threatened,' he said in a low shaken voice. 'have been threatened by vigilantes.'"

Through Confidential Informant [redacted] it was learned that on December 3, 1941, HARRY KRAMER drew a check on the account maintained by him for the operation of the People's World local Communist newspaper, this check being No. 4255 in the amount of $6,000 to the order of "National Committee, Communist Party, U.S.A." This check was signed by HARRY KRAMER and by H. SCHAFF, the latter individual acting in the capacity of Treasurer of the People's World. This office has in its possession a photstatic copy of the cancelled check, written to the order of the National Committee, Communist Party, U.S.A., bears the following printed designation, "People's World, 585 Market Street, San Francisco."

On November 5, 1941, two days after the date of the above-mentioned check, a deposit of $6,000 in $20 bills was made to the account on which the check had been drawn. In an examination of the account carried as "GEORGE R. ANDERSEN, Special," at the Wells Fargo Union Bank of San Francisco, it was ascertained that on December 5, 1941, a check was drawn to cash in the amount of $6,000, this being on the same date that $6,000 in $20 bills was deposited in the HARRY KRAMER account. [redacted] made the observation that this sum of money was obviously being used to cover the check for $6,000 drawn on December 3, 1941, to the order of the "National Committee, Communist Party, U.S.A."

In a telephone conversation between the subject and Special Agent R.L. KING of this office, ANDERSEN stated that in the past year or two, the People's World had printed several things of an uncomplimentary nature concerning the Federal Bureau of Investigation, and ANDERSEN then stated that, however, at the present time and in view of the present War situation, "things are different," and it was the desire of the People's World to do everything in its power to cooperate with the FBI in its present program. There was some other conversation concerning the relationship of this organization to the People's World, and it terminated with ANDERSEN making the statement, "For all we know, six months from now the situation may be back where it was." This statement by ANDERSEN referred to the possibility that six months from now the Communists may be again attacking this Bureau.

Page 64:

Through Confidential Informant [redacted] it was learned that subject was to accompany STEVE NELSON and WALTER LAMBERT, prominent local Communists, to a meeting of the Communist Party on February 26, 1942. At 8 P.M. on this date, Special Agent AUGUSTUS F. SCHERMERHORN and Special Agent QUENTIN H. PLUNKETT parked in their automobile across the street from NELSON's residence at 3720 Grove Street, Oakland, California, and observed three men arrive at this address, enter the house, and a few minutes later, return to their automobiles with another man. The license number of one automobile was 37A 113, which is a Studebaker Six Cylinder registered to GEORGE R. ANDERSEN, 69 Piedmont Street, San Francisco. The other automobile used by these men was a 1936 Chevrolet Coupe Six Cylinder, License 93F 180, registered to Mrs. HAZEL C. WOOD, 924 Fulton Street, San Francisco.

On July 8, 1942, Special Agent A.B. BERRY examined the records of Local Draft Board No. 87, and the following information concerning the subject was secured:

Subject's registration card reflected GEORGE RICHARD ANDERSEN, 69 Piedmont Street, San Francisco, was born September 19, 1900, at Copenhagen, Denmark. He also advised that the individual who would always know of his whereabouts is his wife FRANCES ANDERSEN FOSTER *Andersen*. [Italics denote handwritten text.]

Subject's questionnaire reflected he had no physical or mental defects nor was he an inmate of an institution. He did not have a Social Security number in view of the fact that he is an employer and with regard to his education he stated he had eight years of elementary school, four years of high school, and four years at the San Francisco Law School. ANDERSEN stated he is a member of the firm of ANDERSEN & RESNER, 544 Market Street, and that he has been a practicing attorney for the past fifteen years, averaging from $8,000 to $10,000 yearly income. As to other occupational experience, subject stated he was an apprentice shipfitter and loftsman, making templates for the hull of steel ships from 1916 to 1921. Subject advised he was married

December 24, 1934, at Yuma, Arizona, and that he has three children. As to persons who are dependent upon him, subject listed FRANCES FOSTER, age 38, wife; [redacted] and M. STROUKEL, housekeeper, age?. ANDERSEN later qualified the dependency of his wife by stating she is a practicing physician in San Francisco and has her own income. ANDERSEN also stated he supported Mrs. M.L. PERRY, 65 Belcher Street, who is his mother and who is approximately seventy-one years of age. According to ANDERSEN, he and his wife have approximately $25,000 to $30,000 in assets.

ANDERSEN stated that as to previous military experience he had served in the Air Reserve from 1923 to 1926, from which he had an honorable discharge.

Page 65:

As of December 16, 1942, the subject was placed in Class 3A by his Local Draft Board.

The following physical description of subject was obtained from his registration card, as follows:

Height	6’
Weight	185
Complexion	Light
Eyes	Blue
Hair	Brown
Build	Medium
Race	White
	Wears Glasses

Conf. Inft [Italics denote handwritten text.]

On October 12, 1942 [redacted] advised that information had been received that indicates that the subject has possibly engaged in illicit relations with one [redacted] From the information received, it appears that [redacted] is presently working in a cafe as a waitress somewhere in Berkeley, California, and is in attendance at the University of California, probably as a student in her Freshman year. It is also noted that ANDERSEN recently gave [redacted] a typewriter which appears to have been more or less of a compensatory gesture on his part. The information concerning the typewriter was furnished this office by Confidential Informant [redacted] and this same informant, who is acquainted with [redacted] advised that the subject had told her that although he was born in Denmark, he was not a citizen of that country.

Confidential Informant [redacted] also advised that the subject had told [redacted] that he did not like the way she was contemplating obtaining her tuition money for her education and told her that she should come to his office and he would give her the money. However, she informed [redacted] that she told ANDERSEN that she did not want to take any more tuition money from him. [redacted] further advised that subject made arrangements to take [redacted] to Oregon with him over the week-end of October 15, 1942. This informant did not know whether this trip was actually carried out or not, but he felt fairly certain that in view of the arrangements that were made that it probably was.

Special Agent AUGUSTUS F. SCHERMERHORN, upon checking at the Registrar's Office of the University of California, ascertained that [redacted] applied for admission at the University of California on [redacted] At this time she gave her address as [continued on page 66]

Page 67:

Under date of September 12, 1941, the Bureau advised that a Custodial Detention Card concerning the subject had been issued and subsequently advised that subject had been given a dangerousness classification of A-1.

Confidential Informant [redacted] advised that the subject was a subscriber to the People's World as of June, 1942.

According to Source of Information A, the subject is acquainted with the following prominent Communists in the San Francisco Bay area: LEO BAROWAY, RUDIE LAMBERT, ISAAC FOLKOFF, HARRY KRAMER, MERVYN RATHBONE, WILLIAM SCHNEIDERMAN, LOU McLAIN, Publicity Director for the People's World.

Source of Information B stated that in a conversation between the subject and LOUISE LAMBERT, at which time [redacted] Louise stated that it sounded funny to hear someone praising Russia. ANDERSEN then said that it was wonderful. Source B further stated that subject is the attorney for the INTERNATIONAL WORKERS ORDER.

A review of the files of the San Francisco Field Division revealed the following information:

The U.S. Attorney at San Francisco advised on July 1, 1940, that subject was Chairman and legal adviser for the SCHNEIDERMAN-DARCY Defense Committee.

Confidential Source of Information C advised that the People's World of February 2, 1942, [redacted] stated that the subject handled a suit of the Communist Party against the State of California to compel the state to place the Party on the ballot for the August, 1942, Primary.

Confidential Source of Information D advised that the Western Worker of November 18, 1935, [redacted] stated that the subject was defending ANITA WHITNEY, local Communist Party leader who is on trial for perjury.

Confidential Source of Information E advised that the subject holds a mortgage of $8,125 on land used as a Communist Party Headquarters in San Francisco, and that the legal title to this land is in the name of HARRY SCHAFF, People's World Treasurer.

Page 68:

Records of the San Francisco County Clerk reveal that a copy of an affidavit filed by AL CRAWFORD, attorney for IVAN FRANCIS COX, plaintiff reveals that subject is listed as a defendant in a suit brought by the plaintiff against the Communist Party and WILLIAM SCHNEIDERMAN, HARRY BRIDGES, and other specific Communist Party members.

On December 12, 1942, a sixty-day mail cover was placed on the subject at the law offices of ANDERSEN and RESNER, Room 607, 544 Market Street, San Francisco, California.

By letter of May 12, 1942, the Bureau advised that subject's name had been placed on the Censorship Watch list.

Page 71:

FEDERAL BUREAU OF INVESTIGATION

Case originated at SAN FRANCISCO, CALIFORNIA	FILE NO. 61-146

Report made at	Date Made	Period	Report made by
San Francisco, Calif.	7/14/43	6/22-25, 28-30; 7/ 6.8/43	ARTHUR F. BAIER mfd

Title	Character of case
GEORGE RICHARD ANDERSEN	INTERNAL SECURITY – C;
alias George Anderson	CUSTODIAL DETENTION

SYNOPSIS OF FACTS:

Subject's past connections with INTERNATIONAL LABOR DEFENSE set out; [redacted] additional reported activities of subject on behalf of the Communist Party set out; informants have reported subject as being a Communist Party member; subject acts as legal counsel for Communist Party in California, as well as for its officers and members; represented WILLIAM SCHNEIDERMAN in his citizenship cancellation case which was recently reversed by the United States Supreme Court; allegedly born 9/19/00 Copenhagen, Denmark; now claims United States citizenship through alleged naturalization of his father who entered the United States from Denmark in 1886, returned to Denmark in 1898 where he remained until 1902 during which time subject was born. Subject now alleges his father became naturalized prior to 1898 but that records of same were destroyed in the earthquake and fire of 1906 in San Francisco. San Francisco Superior Court recently denied subject's petition for restoration of alleged records of his father's naturalization for lack of sufficient proof. Investigation conducted in San Francisco failed to reflect any record of or any evidence to indicate subject's father was ever naturalized. Subject father died 1915. Subject presently classified 3-A by Local Board #87 San Francisco; 1942 family income estimated at $25,000; presently residing 69 Piedmont Street and maintains law offices under name of Andersen and Resner at 544 Market Street, San Francisco. Criminal record in San Francisco negative; more recent description set out.

Page 72:

San Fr. 61-146

REFERENCE: Bureau File 100-2865

Report of Special Agent R.E. MAYER, San Francisco, California dated 5/17/41.

Report of Special Agent JAMES L. HAY, San Francisco, California, dated 2/4/43.

DETAILS: AT SAN FRANCISCO, CALIFORNIA:

Subject's name appears on the key figure list maintained in this Field Division inasmuch as he serves as legal counsel for the Communist Party in California, as well as for its individual officers and members. Subject is also known to be consulted with by high Communist Party officials when determining Party policy and he has also been known to have handled considerable funds for the Communist Party in the past.

This report contains information on the subject as obtained from a review of the San Francisco Field Division files and additional investigation. Information set out in this report is in addition to that set out in previous reports on this individual. For the purpose of clarity and organization, the subject matter of this report will be set out under the following headings:

I. Subject's past connections with the INTERNATIONAL LABOR DEFENSE

II. [redacted]

III. Subject's activities in connection with the COMMUNIST PARTY.

IV. Subject's citizenship status.

V. Miscellaneous information.

I. INTERNATIONAL LABOR DEFENSE:

The November 18, 1935 issue of the Western Worker newspaper, the Western organ of the Communist Party, reported that the subject as the ILD defense attorney defended PETE GARCIA and PABLO ESPINOSA, radical trade unionists, on assault charges. The March 16, 1936 issue of the same publication reported that the subject as the ILD attorney was defending MIKE PUDOFF and ALEX LOSCUTOFF, who were pickets arrested in connection with strike events.

The San Francisco Field Division is in possession of a letter-head of the ILD national office in use in 1937, which reflects the name of the subject as a member of its legal advisory committee.

Page 73:

San Fr. 61-146

The San Francisco Field Division also has in its possession a folder announcing a conference of the ILD of the Northern and Southern California Districts of the ILD to be held April 23 and 24, 1938 at San Francisco. Subject's name appears in this folder as an endorser of the conference.

Also on file in the San Francisco Field Division is a letterhead of the ILD, Northern California District, dated January 20, 1940 containing a mimeographed message and signed by MINI CARSON, Executive Secretary, and GEORGE RICHARD ANDERSEN, Trustee of the Bail Fund.

The May 14, 1941 issue of the People's World newspaper reporting on the Third Biannual National Conference of the ILD held at New York City announced that the subject was a member of the National Committee of that organization.

The June 19, 1941 issue of the People's World newspaper reported that the ILD had entered the case of FESTUS COLEMAN, Negro WPA worker at that time recently convicted of rape and robbery in San Francisco, and that the subject as ILD attorney appealed COLEMAN's conviction.

On July 8, 1941 Source A reported that the subject's law firm, Andersen and Resner, represents the ILD and that the fees of that firm are paid by the funds of the ILD.

The September 2, 1941 issue of the People's World newspaper reported that ILD attorneys GEORGE ANDERSEN and HERBERT RESNER have been officially designated as defense counsel for FESTUS COLEMAN, San Francisco Negro, sentenced to San Quentin Prison for rape and robbery.

The People's World newspaper issue of April 8, 1942, reported that the San Francisco chapter of the NATIONAL ASSOCIATION FOR ADVANCEMENT OF COLORED PEOPLE announced the sponsoring of a mass meeting in behalf of FESTUS COLEMAN, convicted Negro, on April 12, 1942. Speakers listed for the mass meeting included the name of the subject as being from the ILD, along with several known Communists.

The October 2, 1942 issue of the People's World newspaper reported the subject as being one of the endorsers for a conference called the COLEMAN DEFENSE COMMITTEE on October 18, 1942 in the interest of securing a pardon for FESTUS COLEMAN. The December 12, 1942 issue of the same newspaper reported the subject as a member of the Delegation Committee preparing a petition to the California State Advisory Board on behalf of Coleman. (Confidential informants of this office have periodically reported that the COLEMAN DEFENSE COMMITTEE was organized and is controlled by the Communist Party.)

Page 74:

San Fr. 61-146

II. [redacted]

Source B reported that [redacted]

Confidential Informant [redacted] in October 1941 advised that the [redacted] On December 19, 1942 this informant furnished the San Francisco Field Division with [redacted]

On December 19, 1942 this informant furnished the San Francisco Field Division with [redacted]

On April 15, 1943 Source C advised that the subject [redacted]

III. SUBJECT'S ACTIVITIES IN CONNECTION WITH THE COMMUNIST PARTY:

Source D advised this office that the subject was one of several attorneys who signed as mentors by the Executive Committee of the Communist Party to guide HARRY BRIDGES in his activities on the waterfront in 1934.

Confidential Informant [redacted] has reported that LOUISE TODD, Executive member of the Communist Party in San Francisco, who had been sentenced in 1935 on a perjury charge in connection with the Communist Party petition, was on December 19, 1936 paroled to GEORGE ANDERSEN.

The San Francisco Call Bulletin, issue of March 19, 1937 reported that subject as attorney represented ANITA WHITNEY, Communist Party figure-head, who was sentenced and fined 25 days or $50.00 for her participation in connection with rioting before the German Consulate in San Francisco.

Source E reports that at the testimony taken on the extradition proceedings in December 1939 of SAMUEL A. DARCY, Communist Party official formerly of California, Docket M-905, United States Federal Court, Eastern District of Pennsylvania, on an indictment of perjury, subject was mentioned as the representative of the Communist Party in California.

Source F on August 24, 1940 advised this office that GEORGE R. ANDERSEN, San Francisco attorney, represented the Communist Party State Secretary in Arizona MORRIS GRAHAM, and all the members of the Communist Party in Arizona had filed for a writ of mandamus in Maricopa County Superior Court in Arizona seeking to compel the Arizona Secretary of State to place the Communist Party on the state primary election ballot.

Page 75:

San Fr. 61-146

The San Francisco office is in possession of a photostatic copy of a letterhead of the "Lambert for Congress Non-Partisan Committee," listing names of sponsors announcing their support, in the body of the letterhead, by a message directed to all members of organized labor of WALTER LAMBERT, candidate on the Communist Party ticket for United States Congress from the Fifth Congressional District. Subject's name appears on this letterhead as one of the sponsors along with many well-known San Francisco Communists.

The San Francisco Field Division also has on file the letterhead of the SCHNEIDERMAN-DARCY DEFENSE COMMITTEE as of June 1940 reflecting the name of subject as its legal advisor. The United States Attorney FRANK J. HENNESSY in San Francisco, California later received the letter from the subject protesting the Governor's action to cancel the citizenship of WILLIAM SCHNEIDERMAN. Also on file in the San Francisco Office is a handbill announcing the meeting of the SCHNEIDERMAN-DARCY DEFENSE COMMITTEE reflecting the name of the subject as one of the speakers. Confidential Informant [redacted] on August 16, 1941 reported attending this meeting given under the auspices of the SCHNEIDERMAN-DARCY DEFENSE COMMITTEE at Sorosis Hall, San Francisco, on August 15, 1941 and stated that the subject was one of the speakers at this meeting.

The San Francisco Field Division has in its possession a printed invitation to a New Year's party at "Nancy and John Pittmans, proceeds for the People's World newspaper." This invitation contains the name of the subject as one of the sponsors of the Party.

The April 2, 1941 issue of the People's World newspaper reported that the WILLIAM SCHNEIDERMAN case was set for the United States Circuit Court of Appeals on April 7, 1941 and that the subject would represent SCHNEIDERMAN. The April 29, 1941 issue of the same newspaper in reporting that the Ninth Circuit Court of Appeals had affirmed the cancellation of the citizenship of WILLIAM SCHNEIDERMAN announced that the subject would petition for a rehearing.

Confidential Informant [redacted] on January 25, 1942 quoted the statement of a well-known Communist HOMER MULLIGAN to the effect that Dr. FRANCES FOSTER and her husband GEORGE ANDERSEN, the well-known lawyer, were members of the Communist Party.

The People's World newspaper of February 2, 1942 reported that the Communist Party had filed suit in Superior Court at Los Angeles, California to compel the California Secretary of State to place the Communist Party on the August primary ballot, and that LEO GALLAGHER of Los Angeles and attorney GEORGE ANDERSEN of San Francisco were handling the suit for the Communist Party.

Page 76:

San Fr. 61-146

Confidential Informant [redacted] has advised this office that the subject's wife, Dr. FRANCES FOSTER, was seen at the State Conference of some 300 YCL delegates held at 136 Valencia Street in March 1942.

Source G advised this office that on November 25, 1942 subject forwarded a check to LEO BAROWAY, State Organizational Secretary and Financial Director of the Communist Party in California at 121 Haight Street. This source was unable to provide any further information concerning the check.

The People's World newspaper of February 18, 1943 reported that the subject filed a petition for a writ of habeas corpus in behalf of Miss ANITA WHITNEY and Mrs. ELSIE CRANE (Communist Party State Chairman and Organizer, respectively) who were arrested in the Fall of 1942 for violation of a Sacramento City ordinance when Miss WHITNEY endeavored to speak in behalf of her Communist Party candidacy for State Comptroller.

On March 20, 1943 Confidential Informant [redacted] stated that he was present at a general meeting of the Communist Party at California Hall in San Francisco in 1935 or 1936, at which time GEORGE R. ANDERSEN, subject, turned in his application to become a member of the Communist Party. This informant stated he was a witness to the above; further, that ANDERSEN at that time began to handle legal matters for the Communist Party.

Source H advised that the subject acted as legal counsel for WILLIAM SCHNEIDERMAN in his citizenship cancellation trial in the United States District Court, Northern California; also in the appeal of the decision before the United States Circuit Court of Appeals, and that subject collaborated with attorney CAROL KING of New York as the legal counsel for SCHNEIDERMAN when WENDELL WILLKIE argued the appeal before the United States Supreme Court. In June 1943 the United States Supreme Court reversed the decision in the SCHNEIDERMAN case and the San Francisco Chronicle in reporting same stated that ANDERSEN and RESNER, who defended SCHNEIDERMAN in the local courts declared the "case started at a period when redbaiting was rampant and when reactionary elements were sowing the seeds of disunity."

This article also quoted ANDERSEN and RESNER as follows: "This decision is a victory for the win-the-war forces. It will be shared in the capitols of Democracy. It will find no rejoicing in Berlin."

Source I, who is in a position to observe the activities of subject, reports that subject continues in frequent contact with such Communist Party officials as CARL WINTER, LEO BAROWAY, LOUISE TODD, OLETA O'CONNOR, and RUDIE LAMBERT.

Page 82:

San Fr. 61-146

The records of the San Francisco County Clerk in Volume II of the Civil indices reflects the name of JOHN L.C. ANDERSEN, a defendant in a divorce suit with LYDIA J. ANDERSEN as plaintiff, filed September 6, 1911 with judgment entered October 5, 1912. An examination of these divorce papers reflects no information concerning the citizenship status of the subject's father.

The files of the Department of Public Health, Vital Statistics Division, San Francisco, contain a recortd of the death of the the subject's father under the name of JOHN L. ANDESEN, indicating that he died on June 13, 1915 of pulmonary tuberculosis while at the tuberculosis hospital in San Francisco. This record also reflects that the subject's father was born December 22, 1865 in Denmark, his father's name being MICHAEL ANDERSEN and his mother's maiden name being JOHANNA HANSEN. It also indicates that the subject's father's occupation was that of a spotter in a dyeing works and that his residence previous to the time of hospitalization was 243 Noe Street, San Francisco, and at the time of his death his marital status was divorced. No mention is made of the citizenship status of this individual.

Dr. L.M. WILBOR, Superintendent of the San Francisco County Hospital, located the records of the subject's father's hospitalization in 1915 which record, when searched, failed to reflect any mention as to the citizenship status of the patient.

Source K on May 19, 1943 advised that the subject intends to file another petition requesting the Superior Court in San Francisco Count to restore the alleged record of his father's alleged naturalization.

V. MISCELLANEOUS INFORMATION:

The subject's file was reviewed at Local Board #87, 2290 Market Street, which reflects no information in addition to that previously reported, but indicates the following classifications:

August 13, 1942	3-A
February 1, 1943	4-H
May 27, 1943	3-A

His Order is #T-11284.

The files of the San Francisco County Civilian Defense contain a registration of enrollment for civilian defense duty by the subject volunteering as an auxiliary fireman. In this registration the subject gave his description and indicated that he had relatives consisting of cousins living in Denmark. It may be noted that subject objected to being fingerprinted at the time of this registration.

Page 88:

OFFICE OF THE ATTORNEY GENERAL
WASHINGTON, D.C.

July 16, 1943

MEMORANDUM FOR
HUGH B. COX, ASSISTANT ATTORNEY GENERAL
AND
J. EDGAR HOOVER, DIRECTOR
FEDERAL BUREAU OF INVESTIGATION

I refer to Mr. L.M.C Smith's memorandum to me dated June 28, 1943, which reviews the history, development, and meaning of the Special Case work and of the danger classifications that were made as a part of that work.

After full re-consideration of these individual danger classifications, I am satisfied that they serve no useful purpose. The detention of alien enemies is being dealt with under the procedures established by the Alien Enemy Control Unit The Special Case procedure has been found to be valueless and is not used in that connection. There is no statutory authorization or other present justification for keeping a "custodial detention" list of citizens. The Department fulfills its proper functions by investigating the activities of persons who may have violated the law. It is not aided in this work by classifying persons as to dangerousness.

Apart from these general considerations, it is now clear to me that this classification system is inherently unreliable. The evidence used for the purpose of making the classifications was inadequate; the standards applied to the evidence for the purpose of making the classifications were defective; and finally, the notion that it is possible to make a valid determination as to how dangerous a person is in the abstract and without reference to time, environment, and other relevant circumstances, is impractical, unwise, and dangerous.

For the foregoing reasons I am satisfied that the adoption of this classification system was a mistake that should be rectified for the future. Accordingly, I direct that the classifications heretofore made should not be regarded as classifications of dangerousness or as a

100-2865 [Italics denote handwritten text.]

Page 89:

Federal Bureau of Investigation
United States Department of Justice
Suite 1729 – 111 Sutter Street
San Francisco, California
August 12, 1943

Director, FBI

Dear Sir:

The following is a summary of the information obtained from Confidential Informant [redacted] for period July 28 to August 1, 1943, in regard to the above-captioned matter:

This informant advised that during the above period, GEORGE ANDERSEN was very much interested in aiding the position of the Negroes in Welders Union Local 81. It was learned that thirty-five to forty-five per cent of the welders at the Bethlehem Shipyards are Negroes and that fifty per cent of the entire production line is colored. ANDERSEN is aiding this union because of its sympathy for Negroes and believes that with his assistance, the union will be able to obtain working control of Labor at the Bethlehem Yards.

Information was also received from this source concerning the activities of ANDERSEN and RESNER in their campaign to have the Dilworth Bill declared unconstitutional by the California State Supreme Court.

Very truly yours,
[signed] *N.J.L Pieper*
N.J.L Pieper

George Andersen FBI File: HQ-100-2865 Section 3

Page 6:

FEDERAL BUREAU OF INVESTIGATION

THIS CASE ORIGINATED AT SAN FRANCISCO, CALIFORNIA	FILE NO. 61-146	
REPORT MADE AT	DATE WHEN MADE	PERIOD FOR WHICH MADE
SAN FRANCISCO	8/8/45	7/17, 19, 20; 8/1, 2/45

TITLE "CHANGED"	CHARACTER OF CASE
GEORGE RICHARD ANDERSEN, with aliases, George Anderson, George Carl Andersen	INTERNAL SECURITY - C

SYNOPSIS OF FACTS: Subject continues to reside at 579 El Camino Del Mar, San Francisco, and to maintain his law practice at 544 Market Street, San Francisco. He recently transferred from the North Side Professional Club to the Richmond Club of the CPA. He is closely associated with CPA functionaries and members. He recently discussed with LEO BAROWAY of CPA headquarters a "9,000 odd dollar check" which he gave to BAROWAY, which possibly is identical with the funds received from the Bank of Foreign Trade, Moscow.

REFERENCE: Bureau File 100-2865.

Report of Special Agent ROBERT LEO BRUGGEMAN, dated 3/22/45 at San Francisco, Calif.

DETAILS: Subject is considered a key figure in Communist activities in the Bay Area.

It is to be noted that the title of instant report has been marked changed to reflect the name of GEORGE CARL ANDERSEN as an alias inasmuch as Source A reported that the subject was referred to by LEO BAROWAY of CPA headquarters in San Francisco by that name.

Page 8:

San Francisco File 61-146

AT SAN FRANCISCO, CALIFORNIA.

Source A submitted periodic reports to the San Francisco Field Division regarding the following activities of the subject.

This source stated that ANDERSEN is contacted frequently by CPA functionaries and members and also disclosed that ANDERSEN is known to have been referred to by LEO BAROWAY of CPA headquarters in San Francisco as GEORGE CARL ANDERSEN.

On March 2, 1945, Source A overheard ANDERSEN ask LEO BAROWAY of CPA headquarters whether he had given LEO that "921 figure" check, that '9,000 odd dollar check.' In view of the fact that the check from the Bank of Foreign Trade, Moscow, to the firm of ANDERSEN and RESNER was in the amount of $9,662.91, it is believed that the transfer to the CPA may have been referred to in this conversation.

On or about January 19, 1945, ANDERSEN is known by Source A to have loaned $1,000.00 to the CPA for publicity purposes.

On March 3, 1945, ANDERSEN held a meeting at his home for the purpose of discussing the Big Three Conference. This meeting was attended by approximately twenty-five to thirty-five persons, among whom were LEO BAROWAY, LEE LEVY, and HAL SAWYER, all of whom are known CPA members in the San Francisco Field area.

ANDERSEN was selected by CPA headquarters to attend the state CPA school for the week of April 8 to 15, 1945, but he declined the invitation, inasmuch as he was too busy to attend.

On April 12, 1945, ANDERSEN attended a meeting of the RICHMOND CPA Club.

On April 23, 1945, he met with LEO BAROWAY of CPA headquarters at his office at 544 Market Street.

On May 16, 1945, ANDERSEN addressed the Eureka Valley Club of the CPA at the request of CLEMMIE BARRY of CPA headquarters in San Francisco.

On June 11, 1945, ANDERSEN discussed with RUDIE LAMBERT of CPA headquarters the propriety of instigating litigation in the negro situation.

It was ascertained by Source A that ANDERSEN was a delegate from the Richmond CPA Club to the CPA State Convention and that he attended the meeting on July 14, 1945, at Moose Hall in San Francisco.

Page 9:

San Francisco File 61-146

This source also reported that he had learned that ANDERSEN did not favor the idea of going into an open neighborhood club of the CPA, but expressed a willingness to cooperate and to do so if necessary.

Source B informed the San Francisco Field Division of the following CPA activities of the subject.

ANDERSEN attended meetings of the North Side CPA Club on February 15, 1945, March 1, 1945, and March 15, 1945. At these meetings he indicated that he was transferring to the Richmond Club as soon as he had found someone to fill his position as president in the North Side Club. On March 15, 1945, he announced that that would be his last meeting at the North Side Club and that he would thereafter attend the meetings of the Richmond Club.

Source B also reported that ANDERSEN attended a meeting of the San Francisco County Committee of the CPA on March 15, 1945, for the purpose of discussing the reshuffling of the membership in the various clubs.

Source C advised on January 23, 1945, that ANDERSEN attended a meeting of the CPA headquarters on that date for the purpose of discussing the work of the CPA professional clubs.

This source also reported on March 19, 1945, that ANDERSEN was mentioned as a possible student for the CPA training school by members of CPA headquarters in one of their meetings.

Source D informed the San Francisco Field Division that ANDERSEN attended a meeting of the North Side Club at 2626 Green Street, San Francisco, on March 1, 1945, at which time it was announced that he was transferring into a neighborhood club and would attend no more meetings of the North Side Club.

Source E ascertained on March 9, 1945, that the BROWNLEE-SHERICK case was referred to ANDERSEN by STEVE NELSON, prominent CPA member in the East Bay.

Source F reported on May 7, 1945, that ANDERSEN contemplated enrollment in a CPA Spanish class which meets every Thursday night for approximately two hours.

Source G revealed on May 7, 1945, that ANDERSEN received a letter and a picture from one KOZLOV of Hollywood, California, which picture was to be delivered to MOLOTOV during his stay in San Francisco. The nature of this picture could not be ascertained by this source.

Page 10:

San Francisco File 61-146

Source H reported on May 22, 1945, that ANDERSEN holds important conferences with various members of the CPA in the mimeograph room of CPA headquarters in San Francisco.

Source I advised that ANDERSEN and his wife attended the ARI banquet on May 27, 1945.

With the cooperation of Source J, the San Francisco Field Division obtained a copy of a receipt issued to ANDERSEN by the CPA which receipt reflects that the amount of $10.00 was paid by ANDERSEN to cover his dues for FEBRUARY and March. This receipt is being retained in the exhibit files in the San Francisco Field Division.

Source K advised on June 22, 1945, that ANDERSEN was in contact with one OLAF NICHOLAS OLSON, a sawmill operator in the vicinity of Anchorage, Alaska, during June of 1945. OLSON is believed to be identical to one O.N. OLSON, who is regarded as an ultra radical in the State of Washington, having signed referendum petitions allegedly circulated by the IWW for the repeal of the State Criminal Syndicalism Law.

Source L reported on March 10, 1945, that he had an opportunity to see a list of CPA club presidents and that the name of GEORGE ANDERSEN appeared thereon.

Source M advised on March 23, 1945, that ANDERSEN discussed future legal steps in regard to the boilermakers union at a special meeting of all the members of the County Committee of the CPA on March 23, 1945. This source also reported that ANDERSEN, as attorney for the CPA, was scheduled to appear before the Fillmore Club of the CPA to discuss the meaning of the boilermakers' decision in regard to the negroes. This source also ascertained on April 23, 1945, that ANDERSEN was among the CPA members designated by CPA headquarters for attendance at the 1945 State CPA school.

On May 14, 1945, Source N saw a letter which was written by LEO BAROWAY of CPA headquarters and dated May 10, 1945. This letter invited CPA members to an informal social discussion at the home of the subject on May 19, 1945.

On May 22, 1945, Source O reported that ANDERSEN participated in the press-membership drive of the CPA.

Source P advised on January 21, 1945, that ANDERSEN was invited to a meeting of the State Finance Committee at the home of [continued on page 11]

Page 11:

San Francisco File 61-146

[continued from page 10] ANITA WHITNEY, prominent CPA member on February 2, 1945. This source also obtained a copy of a letter, dated January 9, 1945, written by LEO BAROWAY extending an invitation to an informal social gathering at the home of subject on March 3, 1945. This letter stated that WILLIAM SCHNEIDERMAN, State president of the CPA, was scheduled to speak regarding the Big Three Conference at this meeting.

This source also reported that ANDERSEN was a member of the new officers class as a representative of the North Side Club.

Source P also furnished this office with a copy of the Northern California Political Prisoners Bulletin of 1934, which revealed that GEORGE ANDERSEN spoke at a meeting held at the home of Mrs. KENNETH HAYES in Berkeley on April 19, 1934.

Source Q obtained a copy of an engraved invitation which read as follows:

> "Mr. and Mrs. GEORGE ANDERSEN invite you to a New Years Eve Party at their home, 570 El Camino del Mar at China Beach, Sunday, December 31, from 8:30 p.m. benefit California Labor School."

This evidence is being retained in the exhibit files of the San Francisco Field Division.

Source R reported on September 18, 1944, that he had an opportunity to see a letter sent by the firm of ANDERSEN and RESNER to Mr. BENJAMIN B. KNIGHT, dated January 15, 1943, regarding the estate of MICHAEL D. LAWLER. In this letter ANDERSEN stated, "I, of course, represent the Communist Party." A notation on the letter indicated that a carbon copy was sent to the Communist Party at 121 Haight Street, San Francisco. This source also ascertained that ANDERSEN sent a $100.00 check to LEO BAROWAY at Communist Party headquarters in San Francisco.

Source S on December 9, 1944, reported that ANDERSEN wrote a check on behalf of the Committee for Citizenship Rights in the amount of $50.00. He also reported that he had seen a check which was payable to ANDERSEN and signed by the SCHNEIDERMAN-DARCY Defense Committee by HERBERT NUGENT.

This source also furnished the San Francisco Field Division with a copy of the Daily Worker of August 10, 1934, entitled, "The Frisco Court Grinds Out Justice for Jailed Workers." The article criticized Judge STEIGER for his treatment of subject as the attorney for the International Labor Defense and the defendant strikers. This source [continued on page 12]

Page 12:

San Francisco File 61-146

[continued from page 11] also furnished a clipping from the Western Worker of February 11, 1935, which publicized the fact that ANDERSEN represented LOUISE TODD when she was charged with perjury arising out of the circulation of petitions for the purpose of placing the Communist Party on the ballot. These items are being retained in the exhibit folder of the San Francisco Field Division.

On December 9, 1944, Source T reported that he had seen a pamphlet which was issued in behalf of ARCHIE BROWN as a write-in candidate for Congress, Fourth District. GEORGE ANDERSEN's name, along with the names of other prominent and known Communists in the Bay Area, appeared as one of the sponsors for ARCHIE BROWN.

On May 29, 1945, ANDERSEN wrote to the San Francisco Field Division in connection with a Hatch Act investigation, demanding a right to appear with the subject on interview.

The May, 1945 Telephone Directory reflects that subject and his wife continue to reside at 570 El Camino del Mar, San Francisco, and to practice law at 544 Market Street, San Francisco.

Page 26:

An article appearing in the DISPATCHER on February 8, 1946, reflects the following information concerning the subject:

"During the 1934 West Coast Maritime strike, it was GEORGE ANDERSEN, another member of the firm, who represented the thousands of arrested strikers in San Francisco. In less than three months he handled the cases of some 700 arrested longshoremen alone before the police courts of the city.'"

"For his efforts, he was threatened with 'hanging,' and additional promises to blow his office to smithereens. This last threat was regarded with sufficient seriousness by the owners of the building in which he was located to prompt them to remove his name from the building index.

"Andersen was chief defense counsel in the notorious KING, RAMSEY, CONNOR ship murder frameup of 1936. His partner, HERBERT RESNER represented CONNOR. This was the period when the 'bust-the-unions' campaign had reached a particularly high pitch, and incorruptible labor leaders were necessitating new techniques of attack by their enemies."

"The battle against racial discrimination took a great step forward last year when GEORGE ANDERSEN and HERBERT RESNER won a California Supreme Court decision ruling that any union which does not admit Negro workers to full union membership cannot enforce a closed shop contract......"

An article in the DAILY PEOPLES WORLD on March 29, 1946, under the caption "Cops Stop FEPers in Park" is quoted in part as follows:

"San Francisco, March 28. City police are not permitting citizens to circulate petitions in Golden Gate Park for a fair employment practices act."

The subject is quoted in this article as having stated "There is absolutely no law or ordinance prohibiting such activity."

The article indicates that the subject is the attorney for the fair employment committee. The subject further said, according to the article, that he has not found "one city or police official who has read the ordinance the police claim to be enforcing in the park." The article further said that the subject said "I am attempting to get assurance from police officials that FEP workers this coming Sunday will not be molested."

The February 1946 telephone directory for the City of San Francisco indicates that the subject continues to reside at 579 El Camino Del Mar, San Francisco, California.

Page 28:

SF 61-146

Also in August 1945 confidential source c advised that at a of [sic] the Seamen's Club in San Francisco WALTER STACK said in a discussion of the State Convention that "GEORGE ANDERSEN was chairman of the Balloting Committee", and also, "When a Communist convention becomes dominated by lawyers and super-intellectuals, something is wrong."

In September 1945 source of information D advised that CLEMMIE BARRY asked the subject to call CAMERON KING (San Francisco City Registrar's Office) and have him straighten out his registrars regarding people registering as Communists. CLEMMIE BARRY said that they were telling people that they have to register either as Republicans or Democrats. The subject agreed to call KING in this matter. CLEMMIE BARRY said she understood that RUDY (probably RUDY LAMBERT, then State labor director of the Communist Party in San Francisco) "had a little dough cooking with GEORGE." The subject then advised that RUDY must be meaning that Santa Rosa matter, and that it was not settled as yet. Subject also advised that he had given RUDY most of the money and did not see him before he left.

In October 1945 confidential source of information D that [sic] DECCA TRUEHAFT had advised HERB NUGENT that she had been advised by the San Francisco Park Commission that they would not grant the use of loud speakers in the parks in San Francisco for political purposes. The matter was placed in the hands of the subject.

During November 1945 confidential source D advised that WILLIAM SCHNEIDERMAN spoke to the subject concerning the then proposed merger of the subject and his law partner, HERB RESNER, with the law firm of RICHARD J. GLADSTEIN, HAROLD M. SAWYER, and EDISES, with law offices at 240 Montgomery Street in San Francisco. SCHNEIDERMAN was interested in discussing it with them before the merger took place. It is noted that soon after this date the above mentioned merger did, in fact, take place.

Source of information D advised in December 1945 that a meeting of the Party was scheduled to be held at the home of the subject on December 15, 1945, at which ANITA WHITNEY was to be a principle speaker.

The same source advised that DECCA TRUEHAFT had inquired of the subject if he could think of anyone who could contribute some money to the Party? Subject replied that he could think of no one but that he personally would forward a check for $100 and indicated that perhaps he could do something for the Party monthly.

Page 30:

SAC, San Francisco July 24, 1945

Director, FBI
George Richard Andersen, with alias
Internal Security-C

Reference is made to the pending report of Special Agent G. Allison Driskell, dated June 13, 1946. It is desired that a prosecutive summary report be prepared incorporating all information which might be classified as legally admissible evidence tending to establish subject's Communist Party membership or affiliation and his knowledge of the revolutionary aims and purposes of the party. This information should be attributed to original sources and not to previously submitted reports. Confidential informants and sources should be appropriately protected by symbol.

Page 33:

S.F. File No. 61-146

accounts maintained by subject GEORGE RICHARD ANDERSEN. On December 5, 1941 on the account of "GEORGE R. ANDERSEN, SPECIAL" at the Wells Fargo Union Bank of San Francisco, a check was drawn to "cash" in the amount of $6,000. This check was written on the same date that $6,000 in $20 bills was deposited to the HARRY KRAMER account. It is quite apparent, therefore, that this amount of money was used to give the check drawn for $6,000 to the order of the National Committee, Communist Party, USA.

[redacted]

During 1943, it was observed that subject was in frequent contact with Communist Party officials, such as CARL WINTER, LOUISE TODD, OLETA O'CONNOR YATES, and RUDY LAMBERT. ANDERSEN was extended an invitation to attend the 1943 State Communist Party Convention held at 121 Haight Street, San Francisco, on June 27, 1943. In connection with the election on November 11, 1942, the name of GEORGE R. ANDERSEN, attorney, appeared as a sponsor on an election flyer circulated by the Non-Partisan League to elect ARCHIE BROWN, a well known Communist. During 1943, it is known that the firm of ANDERSEN and RESNER was a subscriber to the "Daily Worker", a Communist organ.

On May 7, 1944, ANDERSEN attended the State Convention of the Communist Party at 121 Haight Street, San Francisco. In June of 1944, the Party gave a banquet for ARCHIE BROWN, well known Communist Party functionary in San Francisco in honor of his induction into the Armed Forces of the United States. ANDERSEN is known to have received an invitation to this banquet. In September, 1943, ANDERSEN was invited to speak on the Bill of Rights at the meeting of the Twin Peaks Club of the Communist Party which was held at 1748 Haight Street on December 16, 1943.

[redacted]

Subject GEORGE RICHARD ANDERSEN was a subscriber to the "Peoples World" newspaper, Communist-controlled publication, during 1943 in the name of ANDERSEN and RESNER, 544 Market Street, and also in the name of GEORGE R. ANDERSEN, 69 Piedmont Street, which was the subject's residence at that time.

[redacted]

On December 2, 1943, ANDERSEN attended a closed meeting of the Professional Section of the Communist Party held at the home of JACK PATTEN, 60 Alpine Terrace, San Francisco. This section meeting was [continued on page 34]

Page 34:

S.F. File No. 61-146

[continued from page 33] composed of members from the Government workers, Architects, Multi-professional and Lawyers Branches. Other prominent Communists in attendance included AUBREY GROSSMAN, organizer of the Professional Section, RICHARD GLADSTEIN, MARJORIE LEONARD, BERTRAM EDISES and HERBERT RESNER.

In December 1943, ANDERSEN attended a meeting of the Communist Party, USA, as a member of the Lawyers Branch of the Party. Also in December, 1943, an Executive Committee meeting of the South side Club of the Communist Party was held at which time it was decided that the subject should be designated as the Drive Director for the club in connection with the financial drive of the Peoples World, Communist-controlled newspaper published in San Francisco. ANDERSEN recently had transferred from the Lawyers Branch to the Southside Club of the Party. In January and February 1944, ANDERSEN attended meetings of the Professional Section of the Communist Party.

ANDERSEN is known to have paid $10 to the Communist Party to cover his dues for February and March, 1945.

[redacted]

In October 1944, it was decided by the Communist Party that subject GEORGE ANDERSEN could conveniently transfer from the Professional Section of the Party into a neighborhood club. Informant learned that ANDERSEN promised that he would go into a neighborhood club as soon as he was able to ascertain the proper club.

In December 1944, ANDERSEN attended a meeting of the Northside Club of the Communist Party and was nominated to serve on the Peoples World Committee of that Club.

SOURCE D

On January 25, 1944, ANDERSEN is believed to have attended a general Communist Party meeting at Druids Hall in San Francisco. At this meeting, there was a report on the results of the meeting of the National Committee of the Communist Party.

In January of 1945, ANDERSEN and RESNER received instructions from Communist Political Association Functionaries to prepare a synopsis of the 32-page decision which was rendered by the State Supreme Court in a case involving Negro employees and a closed shop contract. ANDERSEN is known to have contributed sufficient funds to the Communist Political Association in 1944 to enable it to obtain office equipment for its new headquarters at 942 Market Street, San Francisco. On January 23, 1945, ANDERSEN attended a meeting at Communist Party headquarters at which time [continued on page 35]

Page 35:

S.F. File No. 61-146

[Continued from page 34] there was a discussion of the work of the Professional Clubs of the Party.

On March 19, 1945, ANDERSEN was suggested as a possible student for the CPA Training School by members of the CPA Headquarters in one of their meetings. In March, 1946, ANDERSEN attended a meeting of the President's Council held at Communist Party headquarters in San Francisco. At this meeting, OLETA O'CONNOR YATES stated that ANDERSEN was the person who could advise the Party of the possible ways of getting the Communist delegates on the ballot in 1946. ANDERSEN then explained the manner in which this might be done.

SOURCE E

A letter from ANDERSEN to the Bank of Foreign Trade, Moscow, Russia, acknowledged receipt of a letter from the Bank of Foreign Trade in April, 1944. This letter advised ANDERSEN of a deposit in the Bank of Foreign Trade, Russia, to the account of ANDERSEN in the amount of $9,662.91. ANDERSEN in his letter requested the addressee to transfer to the sender's account in this country, the above amount of money through the sender's banking connections in the United States or the Bank of America, Palace Hotel Branch, San Francisco, California. In December 1944, the Chase National Bank in New York received instructions from the Bank of Foreign Trade in Moscow to effect a payment of $9,643.00 to GEORGE ANDERSEN and/or HERBERT RESNER, 544 Market Street, San Francisco, California.

[redacted]

ANDERSEN was a member of the Civil Liberties Union which sought to establish the right in California to the use of school buildings by political parties. This committee also was requested for its recommendation for action in the case of FESTUS COLEMAN, an alleged victim of deprivation of civil rights.

[redacted]

It is known to informant that ANDERSEN held important conferences with various members of the Communist Political Association at CPA Headquarters in San Francisco during the earlier part of 1945.

[redacted]

ANDERSEN is known to have served as President of a San Francisco Branch of the Communist Political Association. During May 1945, ANDERSEN received an invitation written by LEO BAROWAY of CPA headquarters inviting him to attend an informal social discussion on [continued on page 36]

Page 36:

S.F. File No. 61-146

[Continued from page 35] May 19, 1945. On May 22, 1945, ANDERSEN participated in the Press Membership Drive of the CPA. On January 21, 1945, ANDERSEN was invited to a meeting of the State Finance Committee at the home of ANITA WHITNEY, prominent CPA member, on February 2, 1945.

On March 3, 1945, invitations were extended by LEO BARAWAY of CPA Headquarters to an informal social gathering at the home of the subject at which meeting WILLIAM SCHNEIDERMAN, State President of the CPA, was scheduled to speak regarding the "Big Three" conference, ANDERSEN was a member of the New Officers Class of the Communist Party as a representative of the Northside Club during the early part of 1945. During December, 1945, CPA Headquarters issued engraved invitations which read as follows:

> "Mr. and Mrs. GEORGE ANDERSEN Invite You To a New Year's Eve Party at Their Home 570 El Camino Del Mar at China Beach, Sunday, December 31 from 8:30 PM Benefit California Labor School"

This invitation is being retained in the exhibit files of the San Francisco Field Division.

On August 19, 1945, ANDERSEN was on the Balloting Committee of the Communist Party at their State Convention held at Sacramento, California.

[redacted]

At a meeting of the Seamen's Club in San Francisco during August of 1945, WALTER STACK reported that "GEORGE ANDERSEN was Chairman of the Balloting Committee and when a Communist Convention becomes dominated by lawyers and super intelligence, something is wrong".

[redacted]

In 1941, ANDERSEN maintained six separate bank accounts in San Francisco. These accounts were as follows:

1. GEORGE R. ANDERSEN, Special Account; Savings Account #17435 – Wells Fargo Bank and Union Trust Company, Main Office.

Page 37:

S.F. File No. 61-146

2. GEORGE R. ANDERSEN, Trustee – Checking Account, Bank of America, Day and Night Branch.
3. ANDERSEN & RESNER, Special Account – Checking Account – American Trust Company, Palace Hotel Branch.
4. ANDERSEN & RESNER, General Account – Checking Account – American Trust Company, Palace Hotel Branch.
5. GEORGE R. ANDERSEN, Special Account – Checking Account – American Trust Company, Palace Hotel Branch."
6. GEORGE R. ANDERSEN or FRANCES FOSTER – Checking Account – American Trust Company, Palace Hotel Branch.

On November 9, 1940, a check was written in the amount of $4,000 to ELAINE BLACK, well known Communist and active worker of the International Labor Defense. This check was written against the account of GEORGE R. ANDERSEN, Trustee. Signatures to this account are any two of the following individuals: GEORGE R. ANDERSEN, Trustee, HELEN K. PELL, Trustee, MINNIE CARSON, and ELEANOR FAUROT. HELEN PELL was Executive Secretary of the Inter-professional Association, a Communist Front group and also organizational director of the American Peace Mobilization, another Communist front group. MINNIE CARSON was a registered Communist Party voter for the election year 1940, a member of the Communist Party State Central Committee in 1938 and engaged actively in the support of the defense of SAM DARCY. ELEANOR FAUROT was connected with the International Labor Defense in Oakland, California. Signatures to the account entitled "ANDERSEN & RESNER, Special Account.", included subject, his law partner, HERBERT RESNER, and his secretary, ESTHER BROWN. The latter is the wife of ARCHIE BROWN, a member of the Communist Party State Central Committee for 1940 and candidate on the Communist Party ticket for State Treasurer, State Assemblyman and U.S. Congressman for the election years 1934, 1936 and 1940, respectively.

"Western Worker" Issue of Nov. 18, 1935

This issue reported that ANDERSEN, as the ILD Attorney, defended PETE GARCIA and PABLO ESPINOSA, radical trade unionists, on assault charges.

Page 38:

S.F. File No. 61-146

Peoples World Issue of Feb. 2, 1942

This issue disclosed that ANDERSEN was the attorney for the Communist Party in a suit against the State of California to place the Communist Party on the ballot in the August 1942 primary elections.

Western Worker Issue of July 22, 1935

This issue reported that ANDERSEN had been proposed by the Labor Party as a candidate for Municipal Judge.

Western Worker Issue of Nov. 11, 1935

This issue disclosed that ANDERSEN received 37,673 votes for Judge of Municipal Court on the United Labor Party ticket.

Western Worker Issue of Nov. 14, 1935

This issue disclosed that ANDERSEN was engaged in defending ANITA WHITNEY, Communist Party figure-head in California on perjury charges.

Western Worker Issue of May 27, 1937

This issue reported that ANDERSEN had been appointed official attorney for the Alaska Cannery Workers Union, a Communist-dominated organization.

Western Worker Issue of Aug. 23, 1937

This issue disclosed that ANDERSEN was a sponsor of the California Branch of the Friends of the Abraham Lincoln Brigade, a Communist-front organization.

Western Worker Issue of Nov. 4, 1937

ANDERSEN was disclosed as the speaker on behalf of the Abraham Lincoln Brigade at a mass meeting of waterfront workers at 32 Clay Street, San Francisco on Nov. 3, 1937.

Peoples World Issue of April 7, 1939

This issue reported that ANDERSEN when asked if he were a registered member of the Communist Party answered, 'No, but if I chose to be a member I would be, and I don't think that membership in the Communist Party should prevent a man from exercising his right of free speech.' This statement was made in Sacramento on April 6, 1939 in connection with the repeal of the C.S. Act. (Criminal Syndicalism Act).

Page 39:

S.F. File No. 61-146

Peoples World Issue of Mar. 30, 1940

This issue disclosed that ANDERSEN was one of the fifty prominent California citizens who signed a proclamation issued Marcy 29, 1940 condemning the "persecution" of WILLIAM SCHNEIDERMAN and SAM DARCY, Communist leaders and "pledge support to efforts of the SCHNEIDERMAN-DARCY Committee to prevent a blackout of civil liberties."

Peoples World Issue of April 11, 1940

This issue reported that GEORGE ANDERSEN and LEO GALLAGHER were the leading speakers at a SCHNEIDERMAN-DARCY Defense Committee mass meeting scheduled for April 12, 1940 at Jenny Lind Hall, 229 Telegraph Avenue, Oakland, California.

Peoples World Issue of April 8, 1942

This issue disclosed that the San Francisco chapter of the National Association for Advancement of Colored People, a Communist-front organization, announced the sponsoring of a mass meeting on behalf of FESTUS COLEMAN, convicted Negro on April 12, 1942. Speakers listed for the mass meeting included the name of subject as a representative of the ILD along with several other known Communists.

Peoples World Issue of Sept. 21, 1943

ANDERSEN was listed in this issue as one of the sponsors of the candidacy of OLETA O'CONNOR YATES as supervisor of San Francisco County; although San Francisco County and City elections are not partisan in nature, this article mentioned that Mrs. YATES also had the sponsorship of the Communist Party.

Peoples World Issue of Oct. 21, 1943

This issue reported that ANDERSEN was engaged in writing letters to his neighbors enclosing a pamphlet on OLETA O'CONNOR YATES. The contents of these letters written by subject were printed in the paper and is quoted as stating, "The candidate is a Communist who urges that her Party affiliation in this non-partisan election should not dissuade them from giving their support."

The San Francisco Field Division is in possession of a printed folder announcing the 1943 summer term of the Tom Mooney Labor School, Communist-sponsored organization, which folder reflects that ANDERSEN was an instructor in a class on citizenship at that school.

Page 40:

S.F. File No. 61-146

At a meeting of the Northside Club of the professional group of the CPA during September 1944, it was decided that ANDERSEN should be accepted into that club. ANDERSEN is believed to have transferred from the Southside to the Northside Club because of his change in residence to 570 El Camino Del Mar, San Francisco. ANDERSEN attended his first meeting of the Northside Club in the early part of October 1944 and continued to attend meetings of the club during 1944. It was noted by informant that ANDERSEN did not agree entirely on the theory of Marxism with other members of the club and was arguing continually at the club meetings.

In January 1945, ANDERSEN was elected President of the Northside Club to serve during the year 1945. On February 15, March 1 and March 15, 1945, ANDERSEN attended meetings of the Northside Club at which time he indicated that he was transferring to the Richmond Club of the CPA as soon as he found some one to fill his position as President of the Northside Club. On March 15, 1945, he announced that he would no longer attend meetings of the Northside Club inasmuch as he would thereafter attend meetings of the Richmond Club. On March 15, 1945, ANDERSEN also attended a meeting of the San Francisco County Committee of the CPA for the purpose of discussing the reshuffling of the membership of the various clubs.

Page 41:

S.F. File No. 61-146

The following informants who are known to be highly reliable can furnish the following information as to subject's Communist Party membership and activities, but the admissibility of the evidence is questionable:

[redacted]

In 1934, ANDERSEN was the official attorney for the Communist Party retained at $150.00 per month plus court fees. As of August 1934, he was an executive member of the San Francisco District Communist Party. As of September 1935, he was a member of the down-town section of the Communist Party. As of October 1935, he was member No. 3 of the Inner Circl [sic] of Ten of the Communist Party. During 1936, he was legal advisor of the Executive Committee of the Communist Party and Member No. 6 of the Political Committee of District No. 13 of the Communist Party.

On December 22, 1936, LOUISE TODD, a well known Communist, was paroled to the custody of GEORGE ANDERSEN. In 1937, he was a candidate for San Francisco supervisor on the Communist Party ticket. In 1938, he was State Chairman of the Friends of the Abraham Lincoln Brigade, a Communist front organization.

At a meeting of the Russian American Society on November 3, 1941, it was announced that GEORGE ANDERSEN would handle the affairs of incorporation of this society.

[redacted]

In 1934, ANDERSEN was the official attorney of the Communist Party, a member of the Executive Committee of the Emergency Defense Committee and an executive member of the San Francisco District Communist Party. In his legal capacity, he is known to have attended all secret meetings of the Communist Party in 1935 and to have given his legal advice to the progress of the movement. He was reported to be one of the brains behind HARRY BRIDGES and member No. 2 of the Inner Circle of Ten of the Communist Party.

In 1938, the complaint of Ivan F. COX alleged that ANDERSEN was a member of the 13th District of the Communist Party, and legal advisor of its inner group and also the legal advisor for HARRY BRIDGES and other leading Communists. As of June 1942, he was a subscriber to the Peoples World Communist newspaper published in San Francisco.

[redacted]

On February 26, 1942, ANDERSEN was to accompany STEVE NELSON [continued on page 42]

Page 42:

S.F. File No. 61-146

[continued from page 41] and WALTER LAMBERT, prominent local Communists, to a meeting of the Communist Party in Oakland, California. In March 1944, ANDERSEN was under consideration as a member of the County Committee in San Francisco. ADA SMOLAN expressed the belief that ANDERSEN should not be elected to the County Committee because there was some question of his not being known generally as a member of the Communist Party. In May 1944, ANDERSEN was invited to the State Convention of the Communist Party. In October 1944, ANDERSEN endeavored to obtain the use of the San Francisco Opera House for a mass meeting at which ROBERT MINOR, Vice President of the CPA, was to speak.

In January 1944, ANDERSEN obtained $100 from a man who had come to his office for the purpose of turning this money over to the Communist Party. ANDERSEN was one of a few to whom the Communist Party had given books as a token of their appreciation for contributions to the Party. In May 1944, ANDERSEN made a substantial donation to the Communist Political Association in an effort to help balance the budget of that organization.

In July 1944, ANDERSEN obtained another donation for the CPA from one of his friends.

On or about January 19, 1945, ANDERSEN is known to have loaned $1,000 to the CPA for publicity purposes. He was selected to attend the State CPA School for the week April 8 to 15, 1945 but declined the invitation on the excuse that he was too busy to attend. On April 12, 1945, he attended a meeting of the Richmond CPA Club. On April 23, 1945, he met with LEO BAROWAY of the CPA Headquarters at his office at 544 Market Street. On May 16, 1945, he addressed the Eureka Valley Club of the CPA at the request of CLEMMIE BARRY of CPA Headquarters at San Francisco. On June 11, 1945, he discussed with RUDY LAMBERT of CPA Headquarters the matter of instigating litigation in the Negro situation. During November, 1945, he spoke to WILLIAM SCHNEIDERMAN, State Secretary of the Communist Party, concerning the proposed merger of himself and his law partner, HERBERT RESNER with the law firm of GLADSTEIN, SAWYER and EDISES. It is noted that soon after the date of this discussion the proposed merger did, in fact, take place. In January 1946, ANDERSEN attended a meeting of the Finance Committee of the Communist Party at the home of ANITA WHITNEY.

[redacted]

During October of 1943, ANDERSEN formed a $10 Bill Fund and contacted approximately one hundred persons requesting a $10 contribution from each individual to be used for radio time in the election campaign of OLETA O'CONNOR YATES, Communist Party functionary. ANDERSEN also was active in making speeches in behalf of OLETA O'CONNOR [continued on page 43]

Page 43:

S.F. File No. 61-146

[contined from page 42] Yates during the fall of 1943. During the early part of October, 1944, ANDERSEN was invited to a meeting of the Northside Club of the CPA by HAROLD SAWYER, President of that Club. On October 14, 1944, ANDERSEN received an invitation to a small meeting of Communists who had helped the CPA financially which meeting was held at the home of WESLEY DE LAPPE and attended by ROBERT MINOR, national functionary of the CPA. During May of 1944, ANDERSEN was in contact with LEO BAROWAY, State Financial Secretary of the Communist Party in connection with some funds received from a "foreign bank."

[redacted]

A meeting of the Northside Club of the CPA was held at ANDERSEN's home on November 30, 1944.

[redacted]

On December 31, 1944, ANDERSEN held a New Year's Eve Party at his home for the benefit of the California Labor School. In November 1943, ANDERSEN is believed to have attended a meeting at 121 Haight Street at which a report on elections was to be given by WILLIAM SCHNEIDERMAN who at that time was secretary of District 13 of the Communist Party.

[redacted]

Informant knows that subject and his law partner, HERBERT RESNER, are members of the Communist Party and have been for several years. On January 25, 1944, ANDERSEN attended a general Communist Party meeting at the Druids Hall in San Francisco.

[redacted]

In September 1943, ANDERSEN was invited to speak on the Bill of Rights at a meeting of the Twin Peaks Communist Party Club.

[redacted]

ANDERSEN attended a meeting of the Northside Club at 2626

Page 49:

SF 61-146

Confidential Informant T-5 has stated that GEORGE ANDERSEN in March of 1947 loaned People's World newspaper $1,000.00

Confidential Informant T-6 has reported that the subject, GEORGE ANDERSEN, regularly attends meetings of the Board of Directors of the People's World newspaper and is believed to be a member of that board. The People's World newspaper is a daily paper published in San Francisco that is controlled by the Communist Party.

Confidential Informant T-7 has made available to this office a list of contributors to the Communist Party in the year of 1946. On this list appears the name GEORGE ANDERSEN with the total contribution of $1450.00. Also on the list was a notation that ANDERSEN's law partners HERB RESNER and RICHARD GLADSTEIN had donated to the Party, Resner donating $100 and Gladstein $1,350.00 Also a notation was made to the effect that BERT EDISES, another law partner of the subject, had given $3,650.00 to the Party in 1946, and HAL SAWYER, the remaining member of the firm, had donated $2,310.00 to the Party. This informant indicated that the Party functionaries felt, however, that anyone with an income of $45,000 a year should contribute at least $7,000 a year to the Party, and it is believed that ANDERSEN and his law partners have incomes of approximately $40,000 to $45,000 a year.

In November of 1946, city and county of San Francisco held municipal elections, at which time OLETA O'CONNOR YATES, San Francisco

County Chairman of the Communist Party, ran for Supervisor. Among the people listed as endorsers of her candidacy is the subject, GEORGE ANDERSEN. YATES was not elected.

On December 13, 1947, Confidential Informant [redacted] reported to the San Francisco Office that [redacted]

ANDERSEN continues to reside with his wife and children at 570 El Camino Del Mar, San Francisco. He is a partner in the law firm of GLADSTEIN, ANDERSEN, RESNER, SAWYER and EDISES with offices at 240 Montgomery St., San Francisco. All of the partners in this law firm have been reported to be members of the Communist Party in San Francisco. This firm handles all of the Communist Party's legal activities and problems and also specializes in labor law, being retained by some of the left wing unions in San Francisco.

Page 52:

FEDERAL BUREAU OF INVESTIGATION

THIS CASE ORIGINATED AT SAN FRANCISCO, CALIFORNIA			FILE NO. 61-146
REPORT MADE AT	DATE WHEN MADE	PERIOD FOR WHICH MADE	
SAN FRANCISCO	11/3/48	10/19-22, 25, 26, 28/48	

REPORT MADE BY
DONALD J. KENNEDY

TITLE	CHARACTER OF CASE
GEORGE RICHARD ANDERSEN, was. GEORGE CARL ANDERSEN, George Anderson	INTERNAL SECURITY (C)

SYNOPSIS OF FACTS:

Subject was shot in the shoulder during an alleged holdup 1/10/48 in the offices of his law firm, Gladstein, Andersen, Resner and Sawyer; assailant not identified by SFPD. ANDERSEN is in close touch with high officials of the Communst Party, contributes substantially to Communist Party directly and to causes sponsored by CP, and is an official in the Haymarket Branch, Professional Section, Communist Party, San Francisco. Andersen is particularly active in financial affairs of CP. Subject is on bail bond committee of San Francisco Chapter, Civil Rights Congress. He continues to reside at 570 El Camino Del Mar, San Francisco, and to practice law at 240 Montgomery Street, San Francisco.

REFERENCE: Bureau File 100-2865

Report of Special Agent JOSEPH G. LANDIS, San Francisco, dated 1/2/48

DETAILS: AT SAN FRANCISCO, CALIFORNIA

Addresses and Background Information

On October 21, 1948 SA NORMAN FRIE and SA DONALD J. KENNEDY observed GEORGE RICHARD ANDERSEN emerge from the entrance of 240 Montgomery Street at approximately 10 A.M., walk to the parking lot located on the north side of Sutter Street between Montgomery Street and Sansome Street, and drive therefrom a grey 1947 Lincoln Convertible bearing current California license plates 250-571. It was noted that the building directory for 240 Montgomery Street lists the law [continued on page 53]

Page 53:

[continued from page 52] firm Gladstein, Andersen, Resner and Sawyer as occupying the fifth floor of that building.

The records of the San Francisco Police Department contain a report dated January 10, 1948 signed by Inspector ALFRED J. NEDLER reporting the results of an investigation conducted on that date relative to the attempted holdup at the law firm of Gladstein, Andersen, Resner and Sawyer, fifth floor, 240 Montgomery Street, and the shooting of GEORGE R. ANDERSEN, a member of the firm. This report reflects that at about 10 A.M. on January 10, 1948, two armed men entered the reception room of the law firm finding therein ANDERSEN, the switchboard operator, and a client. These three, together with HAROLD M. SAWYER, partner, and another client, were forced to lie down in ANDERSEN's office and told to throw out on the floor their wallets. While one of the robbers was examining ANDERSEN's wallet, ANDERSEN grappled with the man, attempting to reach his gun. ANDERSEN was struck on the head with the butt of his gun by the other robber, and during the melee two shots were fired, one of which penetrated ANDERSEN's right shoulder exiting through the back. The robbers made good their escape, apparently without taking anything, and were not identified by any of the persons who saw them. The report continues that members of the law firm were interviewed and disclosed that they had previously received threats of bodily harm, that they had represented various labor unions and had incurred animosity from exiled members of these unions. The report concludes that although nothing concrete was established, the motive for the offense could have been something other than robbery.

In the issue of the San Francisco Chronicle dated January 13, 1948, there is contained the information that ANDERSEN's law firm had offered a $500 reward "for information leading to the arrest and conviction" of the men who wounded ANDERSEN on Saturday, January 10, 1948.

On January 11, 1948, T-1 reported that RICHARD GLADSTEIN, a law partner of ANDERSEN, had discussed the shooting with ANDERSEN, and that they had come to the conclusion that it was not an ordinary holdup for the following reasons:

1. Too little chance of getting any substantial amount for the risk involved.
2. Only the one elevator to use to get away.
3. Only money in a lawyer's office would be in form of bank drafts or checks.
4. Left wallets on the floor after looking through each one
5. Unprofessional actions of the robbers.

Page 56:

SF # 61-146

being ideal for this position since ANDERSEN already had several bank accounts including an account in which he was the trustee, had large financial interests, and also was close mouthed in this type of matter.

Affiliation With Communist Party Front Organizations

On March 13, 1948 T-7 reported that ABNER GREEN, Executive Secretary of the American Committee for the Protection of Foreign Born, was in correspondence with George R. Andersen relative to the defense of cases involving deportation of alien Communist Party members.

On March 19, 1948 T-8 advised that GEORGE R. ANDERSEN, RICHARD GLADSTEIN, and HERBERT RESNER were on the Bail Bond Committee of the Civil Rights Congress, San Francisco Chapter.

Page 62:

SF 61-146

T-3 advised on October 26, 1948, that the State Communist Party had consulted GEORGE ANDERSEN relative to the subpoenas which were being issued in Los Angeles to officials of the Communist Party in that city.

T-2 advised on October 28, 1948, that WILLIAM SCHNEIDERMAN, State Chairman of the Communist Party, consulted GEORGE ANDERSEN regarding the rights of witnesses in testifying before grand juries.

T-3 advised on March 15, 1949, that SCHNEIDERMAN contacted ANDERSEN for legal advice on the number of days which could elapse before an appeal.

T-3 also advised on May 28, 1949, that SCHNEIDERMAN consulted with ANDERSEN on a legal matter having to do with the Communist Party.

T-4 and T-5 advised that on a number of occasions during the spring of 1949 RUDY LAMBERT, an officer in the State Communist Party, was in frequent contact with GEORGE ANDERSEN relative to financial matters.

Both T-3 and T-4 advised that ANDERSEN would furnish LAMBERT with sums up to two or three thousand dollars as LAMBERT required.

T-2 advised on January 28, 1949, that HARRY KRAMER, Business Manager for the Daily People's World, Communist controlled daily newspaper on the West Coast, contacted GEORGE ANDERSEN relative to securing $5,000 for tax purposes.

T-6 advised on January 4, 1949, that DAVID JENKINS, Director of the California Labor School, consulted with GEORGE ANDERSEN relative to the tax liability of the California Labor School. The same source of information advised that JENKINS and ANDERSEN again consulted concerning the same matter on April 21, 1949.

T-7 advised on October 15, 1948, that GEORGE ANDERSEN was a speaker at a Civil Rights Conference held at the Western Women's Club, 111 O'Farrell Street, on October 15, 1948, one of the other speakers on the program being WILLIAM SCHNEIDERMAN, previously identified.

Page 66:

SAC, San Francisco CONFIDENTIAL September 30, 1949

Director, FBI

GEORGE RICHARD ANDERSEN, was
INTERNAL SECURITY – C
Bureau file 100-2265

Reference is made to Form FB 142 dated September 14, 1949, submitted by your office recommending a technical surveillance on the law office of the subject, 240 Montgomery Street, Fifth Floor, San Francisco, California, telephone Douglas 2-4821 (Bus).

It is noted that the location of that telephone is at the same address as the law firm of Gladstein, Andersen, Resner and Sawyer. Information is not available as to whether this telephone is a private telephone of Andersen's at that address or the main telephone number for the law firm, catering the office through a switch board. If the telephone line goes through a switch board it appears likely that a law firm of this size would have additional trunk lines entering through this same switch board.

You are requested to immediately furnish the details concerning the proposed installation as well as the amount of monitoring necessary if the installation is to cover all incoming communications to the law firm.

Page 67:

Office Memorandum UNITED STATES GOVERNMENT

TO: Director FBI Date: September 14, 1949

FROM: SAC, San Francisco

SUBJECT: RECOMMENDATION FOR INSTALLATION OF TECHNICAL OR MICROPHONE SURVEILLANCE

RE: Title GEORGE RICHARD ANDERSEN, WAS.
(BUFILE 100-2685) *2865* [Italics denote handwritten text.]
Character of Case INTERNAL SECURITY-C
Field Office San Francisco
Symbol Number [redacted]
Type of Surveillance (Technical or Microphone) Technical

1. Name and address of subject:
   GEORGE RICHARD ANDERSEN
   240 Montgomery St., 5th Floor, San Francisco, Telephone
   Douglas 2-4821 (Bus.)
2. Location of technical operation:
   Central Plant
3. Other technical surveillances on same subject:
   None
4. Cost and manpower involved:
   No additional manpower or rental costs involved since Technical will be operated from central location.

Page 68:

6. Type of case involved: INTERNAL SECURITY-C
7. Connection or status of subject in the case:

The subject is believed to be a member of the Haymarket Club of the Professional Section of the Communist Party in San Francisco. This club is composed of attorneys. He is known to be in contact with prominent CP members in San Francisco. He is consulted by high CP officials in regard to legal and financial matters which concern the Communist Party. He is a member of the law firm GLADSTEIN, ANDERSEN, RESNER, and SAWYER. GLADSTEIN is presently in New York City in connection with the trial of the Communist Leaders. It is believed that ANDERSEN acts as the financial agent for the Communist Party in the transmission of funds from National Headquarters to California State Headquarters.

8. Specific information being sought:

Information as to the membership and meeting places of the attorneys, who are Communists, in the San Francisco area. Also to further identify any contacts or associates of the subject.

9. Reasons for believing the specific information will be obtained by the technical surveillance:

The subject is in close contact with high CP officials and is frequently consulted by them on legal and financial matters and inasmuch as the law firm with which the subject is affiliated, is very active in the defense of the Communist leaders in New York City, it is believed that very valuable information will be obtained by a technical surveillance. It is also believed that other attorneys who are communists will be identified. Furthermore, it is hoped that other financial agents of the CP will be identified.

10. Importance of case and subject:

This case is important to the Internal Security of the country.

Page 76:

Office Memorandum UNITED STATES GOVERNMENT

TO: Director, FBI Date: October 12, 1949

FROM: SAC, San Francisco

SUBJECT: GEORGE RICHARD ANDERSEN, was. CONFIDENTIAL

INTERNAL SECURITY – C

(Bureau File 100-2865)

SA P.G. BOWSER ascertained from [redacted] that the telephone number Douglas 2-4821 is the number for the switchboard located in the law firm of Gladstein, Andersen, Resner, and Saywer, 240 Montgomery Street, 5th floor, San Francisco. [redacted] further advised SA BOWSER that five trunk lines enter this switchboard.

The proposed installation will cover all incoming communications to the law firm on the five trunk lines and will be monitored at a central location which has already been established. It is believed that these calls may be monitored by using the present manpower assigned to this location.

DJK: ER
61-146

Page 79:

OBSERVATIONS

Although it would appear that this technical surveillance should prove highly productive because of the number of important Communist subjects using the telephone system in the law office, it also should be noted that information concerning the activities of these subjects has been known to San Francisco for years and that installation of a technical surveillance at this time is not opportune, in view of the trial of Bridges scheduled to start November 14, 1949, and the involvements of Gladstein in the New York trial. It is also pointed out that these subjects are extremely alert to wire tapping and have used that allegation in almost every argument so far before the San Francisco court in the Bridges' case. If this proposed installation was exposed during the trial of Bridges the Bureau would be subject to considerable criticism in view of the importance of the Bridges' case, and could be accused of unethical tactics in covering the activities of defense attorneys which accusation might create adverse public opinion affecting further Bureau investigation.

ACTION

If you approve, there is attached a letter to San Francisco advising them that the requested surveillance is not approved at this time and that another request should be submitted after the Bridges' trial if they believe that such an installation would prove valuable at that time.

Page 81:

SF # 61-146

Communist Party Activities

San Francisco T-1, of known reliability, advised on 6/14/49 that GEORGE ANDERSEN was acting as an attorney for a number of aliens whose deportation for being members of the Communist Party was being sought by the Immigration & Naturalization Service. SF T-1 advised that ANDERSEN consulted with WILLIAM SCHNEIDERMAN, California State Chairman of the Communist Party, regarding the hearings to be held. In this connection San Francisco T-2, of known reliability, advised on 6/24/49 that one of the aliens represented by ANDERSEN was JOHN VOICH. San Francisco T-3 of known reliability, advised on 6/23/49 that ANDERSEN also represented FRANK CARLSON. San Francisco T-4, of known reliability, advised on August 24, 1949, that ANDERSEN was also representing NAT YANISH, another alien.

San Francisco T-5 of known reliability advised that ANDERSEN was in contact with RUDY LAMBERT, chairman of the California State Security Commission for the Communist Party, who also handles financial matters for Communist Party Headquarters, on August 24, 1949; November 23, 1949; and November 28, 1949, T-5 stated that on each occasion LAMBERT contacted ANDERSEN regarding Communist Party funds. T-5 advised that on 9/10/49 LAMBERT was particularly anxious to obtain $750 or $1,000 from ANDERSEN.

San Francisco T-6, of known reliability, advised on September 28, 1949, that HARRY KRAMER, Business Manager of the Daily People's World (West Coast Communist-dominated newspaper), consulted with GEORGE ANDERSEN regarding a check for $13, 210 due to the People's World as part of the settlement of an estate.

SF T-5 advised on 10/4/40 that ARCHIE BROWN, California State Trade Union Director for the Communist Party, consulted with GEORGE ANDERSEN on that day.

San Francisco T-7, of known reliability, advised on 10/31/49 that ROSE ISAAK, Executive Secretary of the American Russian Institute of San Francisco, had consulted on that date with GEORGE ANDERSEN.

San Francisco T-8, of known reliability, advised on July 20, 1949, that ESTHER BROWN, wife of ARCHIE BROWN, had referred IRENE ROBINSON, another member of the Potrero Club of the Communist Party, to GEORGE ANDERSEN.

San Francisco T-9, of known reliability, advised on August 24, 1949, that ALDEN CLARK, Organizer for the Waterfront Section of the Communist Party, had referred a prospective client to GEORGE ANDERSEN.

San Francisco T-3 advised on July 21, 1949, that GEORGE ANDERSEN was a legal representative of the California Labor School.

Page 98:

SF 61-146

Communist Party. T-3 advised that GLADSTEIN is a Communist Party member.

T-3 reported on March 20, 1951, that LAMBERT, SCHNEIDERMAN, GLADSTEIN and ANDERSEN, on March 19, 1951, had discussed what the Supreme Court's decision might be regarding the eleven Communist Party leaders in New York.

On March 23, 1951, SA [redacted] observed HENRY HUFF who is Communist Party Chairman of District 12, according to T-3, in ANDERSEN's office at 240 Montgomery Street. The purpose of their meeting was not known.

San Francisco T-4 of known reliability, advised that GEORGE ANDERSEN spoke at a Protest Rally on March 21, 1951, at 1440 Harrison Street, Oakland. T-4 reported that this meeting was a Protest Rally against "Jail Without Bail" and was sponsored by the Northern California Committee for the Protection of the Foreign Born. There were approximately 100 people in attendance at the meeting.

T-4 advised that ANDERSEN stated that the foreign born were being torn from their homes and family at midnight without warning. He stated that some had been in jail for as long as 100 days without trial or bail. He noted that what had happened to them could happen to any one of the persons in the audience. He stated that one did not have to be a foreign born to have this happen to him and gave as an example the Japanese who had been picked up during the last war. He stated this may happen to the Chinese and many others in the event of a future war.

The Attorney General has declared the Northern California Committee for the Protection of the Foreign Born to be within the purview of Executive Order 9835.

San Francisco T-5 of known reliability, reported on May 7, 1951, that GEORGE ANDERSEN, 570 El Camino Del Mar, has a yearly subscription to the Daily People's World newspaper. This subscription is to expire on December 20, 1951.

T-3 has advised that the Daily People's World newspaper is a West Coast Communist-dominated newspaper.

Page 100:

FEDERAL BUREAU OF INVESTIGATION

THIS CASE ORIGINATED AT SAN FRANCISCO

REPORT MADE AT	DATE WHEN MADE	PERIOD FOR WHICH MADE
SAN FRANCISCO	7/15/52	7/2, 3, 7/52

REPORT MADE BY KHT

TITLE	CHARACTER OF CASE
GEORGE ANDERSEN, was	INTERNAL SECURITY (C)

SYNOPSIS OF FACTS:

Subject resides at 570 El Camino Del Mar, SF, and is member of law firm of Gladstein, Andersen and Leonard 240 Montgomery St., SF. In 1943-1944 subject attended CP meetings in SF; in 1951 made statements that he had defended the CP for 20 years; was a member of Bail Bond Committee of CRC and handled bail funds. Made financial contributions and supported CP front groups. Entertained and associated with CP members.

DETAILS: I. BACKGROUND

(a) Residence

The San Francisco Street Address Directory and Telephone Directory for June, 1952 continues to list subject as residing at 570 El Camino Del Mar.

(b) Employment

SF T-1, of known reliability, advises that subject continues to be a member of the law firm of Gladstein, Andersen and Leonard, 240 Montgomery Street, San Francisco.

Subject continues to be listed as an attorney at 240 [continued on page 101]

Page 101:

SF 61-146

[continued from page 100] Montgomery Street in the June, 1952 Telephone Directory for San Francisco.

II. CONNECTION WITH THE COMMUNIST PARTY

SF T-2, of unknown reliability, an attorney in the community where he resides, advised on March 19, 1951 that he had in 1943 and 1944 been a member of the South Side Club of the Haymarket Branch (which is the lawyers' branch), Communist Party of San Francisco. Among those SF T-2 recalled as having been in attendance at meetings of these Communist Party units were GEORGE ANDERSEN, RICHARD GLADSTEIN, HERBERT RESNER, AND HAROLD SAWYER (law firm partners).

SF T-2 also stated that in the winter of 1950-1951 he had, during a conversation with ANDERSEN, been told by ANDERSEN that RESNER was no longer with the law firm of Gladstein, Andersen and SAWYER because he had stolen $40,000 of the firm's money; that RESNER was no good, and that all Communist Party members should stay away from him.

SF T-3, of known reliability, advised on October 30, 1951 that he had talked with subject on October 25, 1951, at which time Andersen had told him that he, (ANDERSEN), had been a defender of and has legally defended the Communist Party up and down the west coast for 20 years; that he knew the interior workings of the Party because of the fact that he has in the handling of the Communist Party legal affairs been required to know this information, and that he had sat in on their (Communist Party) Executive Board meetings during this time. According to SF T-3, ANDERSEN also stated that in all the period of time that he has been associated with the Communist Party he has never heard any statements by any of the members of the Communist Party which would indicate in any way that this group believes, taught, or advocated any violent overthrow of the United States Government.

III. OTHER ACTIVITIES IN FURTHERANCE OF THE COMMUNIST PARTY

(a) Speeches

Subject gave a speech (which is noted in Section IV) concerning the trial of the California Communist leaders in Los Angeles on February 29, 1952.

(b) Contacts with Communist Party Leaders

SF T-4, of known reliability, advised on December 27, 1951 [continued on page 102]

Page 102:

SF 61-146

[continued from page 101] that GEORGE ANDERSEN had told him this date that he, (ANDERSEN), had invited RUDE LAMBERT and a few friends into his home for New Year's Eve and that LAMBERT was going to be able to go to this party.

RUDE LAMBERT is currently on trial in United States District Court at Los Angeles charged with violation of the Smith Act of 1940.

IV. MISCELLANEOUS

The records of the Secretary of State of the State of California, checked by SA EDWIN P. PARK on June 4, 1951, reflected that articles of incorporation of the American Russian Institute, Inc., (ARI), filed on November 28, 1950 show that the attorneys for the ARI were the law firm of Gladstein, Andersen, Resner and Sawyer, 240 Montgomery Street, San Francisco.

The ARI of San Francisco has been declared a Communist organization by the Attorney General of the United States and as coming within the purview of Executive Order 9835.

SF T-5, of known reliability, advised on June 19, 1951 that the CRC had on August 3, 1951 accepted GEORGE ANDERSEN's resignation from the Bail Bond Committee.

The CRC has been declared a Communist organization and as coming within the purview of Executive Order 9835 by the Attorney General of the United States.

SF T-1 reported on December 28, 1951 that subject had advised him that he had made financial contributions earlier that month to the "Daily People's World" newspaper [redacted]

The "Daily People's World" has been cited as the official organ of the Communist Party on the west coast by the Special Committee on Un-American Activities, United States Congress, Report dated March 29, 1944, on page 95. [redacted]

Page 103:

SF 61-146

[redacted]

SF T-7, of known reliability, advised on March 10, 1952 that GEORGE ANDERSEN had given a speech on February 29, 1952 at the California Labor School (CLS), 321 Divisadero Street, concerning the current trial of fifteen California Communists in the United States District Court at Los Angeles. SF T-7 reported that ANDERSEN's speech was entitled, "The Stool Pigeon" and that the theme of his talk was that the stool pigeon is either a liar or a spy, or is working for a reward.

The CLS has been declared a Communist Party organization by the Attorney General of the United States as coming within the purview of Executive Order 9835.

SF T-8, of known reliability, furnished an invitation on December 5, 1951 for a Russian dinner to be held at the home of Mr. and Mrs. GEORGE ANDERSEN, 570 El Camino Del Mar, on Saturday, November 17, 1951.

This invitation indicates that all the proceeds of the dinner, which would cost $1.50, would go to the Emergency Defense Fund.

SF T-9, of known reliability, has advised that the Emergency Defense Fund is a fund being raised by the California Emergency Defense Fund Committee composed of Communist Party members to finance the defense of fifteen California Communists currently on trial in the United States District Court in Los Angeles, who are charged with violation of the Smith Act of 1940.

The "Daily People's World" newspaper dated January 31, 1952 carries an article on page 3, column 1, regarding EARL DICKENSON, who the article states, is president of the National Lawyers Guild, and indicates that DICKENSON is giving a series of talks on the dangers of the Smith Act for the American people.

DICKENSON's schedule listed in this article reflected that he was to be guest of honor at a reception in the GEORGE R. ANDERSEN home at 570 El Camino Del Mar, San Francisco.

On March 22, 1951 DONALD J. KENNEDY, a former Special Agent of the FBI, who is now a practicing attorney in the San Francisco area, furnished documents which he had received through the mail from an organization known as "Lawyers Against Test Oaths For The Bar". Included in this material was a copy of California State Senate Bill 1666 dated January 23, 1951 which proposes a bill to require every member of the State Bar of California [continued on page 104]

Page 104:

SF 61-146

[continued from page 103] to file with the Board of Governors of the State Bar of California a sworn affidavit that he does not advocate overthrow of the Government of the United States or of the State of California by force or violence or other unlawful means and that within five years immediately preceding the taking of this oath, he has not been a member of any organization that advocated overthrow of the Government of the United States and the State of California by force or violence or other unlawful means. One of the documents furnished was on the letter head of "Lawyers Against Test Oaths for the Bar", dated March 9, 1951. This letter is addressed to "Dear Fellow Member of the Bar" and urges opposition to the aforementioned bill which states, "would, if enacted, seriously interfere with our honorable profession and inevitably with the administration of justice". The letter also solicits funds to fight this bill. Among those listed as sponsors of this organization in Northern California was GEORGE R. ANDERSEN, San Francisco.

The "Voice", official newspaper of the National Union of Marine Cooks and Stewards (NUMCS or MCS), dated May 30, 1952 carried photos on page 7, columns 3-5 reflecting a visit to the MCS hall by PAUL ROBESON. In one photo is shown five men whom the picture sub-heading identifies as "MCS Attorneys GEORGE ANDERSEN and ALLAN BROTSKY, National Officers EDDIE TANGEN and HUGH BRYSON and ROBESON". The sub-heading also indicates that these five men are having a discussion on an attempt to halt a concert (by ROBESON) in Berkeley, California.

The "Washington, D.C. Times Herald" dated July 15, 1949 contains an article entitled "Probers Told ROBESON is Veteran Red". In this article MANNING JOHNSON, an ex-Communist party leader is reported as testifying before the United State Congress on July 14, 1949 that PAUL ROBSESON had been a member of the Communist Party for many years, that he had met ROBESON frequently at Communist Party headquarters in New York where ROBESON held secret meetings with Communist Party National Committee members.

EDDIE TANGEN has been identified as a Communist Party member by SF T-10, of known reliability.

SF T-11, of known reliability, advised on June 28, 1949 that HUGH BRYSON was a member of the Seamen's Branch of the Communist Party in San Francisco.

SF T-12, of known reliability, advised on June 2, 1949 that ALLAN BROTSKY is a Communist Party member active in youth groups.

Page 108:

FEDERAL BUREAU OF INVESTIGATION

THIS CASE ORIGINATED AT SAN FRANCISCO

REPORT MADE AT	DATE WHEN MADE	PERIOD FOR WHICH MADE
SAN FRANCISCO	3/23/53	3/3, 12, 17, 18, 20/53

REPORT MADE BY mtt

TITLE	CHARACTER OF CASE
GEORGE RICHARD ANDERSEN, was	INTERNAL SECURITY (C)

SYNOPSIS OF FACTS: SECURITY INFORMATION - CONFIDENTIAL

Subject resides at 570 El Camino del Mar, San Francisco, California, and is a member of Gladstein, Andersen, and Leonard Law Firm, 240 Montgomery Street, San Francisco. Subject reported member of Lawyers Group, Professional Section, CP, 1952, and advised another attorney that he was one of the 'Communist Party attorneys' in 1953. Subject gave speeches before Committee for Protection of Foreign Born in 1952 and was in contact with ROSE ISAAK. Subject a subscriber to the "Daily Peoples World" 1951, a candidate for IPP 1952. Contributed to the DPW and IPP in 1952. Was noted at Smith Act Trial in Hawaii 1953.

SECURITY INFORMAITON - CONFIDENTIAL

Page 109:

DETAILS:

I. BACKGROUND INFORMATION

a) Residence

The San Francisco Street Address Telephone Directory for March, 1953, continues to list subject as receiving service at 570 El Camino del Mar, San Francisco, California. Neighborhood inquiries on March 20, 1953, ascertained that GEORGE ANDERSEN resides at and is the owner of this residence.

b) Employment

San Francisco T-1, of known reliability, advises that subject continues to be a member of the law firm of Gladstein, Andersen, and Leonard, 240 Montgomery Street, San Francisco.

II. CONNECTIONS WITH THE COMMUNIST PARTY

San Francisco T-2, of known reliability, advised on August 28, 1952, that the Professional Section, Communist Party of San Francisco, was broken down into groups, one of which SF T-2 named as the Lawyers Group. SF T-2 was of the belief that GEORGE ANDERSEN was a member of this Lawyers Group of the Professional Section.

On February 25, 1953, San Francisco T-3, of unknown reliability, but who is an established attorney in the San Francisco area, advised that during a recent conversation on a legal matter with GEORGE ANDERSEN, he

(ANDERSEN) had stated, "You know we (firm of Gladstein, Andersen, and Leonard) are the Communist Party attorneys."

III. OTHER ACTIVITIES IN
FURTHERANCE OF THE
COMUNIST PARTY

(a) Speeches

San Francisco T-4, of known reliability, advised on September 4, 1952, that Attorney GEORGE ANDERSEN was one of the speakers at a meeting of the Committee for the Protection of the Foreign Born on March 21, 1952.

San Francisco T-5, of known reliability, made available on July 23, 1952, a text of the proceedings of the conference of the Northern California Committee for the Protection of the Foreign Born, held June 29, 1952, at Serbian Hall, 225 Valencia Street. This text reflects that the subject addressed the conference.

Page 110:

SF 61-146

The American Committee for Protection of the Foreign Born has been cited by the Attorney General of the United States as an organization coming within the purview of Executive Order 9835.

(B) Contacts with Communist Party Leaders

San Francisco T-6, of known reliability, advised on August 18, 1952, that he learned this date that one of the individuals with whom GEORGE ANDERSEN had an appointment this date was ROSE ISAAK.

San Francisco T-7, of known reliability, has advised that ROSE ISAAK is Secretary of the American Russian Institute of San Francisco (which organization has been cited by the Attorney General as coming within the purview of Executive Order 9835).

San Francisco T-8, of known reliability, advised during the years 1944-1948 that ROSE ISAAK was a frequent visitor at the Russian Consulate in San Francisco until it closed in 1948.

IV. MISCELLANEOUS

San Francisco T-9, of known reliability, advised on November 15, 1951, that GEORGE R. ANDERSEN, 570 El Camino del Mar, San Francisco, California, was a new subscriber to the "Daily Peoples World," West Coast Communist newspaper, and that he held a yearly subscription to expire December 20, 1951.

The records of the San Francisco County Registrar of Voters reflect that for the California State primary election held June 3, 1952, GEORGE R. ANDERSEN was the candidate for member, San Francisco County Central Committee for the Twenty-First Assembly District on the ticket of the Independent Progressive Party (IPP).

The records of the San Francisco Voters Registry also reflect that GEORGE RICHARD ANDERSEN, 570 El Camino del Mar, a lawyer born in Denmark, registered on September 8, 1944, as affiliating with one of the major political parties. This same registration shows that on March 15, 1949, ANDERSEN changed his affiliation to the IPP, and no change has been made since that time in his registration.

The IPP has been characterized as a Communist inspired and dominated organization by San Francisco T-10, of known reliability; and cited by the California Committee on Un-American Activities, Report of 1948, pages 41 and 62 as "among typical mass organizations that are victims of Communist [continued on page 111]

Page 111:

SF 61-146

domination." "One of the basic Communist fronts in a coalition under the banner of the Third Party Movement to elect HENRY WALLACE President of the United States."

SF t-1 advised on June 20, 1952, that he learned on June 5, 1952, that subject and his wife had contributed finances to the "Daily Peoples World."

Again on July 13, 1952, SF T-1 advised that subject had contributed $200 to the IPP of San Francisco. Another contribution of $100 to the IPP of San Francisco early in November, 1952, was reported by SF T-1 on November 28, 1952.

San Francisco T-7, of known reliability, advised on November 7, 1952, that on November 2, 1952, a fund-raising party had been held at subject's home in honor of VINCENT HALLINAN, IPP candidate for President of the United States. SF T-7 advised that subject had pledged $100 for the IPP at this meeting.

The "Daily Peoples World," West Coast Communist newspaper, dated November 5, 1952, carries an article on page 6, columns 4-5, entitled "U.S. Drops Attempt to Deport Unionist." This article relates that (PETE) BONILLA'S attorney, GEORGE R. ANDERSEN, had stated that the Board of Immigration Appeals in Washington, D.C., had entered an order terminating the proceedings against PETE BONILLA, a member of the International Longshoremen's and Warehousemen's Union. The article further states that "the Government charged BONILLA, born in Honduras, with being a member of the Communist Party and advocating overthrow of the Government by force and violence."

During the course of another investigation, Dr. HOLLAND DE WITTE ROBERTS, Director of the California Labor School, which organization has been cited by the Attorney General as coming within the purview of Executive Order 9835, requested that his attorney, GEORGE ANDERSEN, be contacted relative to an interview with him (Dr. ROBERTS).

SA [redacted] telephonically contacted ANDERSEN on January 28, 1953, at which time ANDERSEN stated he had been retained as ROBERTS' attorney and he wished we (the FBI) would not recontact ROBERTS. At this time ANDERSEN refused to permit his client to be interviewed at any place other than his (ANDERSEN's) office. When this was declined, ANDERSEN stated that we (the FBI) were wasting our time. The conversation was then terminated.

Page 112:

SF 61-146

On January 29 and 30, 1953, SA [redacted] observed at the Smith Act trial being heard in U.S. District Court, Honolulu, T.H., that GEORGE ANDERSEN of San Francisco was in the courtroom and frequently conferred with Defense counsel GLADSTEIN and others of the defense counsel, as well as the defendants. SA [redacted] observed that ANDERSEN did not sit at the counsel table, but was in the first row of the spectators' section directly behind the area where the defense counsel and defendants were located in the court room.

It is to be noted that RICHARD GLADSTEIN is a law partner with subject in the firm of Gladstein, Andersen and Leonard, San Francisco. In addition to being on the defense counsel of the present Hawaii Smith Act trial in New York City in 1949 when members of the Communist Party, USA, National Committee, were tried and convicted. During this trial GLADSTEIN was cited and subsequently served a sentence of six months for contempt of court.

Page 116:

FEDERAL BUREAU OF INVESTIGATION

THIS CASE ORIGINATED AT	SAN FRANCISCO	FILE NO.

REPORT MADE AT	DATE WHEN MADE	PERIOD FOR WHICH MADE
SAN FRANCISCO	OCT 12 1953	9-24, 25, 28, 29-53

REPORT MADE BY
MS

TITLE	CHARACTER OF CASE
GEORGE RICHARD ANDERSEN	INTERNAL SECURITY - C

George Anderson

SYNOPSIS OF FACTS:
Subject continues to reside at 570 El Camino Del Mar and to be a member of GLADSTEIN-ANDERSEN-LEONARD Law Firm, 240 Montgomery Street, San Francisco. Subject reported probably member Lawyers Branch, Professional Section, CP of SF, 1949-1950. Reported contributor to CRC, 1950. Active in BRIDGES-ROBERTSON-SCHMIDT Defense Committee; the Russian American Society and the Committee to Secure Justice for the ROSENBERGS, 1953. Advertised in "Daily Peoples World" 1952 and held reception for Dr. W.E.B. DUBOIS. Opposed subpoenaing of Attorneys before House Committee in 1952.

Page 117:

SF 61-146

II. CONNECTIONS WITH THE COMMUNIST PARTY (CP)

San Francisco T-1, of known reliability, advised on March 2, 1953 on a number of persons, all believed to be members of the Attorneys Branch, Professional Section, CP of San Francisco during the period 1949-1950. Among those attorneys named by SF T-1 was GEORGE ANDERSEN.

III. ACTIVITIES IN CP FRONT GROUPS

A. Civil Rights Congress (CRC)

The CRC has been designated by the U.S. Attorney General pursuant to Executive Order 10450.

San Francisco T-2, of unknown reliability, but who was formerly employed by the CRC, advised on February 18, 1952, that numerous persons in San Francisco had contributed to the CRC in 1950. Among those persons named by SF T-2 was GEORGE ANDERSEN.

B. BRIDGES-ROBERTSON-SCHMIDT DEFENSE COMMITTEE (BRSDC)

THE BRSDC has been designated by the U.S. Attorney General pursuant to Executive Order 10450.

San Francisco T-3, of known reliability, advised that the BRSDC held a meeting on May 13, 1953 at 150 Golden Gate Avenue, San Francisco. SF T-3 reported that GEORGE ANDERSEN gave a talk to the assembled group at this meeting concerning the progress of the HARRY BRIDGES case before the United States Supreme Court.

C. RUSSIAN AMERICAN SOCIETY (RAS)

The RAS has been designated by the U.S. Attorney General pursuant to Executive Order 10450.

San Francisco T-4, of known reliability, advised on July 3, 1953 that the 12th annual banquet of the RAS was held June 27, 1953 at 321 Divisadero Street, San Francisco. SF T-4 advised that GEORGE ANDERSEN was present and made a speech at this affair in which he [continued on page 118]

Page 118:

[continued from page 117] praised the Russian people for their cultural contributions to the world and stated that whenever he encounters a reactionary who hates Russia and Russians he advises them to read Russian books or get acquainted with Russian culture.

SFT-4 advised on August 3, 1953 that GEORGE ANDERSEN had attended a meeting of the RAS held July 23, 1953 at 321 Divisadero Street, San Francisco. SF T-4 reported ANDERSEN as advising the RAS that the placing of the RAS on the subversive list by the Attorney General was illegal and would not stand in any court, but that to fight it would cost at least $600. SF T-4 also reported ANDERSEN as advising the RAS that they should not report the names of members and officers to the U.S. Treasury Department on a questionnaire, sent by that department. ANDERSEN did advise the RAS, however, that they should report financial and political activities.

D. "Daily Peoples World"

The "Daily Peoples World" has been cited as "the official organ of the Communist Party on the West Coast" by the Special Committee on Un-American Activities, U.S. Congress, Report March 29, 1944, Page 95.

The "Daily Peoples World" dated September 4, 1953 carries an advertisement on Page 9, Column 4, as follows:

> "Best Wishes from Richard Gladstein, George R. Andersen, Norman Leonard, Lloyd McMurray, Ewing Sibbett, Allan Brotsky."

It is to be noted that the above are all associated with the law firm of which subject is a partner.

E. Committee to Secure Justice for the Rosenbergs (CSJR)

San Francisco T-5, of known reliability, advised on December 15, 1952 that during 1952 the CP leadership in District 13 directed that special attention be devoted to the ROSENBERG case and that full support to the CSJR (aka. Committee to Save the Rosenbergs) be afforded by CP members.

Page 119:

SF 61-146

San Francisco T-6, of known reliability, advised on June 10, 1953 that a meeting of the Bay Area Committee to Save the Rosenbergs was to be held at the GEORGE ANDERSEN residence, 570 El Camino Del Mar, San Francisco, on June 12, 1953.

SF T-6 advised that PAUL ROBESON was to be the guest of honor and that $25 per person was to be charged. SF T-6 advised on June 15, 1953 that the aforementioned party was held as planned.

The "Washington, D.C. Times Herald" dated July 15, 1949 contains an article entitled, "Probers told Robeson is Veteran Red." In this article MANNING JOHNSON, ex Communist Party leader, is reported as testifying before the U.S. Congress on July 14, 1949 that PAUL ROBESON had been a member of the CP for many years; that he had met ROBESON frequently at CP Headquarters in New York where ROBESON held secret meetings with CP National committee members.

F. Committee to Welcome Dr. DUBOIS

San Francisco T-7, of known reliability, advised on February 14, 1953 that WILLIAM KERNER, Director, Northern California Peace Council (NCPC), advised that the northern and southern councils were bringing Dr. DUBOIS to California as head of the World Peace Crusade. KERNER advised SF T-7 that a welcoming committee was being formed and that a meeting was to be held at the Ambassador Ballroom on February 21, 1953.

SF T-7 subsequently advised that KERNER was arranging for DUBOIS's speeches in various Bay Area locations and that promanent [sic] Communists were being asked to lend their names to the sponsoring committee.

San Francisco T-10, of known reliability, advised that the NCRC is Communist dominated and controlled.

The Un-American Activities Committee, California State Legislature, Report 1949, has one chapter entitled, "Important Communist Front Activity," wherein is listed numerous CP fronts and sponsors thereof. W. E. B DUBOIS is listed on Page 499 as having been affiliated with some eleven to twenty Communist front organizations.

Page 120:

SF 61-146

San Francisco T-8, of known reliability, made available on February 18, 1953 the printed invitation to a reception to honor Dr. W. E. B. DUBOIS at the Ambassador Ballroom at 1805 Geary Street, San Francisco, on February 21, 1953. This invitation listed the Committee to Welcome Dr. W. E. B. DUBOIS. The first individual listed thereon was Mr. GEORGE R. ANDERSON.

IV. MISCELLANEOUS

San Francisco T-9, of known reliability, made available on August 27, 1952 a printed "Statement in Opposition to Subpeonaing [sic] of Attorneys by the House Committee on Un-American Activities."

This printed sheet states, "The House Committee on Un-American Activities has issued subpoenas to over twenty-one Los Angeles attorneys, ordering them to appear and to testify at a hearing to be held in December, 1952." This sheet goes on to state that, "because of the questions recently put by the House Committee to attorneys subpeonaed [sic] before it as witnesses, we seriously apprehend that it proposes to inquire into the personal associations and beliefs of these lawyers. Such inquiries addressed to members of the Bar have a dangerous and injurious affect, [sic] especially at this time, because they can no fail to lessen the readiness of the Bar to fulfil [sic] its duties of representing all clients, including the unpopular." The form further states that, "The published reports of the House Committee show that it has regarded attorneys appearing before it as 'subversive' if their clients decline to answer questions relating to association with the Communist Party in reliance on the constitutional privilege against self-incrimination. It has published familiar characterizations of the conduct of attorneys in filing Briefs as friend of the Court, in cases involving the constitutionality of the resolution criticizing the House Committee or of the Smith Act," and "the very issuance of subpoenas [sic] to these attorneys tends to create doubt in public mind concerning their loyalty. Their availability to serve clients is thus seriously affected, other attorneys fearing that they too might be called as witnesses and perhaps characterized as 'subversive' on account of their clients, and would find it most difficult to accept such cases risking their practice and positions."

This form goes on to attack the projected hearings and urges their discontinuance. The first individual listed among numerous persons is GEORGE R. ANDERSEN, San Francisco.

George Andersen FBI File: HQ-100-2865 Section 4

Page 20:

SF 61-146
DDR: Iq

San Francisco T-18, of known reliability, advised on April 1, 1951 that GEORGE ANDERSEN, a lawyer, gave a talk at a meeting of the Northern California Committee for the Protection of the Foreign Born held March 21, 1951 at 1440 Harrison Street, Oakland, California.

SF T-18 reported ANDERSEN as claiming that the Mc Carran Act is a menace to the civil rights and people should mass to block it. ANDERSEN criticized loyalty oaths and also stated that he expected the Government to declare a state of emergency and start rounding people up.

It is to be noted that the American Committee for the Protection of the Foreign Born has been designated by the Attorney General pursuant to Executive Order 10450.

San Francisco T-19, of known reliability, advised that the California Labor School, 321 Divisadero Street, held a meeting on February 29, 1952 to hear a lecture by GEORGE ANDERSEN entitled a "Stool Pigeon." SF T-19 reported ANDERSEN as giving a dissertation on how to identify an agent provocateur, a stool pigeon and a spy.

SF T-19 reported ANDERSEN as discussing the trials of Communist leaders as seen through a Communist lawyer's eyes and that he paid special attention to the problem of educating working class Communists to the importance of identifying the three groups of people on whom the FBI depend to supply evidence, real and manufactured, against the leaders of the working class. SF T-19 reported subject's speech was mainly concerning the three above-named informants and that he described agent provocateurs as persons who attempt to stir up, incite, and lead members of the working class into committing criminal acts, in order that these people may be jailed on criminal charges and therefore be cut off from public support and that these may be distinguished by their excessive militancy, which takes the form of advocating and assisting in acts of violence and terror against the persons and property of the bourgeoisie and capitalists.

SF T-19 reported ANDERSEN as stating that agent provocateurs are usually people of low character and mentality and are not as a group as dangerous as the most numerous group of police agents.

Page 46:

SF 61-146

JBB: jer

The IPP has been cited by the California Committee on Un-American Activities, Report 1948, pages 41 and 62, as among typical mass organizations that are victims of Communist domination.

E. International Longshoremen's and Warehousemen's Union (ILWU)

San Francisco T-5, of known reliability, advised on July 20, 1954 that the subject continues to be regarded by the leadership of the ILWU in San Francisco as one of their consulting attorneys.

The ILWU was ousted from the CIO on August 29, 1950 on charges of adhering to CP policies rather than following the objectives and policies set forth in the constitution of the CIO.

F. American-Russian Institute (ARI)

San Francisco T-6, of known reliability, advised on June 29, 1954 that the subject was in contact with ROSE ISAAK, Secretary of the ARI in San Francisco, California.

The ARI, San Francisco, has been designated by the Attorney General of the United States pursuant to Executive Order 10450.

Page 56:

Letter to Bureau (100-2865) from SAC, SF (61-146)
RE: GEORGE RICHARD ANDERSEN
JBB: pag

Subject stated to [redacted] protect source), in October 1952 that he has been representing the CP up and down the West Coast for 20 years.

Subject was defeated in his attempt to become a US Representative from the Fourth Congressional District of California in the 1954 election on the Independent Progressive Party ticket in California.

Subject as of May 19, 1955, was acting as one of the counsels for HUGH BRYSON, who is currently being tried in USDC in San Francisco, California, for violation of the Taft-Hartley Act.

II. Recommendation

In view of the subject's position of furnishing the legal talent for the CP in California since 1935 to the present, it is requested that he be retained on the Security Index. It is noted that he has been reliably reported to be a CP member of the highly secret Professional Section of the SFCP by [redacted] in the 1940s.

It is also pointed out that subject has attempted to become a US Representative in the 1954 California elections on the IPP ticket. Subject has shown no defection from the CP line and it is believed that he represents a threat to the internal security of the nation.

III. Detcom Tabbing

Subject is tabbed Detcom.

Subject's new SI card with large red letters stamped Detcom has been received by San Francisco.

George Andersen FBI File: 100-2865 Section 6

Page 42:

UNITED STATES DEPARTMENT OF JUSTICE
FEDERAL BUREAU OF INVESTIGATION

SF 61-146

BUFILE: 100-2865 San Francisco, California

May 1, 1964

CONFIDENTIAL

GEORGE RICHARD ANDERSON

The following individual may be of interest to the Secret Service in the event the President of the United States travels in the Northern Judicial District of California.

1. DESCRPTION

Name	GEORGE RICHARD ANDERSON
Aliases	George Anderson, George Carl Andersen
Sex	Male
Race	White
Birth Data	September 27, 1900,
	Copenhagen, Denmark
Height	6'
Weight	185 pounds
Build	Medium
Hair	Grey
Eyes	Blue, wears glasses

Complexion	Light
Scars and Marks	None known
Peculiarities	None noted...Very arrogant when excited or things do not go his way.
Marital Status	Married, FRANCES ANDERSON, nee Frances Foster
Relatives	[redacted]

Page 44:

CONFIDENTIAL

GEORGE RICHARD ANDERSEN

Nationality	United States, Claims citizenship thru father.
Birth Place	Copenhagen, Denmark
Fingerprint	
Classification	Noee [sic] known
FBI or PD No.	None
Social Security No.	None
Residence	570 El Camino Del Mar,
	San Francisco
Employment	Attorney at Law, Senior Partner in firm of GLADSTEIN, ANDERSEN, and LEONARD, 240 Montgomery Street, San Francisco, California

2. BACKGROUND DATA

ANDERSEN worked from 1916 to 1921 at Bethlehem Steel Company, 22nd and Illinois Street, San Francisco. He attended San Francisco Law School from 1923-1927, and admitted to California Bar, October 7, 1927 and has been practicing as an attorney since said date. Married FRANCES FOSTER at Yuma, Arizona, December 24, 1934. ANDERSEN served in Air Reserve from 1923-1926 and had honorable discharge, but not called into military service due to his age, marital status, and dependents. He is not known to have served in World War II. ANDERSEN is not known to have any mental or physical defects.

3. FACTORS INDICATING A PROPENSITY FOR VIOLENCE

As a practicing attorney he has defended many communist and Communist Party front defenses before Courts of Law and Administrative Boards. When attacks are made on the Communist Party, its fronts and membership, ANDERSEN has displayed a violent temper in defending such groups and becomes most arrogant to Judges and Hearing Officers. However, he has not been known to use physical violence.

4. INFORMATION INDICATING SUBJECT IN POSSESSION OF FIREARMS

Not known. No information has been reported that Subject uses firearms.

Page 47:

1. X Subject's name is included in the Security Index.
2. X The data appearing on the Security Index card are current.
3. Changes on the Security Index card are necessary and Form FD-122 has been submitted to the Bureau.
4. X A suitable photograph X is is not available
5. Subject is employed in a key facility and is charged with security responsibility. Interested agencies are .
6. This report is classified CONFIDENTIAL because (state reason). Information furnished by SF T-1 through SF T-7 could reasonably result in the identification of confidential informants of continuing value and compromise future effectiveness thereof.
7. Subject previously interviewed (dates) . X Subject was not reinterviewed because (state reason) he is a Communist Party attorney and an interview would embarrass the Bureau in view of his hostility.
8. This case no longer meets the Security Index criteria and a letter has been directed to the Bureau recommending cancellation of the Security Index card.
9. X This case has been re-evaluated in the light of the Security Index criteria and it continues to fall within such criteria because (state reason) he is an attorney for the Communist Party and front groups and gives both financial and moral support to these groups.
10. X Subject's SI card X is not tabbed Detcom. X Subject's activities warrant Detcom tabbing because (state reasons) he is devoted to the Communist Party and front groups and is in control of funds earmarked for the advancement of these groups.

Page 48:

UNITED STATES DEPARTMENT OF JUSTICE
FEDERAL BUREAU OF INVESTIGATION
CONFIDENTIAL

Report of:	SA [redacted]	Office: San Francisco, California
Date:	2/26/65	

Field Office File No.: 61-146   Bureau File No.: 100-2865

Title: GEORGE RICHARD ANDERSEN

Character: INTERNAL SECURITY – C

Synopsis:

> ANDERSEN continues to reside at 570 El Camino Del Mar, San Francisco and is a law partner in the firm of Gladstein, Andersen, Leonard and Sibett. 240 Montgomery Street, San Francisco. [redacted] He is a sponsor for the ACPFB. Listed among contacts of W.E.B. Du Bois Clubs. Attended meeting of NCCPFB and as trustee of trust account made $500 donation to this committee. As an attorney for PW interested in securing assignment of funds from a deceased's estate for the PW. As trustee, made a check payable to W.E.B. Du Bois Club of America.

DETAILS:

AT SAN FRANCISCO, CALIFORNIA

I. BACKGROUND

A. Residence

GEORGE RICHARD ANDERSEN continues to reside at 570 El Camino Del Mar, San Francisco, California.

SF T-1 on 2/1/65

Page 49:

SF 61-146
LHJ: dje

B. Employment

ANDERSEN is a partner in the law firm of Gladstein, Andersen, Leonard and Sibbett, with offices at 240 Montgomery Street, San Francisco, California.

SF T-1 on 2/1/65

II. CONNECTIONS WITH THE COMMUNIST PARTY (CP) AND/OR FRONT GROUPS

[redacted]

SF T-2 on 9/17/64

[redacted]

The ACPFB has been designated by the Attorney General of the United States pursuant to Executive Order 10450.

According to the records of the W.E.B. Du Bois Club, with headquarters at 1007 McAllister Street, San Francisco, California, GEORGE ANDERSEN was listed as a contact of the Du Bois Clubs of America.

SF T-4 on 10/15/64

See appendix for documentation of the W.E.B. Du Bois Clubs.

Page 50:

SF 61-146
LHJ: dje

[Italics denote handwritten text.] *American Committee* A meeting of the Northern California Committee for the Protection of Foreign Born (NCCPFB) was held on November 23, 1964, at 830 St. Marys Avenue, San Leandro, California, which was attended by the Subject. The purpose of this meeting was to hear a report from a representative of the ACPFB, [redacted] outlined the Committee's legal problem to prevent them from registering as a representative of a foreign government with the Subversive Activities Control Board. She announced that the Committee's case before the United States Supreme Court would be heard on December 7, 1964, and stated that if the ACPFB lost its case in the United States Supreme Court and was ordered to register as a communist front, then all the committees affiliated with the ACPFB would have to register.

SF T-5 on 12/7/64

See appendix for documentation of the NCCPFB.

GEORGE RICHARD ANDERSEN, writing on the stationery of the law firm of Gladstein, Andersen, Leonard and Sibbett, to the NCCPFB, made a grant of $500 to this organization. The letter written by ANDERSEN is as follows:

> "I acknowledge receipt of your letter of December 11, and on behalf of the E.E. Long Trust I enclose herewith a check to your order in the sum of $500.00, which is a grant to your organization for your continued efforts on behalf of the education of minorities in relation to the Constitution of the United States."
>
> SF T-6 on 12/18/64

GEORGE RICHARD ANDERSEN, as attorney for the Pacific Publishing Foundation, 81 Clementina Street, San Francisco, California, which publishes the "People's World" newspaper, was in contact with an attorney at Minot, North Dakota, namely, [redacted] concerning the estate of one CHRISTENSEN. CHRISTENSEN during his lifetime made an [continued on page 51]

Page 51:

SF 61-146
LHJ: dje

assignment of funds to ANDERSEN's client, the Pacific Publishing Foundation. The funds were on deposit with the Equitable Savings and Loan Association of Long Beach, California, and according to ANDERSEN this association attested to the evidence of an account to which the Pacific Publishing Foundation was a beneficiary at the time of the death of CHRISTENSEN. ANDERSEN was urging Attorney BERKOM to make payment of the funds in the above account to the "People's World" newspaper.

SF T-7 on 12/18/64

The "People's World" is a west coast communist newspaper.

NOTES

The pages correspond to the pages in the pdf file.

1. Page 7 in the .pdf file is a continuation from page 9. Thus, page 7 is out of order and it should be in the spot that is occupied by page 10 in the file. The remaining pages appear to be in order—page 8 is a continuation of page 7 and page 9 is a continuation of page 8.

Appendix C

Norman Leonard FBI File

Page 1:

FEDERAL BUREAU OF INVESTIGATION

THIS CASE ORIGINATED AT SAN FRANCISCO	FILE NO. 100-18773

REPORT MADE AT	DATE WHEN MADE	PERIOD FOR WHICH MADE
WASHINGTON, D.C.	8-29-47	8-13, 22, 27-47

REPORT MADE BY
GUY HOTTEL, SAC HPS:mjm

TITLE	CHARACTER OF CASE
NORMAN LEONARD	SECURITY MATTER - C

SYNOPSIS OF FACTS: Naval Officer's File pertaining to NORMAN LEONARD, NSW 230752, reveals commissioned

Ensign 11-16-42, born 2-27-14 at New York City, matriculated at University of California and Columbia University, New York. Employed as Research Assistant at Columbia University. Upon entrance in Navy was member of law firm of GLADSTEIN, GROSSMAN, MARGOLIS, and Sawyer in San Francisco. Father, SAMUEL LEONARD, born Russia, 1887; mother, ANNA GHINGER, born Austria, 1889. Religion, Hebrew. Member California State Bar and National Lawyers Guild. During tour of duty with Navy served as Legal Officer. Relieved of active duty in rank of Full Lieutenant, 11-24-45 at Los Angeles.

-RUC-

Reference: Letter from San Francisco to Washington Field dated 6-4-47

Details: AT WASHINGTON, D.C.:

This investigation was conducted by Special Employee [redacted] who is assigned to the Washington Field Office.

Page 2:

WFO 100-18773

Mrs. ELIZABETH T. MAGUIRE, Officers' Records, Bureau of Naval Personnel, Navy Department, Arlington, Virginia, annex, made available the Naval Officer's File pertaining to NORMAN LEONARD, Navy Serial No. 230752, an examination of which file revealed that LEONARD had placed an application for a commission with the U.S. Naval Reserve on September 22, 1942, at San Francisco, California.

The following information was obtained from LEONARD's application:

He was born on February 27, 1914, at New York City, attended the University of California, graduating with a Bachelor of Arts degree in 1934, and obtained his Master of Arts degree in 1935 at Columbia University, graduating with an LL. B. from Columbia University in 1938. He was employed as a research assistant to Dr. PHILIP C. JESSUP at Columbia University from 1934 until 1938, and as a Research Assistant to Dr. NOEL T. DOWLING at Columbia University from 1937 until his graduation from Columbia. At the time of his entrance in the Navy he stated that he was a member of the law firm of GLADSTEIN, GROSSMAN, MARGOLIS, and SAWYER in San Francisco. He is a member of the California State Bar and the National Lawyers Guild. His father, SAMUEL LEONARD, was born in

Russia in 1887, and his mother, ANNA GHINGER LEONARD, was born in Austria in 1869. LEONARD stated his wife to be MARJORIE H. LEONARD, residing at 267 Liberty Street, San Franicsco, California. LEONARD's religion is Hebrew.

LEONARD was commissioned an Ensign on November 16, 1942, was advanced to Lieutenant, J.G., on March 1, 1944, and to Full Lieutenant on August 1, 1945. During his tour of duty with the Navy, he had served as Legal Officer on Navy general court martials. It was noted that in his efficiency reports he had an outstanding record as a defense attorney. He was relieved of active duty on November 24, 1945, at Los Angeles, California.

REFERRED UPON COMPLETION TO THE OFFICE OF ORIGIN

Page 4:

FEDERAL BUREAU OF INVESTIGATION

THIS CASE ORIGINATED AT SAN FRANCISCO — FILE NO. 100-17334

REPORT MADE AT	DATE WHEN MADE	PERIOD FOR WHICH MADE
SAN FRANCISCO	12/16/47	12/10,11/47

REPORT MADE BY
JOSEPH G. LANDIS - blw

TITLE	CHARACTER OF CASE
NORMAN LEONARD	SECURITY MATTER- C

SYNOPSIS OF FACTS: Subject reported by informants to be member of the Communist Party in San Francisco. Is active in AVC and in contact with Communist Party officials in the Bay Area. Member of law firm of GLADSTEIN, ANDERSEN, RESNER, SAWYER and EDISSES [sic], 240 Montgomery Street, San Francisco, and resides at 273 Liberty

Street, San Francisco. Background information and description set out.

-C-

REFERENCE — Report of SAC GUY HOTTEL, dated 8/29/47 at Washington, D.C.

DETAILS — AT SAN FRANCISCO, CALIFORNIA

A highly confidential source of information advised the San Francisco Office that the subject is a member of the Hay-Market Branch of the Communist Party in San Francisco and in 1946, pledged $50.00 per month as a sustainer to the Party through this Club. Confidential Informant T-1 also was advised that the subject was a member of the Hay-Market Branch and is believed to be literature director of that club. With reference to the Hay-Market Branch of the Communist Party in San Francisco, it might be stated that this branch is composed almost entirely of lawyers and is considered a professional branch of the Party.

Confidential Informant T-2 advised that the subject is a member of the American Veterans Committee and is believed to be on the State Executive Board of that organization and as a member of the Board, attempts to follow the Party line whenever possible.

Page 5:

JGL: BIW
100-17334

Confidential Informant T-3 advised that the subject is contacted from time to time by leading functionaries of the Party in Alameda County and in San Francisco, with reference to legal matters in the Party that have come up. Subject is a member of the law firm of GLADSTEIN, ANDERSEN, RESNER, SAWYER and EDISSES [sic] with offices at 240 Montgomery Street, San Francisco. This law firm is composed almost entirely of members of the Communist Party and specializes in labor law. They also handle all of the legal work of the Communist Party. Subject resides at 273 Liberty Street in San Francisco. Subject was born February 27, 1914 at New York City, the son of ANNA GHINGER and SAMUEL LEONARD. His parents now reside at 2141 South Orange Drive, Los Angeles, California. Subject's mother, according to information received from [redacted] was born in Austria and his father in Russia. LEONARD attended the University of California at Los Angeles from 1930 to 1934 and received his LLB. From Columbia University Law School in New York City in 1938. Thereafter he came to San Francisco to make his home and later became associated with the law firm with which he is now working. LEONARD was commissioned as an Ensign in the U.S. Naval Reserve at the DNOP, 12th Naval District, on December 1, 1942, and was ordered to report for active duty training at the University of Arizona, Tucson, Arizona, on January 15, 1943. He was detached from active duty as a Lieutenant, USNR on November 24, 1945.

The following is a description of the subject as obtained from the Voters Registration and Office of Civilian Defense in San Francisco:

Name	NORMAN LEONARD
Address	273 Liberty Street, San Francisco
Sex	Male
Race	White
Citizenship	U.S.
Date of birth & place	2/27/14, New York City, New York
Height	6'1"
Weight	160 lbs.
Hair	Brown
Eyes	Brown
Complexion	Fair
Build	Tall and thin
Occupation	Attorney
Business Address	Room 560, Mills Building, 240 Montgomery Street, San Francisco
Social Security No.	551-26-2856
Marital Status	Married, wife MARJORIE FRIEDMAN LEONARD.

Page 9:

FEDERAL BUREAU OF INVESTIGATION

THIS CASE ORIGINATED AT	SAN FRANCISCO	FILE NO. 100-17334
REPORT MADE AT	DATE WHEN MADE	PERIOD FOR WHICH MADE
SAN FRANCISCO	6/10/49	5/16, 17; 6/1/49

REPORT MADE BY

DONALD J. KENNEDY - toc

TITLE	CHARACTER OF CASE
NORMAN LEONARD	SECURITY MATTER - C

SYNOPSIS OF FACTS: Subject resides 750 Sanchez Street with his wife, MARJORIE FRIEDMAN LEONARD. Is employed as attorney in firm of GLADSTEIN, ANDERSEN, RESNER and SAWYER, 240 Montgomery Street, San Francisco. LEONARD believed to be member Hay Market Club, Lawyers Branch, Professional Section, San Francisco County Communist Party. Represented ILWU before Kersten Committee in October 1948. Subject is active in San Francisco Chapter, Civil Rights Congress.

-C-

REFERENCE: Bureau file 100-352441

Report of Special Agent JOSEPH G. LANDIS at San Francisco dated 12/16/47

DETAILS: AT SAN FRANCISCO, CALIFORNIA

Miss HELEN TREWICK, Main San Francisco Post Office, Seventh and Mission, advised that NORMAN and MARJORIE LEONARD submitted a change of address from 273 Liberty Street, San Francisco to 750 Sanchez Street, as of 10/1/48.

Special Employee [redacted] ascertained from the records of the Retailers Credit Association, 15 Stockton Street, that NORMAN and MARJORIE LEONARD had filed a homestead on the Sanchez Street property October 28, 1948.

The June 1949 Telephone Street Directory lists as subscriber at 750 Sanchez Street, NORMAN LEONARD.

Page 10:

100-17334

The building directory at 240 Montgomery Street lists NORMAN LEONARD as employed in the law firm of GLADSTEIN, ANDERSEN, RESNER and SAWYER.

The Registrar of Voters records for San Francisco reflect that NORMAN LEONARD registered on September 13, 1946 giving his address as 272 Liberty Street, formerly 267 Liberty Street, his occupation attorney, born in New York, height 6'1". The same records disclosed that Mrs. MARJORIE HELEN LEONARD registered 8/22/46 from 273 Liberty Street, occupation attorney, born in New York, height 5'5 ½", registration as of 3/18/48 Independent Progressive Party.

The San Francisco Call Bulletin on October 22, 1948 carried an article to the effect that NORMAN LEONARD, representing the International Longshoremen's and Warehousemen's Union, was removed from the court room by the United States Marshal during a hearing conducted by representative CHARLES KERSTEN.

COMMUNIST PARTY ACTIVITIES

> T-1 advised 1/13/49 that HELEN MILLER and LOUISE GARRY, members of the New Era Club, Communist Party mentioned that their husbands, who are attornies [sic], attended meetings of the Lawyers Club, Communist Party on the same evenings as the New Era Club met.

T-1 advised reporting agent that a meeting of the New Era Club would be held at the home of HUGH and HELEN MILLER on 1/27/49. A physical surveillance was conducted on the MILLER residence, 1235 Kirkun Street, San Francisco on the evening of 1/27/49 by Special Agent DONALD W. KUNO and the reporting agent. At approximately 7:54 PM HUGH MILLER was observed to leave the residence and enter a green Dodge sedan bearing California license 33G698 registered to HUGH MILLER. He was surveilled by Special Agent KUNO as he drove off and Special Agent KUNO observed MILLER park his car at 2235 Lake Street, the residence of BENJAMIN (BARNEY) DREYFUS. At approximately 8:00 PM MILLER entered this residence. Special Agent KUNO noted parked in front of 2235 Lake Street at this time a Plymouth Sedan bearing current California license 78F360 registered to NORMAN and MARJORIE LEONARD, 273 Liberty Street, San Francisco. DREYFUS has been identified as a member of the Hay Market Branch by T-2 and MILLER a member of the same branch by T-1.

Page 11:

100-17334

T-3 advised that GEORGE WILLETT, prominent water front Communist was in touch with NORMAN LEONARD during March and April 1949.

T-4 advised May 13, 1947 that NORMAN LEONARD, 273 Liberty Street was a subscriber to the Daily People's World, Communist dominated newspaper on the West Coast.

> T-5 advised that a meeting of the San Francisco Chapter of the Civil Rights Congress was held on December 4, 1948 at 255 Ninth Street, San Francisco, and identified NORMAN LEONARD as being one of the persons in attendance.

T-6 advised that at the conference above mentioned, NORMAN LEONARD was named reporter of the Legislative Committee and People's Organizations of the San Francisco Chapter of the Civil Rights Congress.

CLOSED

Page 16:

cc—Liaison Section

100-352241 PERSONAL AND CONFIDENTIAL

VIA LIAISON

Date: November 20, 1950

To: Director of Naval Intelligence
Department of the Navy
The Pentagon
Washington, D.C.

From: John Edgar Hoover, Director
Federal Bureau of Investigation

Subject: NORMAN LEONARD, LT. S(L)
USNR 230752
SECURITY MATTER – C

For your confidential information the above-captioned individual, who is a member of the USNR, is scheduled for apprehension by this Bureau in the event of a national emergency.

You are requested to furnish a summary of information available concerning the above-captioned individual.

JRM: bjc

NOTE: Subject Leonard is on the Navy suspect list. When the Navy summary is received it should be furnished to the field with a request that the field check subject's current activities.

Page 18:

FEDERAL BUREAU OF INVESTIGATION

THIS CASE ORIGINATED AT	SAN FRANCISCO	FILE NO. 100-17334

REPORT MADE AT	DATE WHEN MADE	PERIOD FOR WHICH MADE
SAN FRANCISCO	5/14/51	4/26/51

REPORT MADE BY

ROBERT E. THAU - dvb

TITLE	CHARACTER OF CASE
NORMAN LEONARD	SECURITY MATTER - C

SYNOPSIS OF FACTS	LEONARD resides at 750 Sanchez Street, San Francisco, and is employed as an attorney in law firm of GLADSTEIN, ANDERSEN and LEONARD, 240 Montgomery Street, San Francisco. Subject was

active in CP youth groups in 1949, and was in contact with CP functionaries in 1949-50. Subject was defense attorney for HARRY BRIDGES, JAMES R. ROBERSON and HENRY SCHMIDT. Subject participated in course "How to Defend Yourself" at California Labor School. [redacted] subscribes to Daily People's World.

DETAILS:

AT SAN FRANCISCO, CALFORNIA

RESIDENCE AND EMPLOYMENT

The April 1951 street address telephone directory lists the subject's wife, MARJORIE LEONARD, 750 Sanchez Street, as a subscriber. This directory lists NORMAN LEONARD, attorney, as a subscriber at 240 Montgomery Street. The building directory at 240 Montgomery Street lists the subject as employed in the law firm of GLADSTEIN, ANDERSON[sic] and LEONARD.

COMMUNIST PARTY AND RELATED ACTIVITIES

San Francisco T-1, of known reliability, advised on June 2, 1949 that the subject was active in youth groups of the Communist Party and was forming academic freedom groups in the various law schools in the San Francisco Bay area.

Page 19:

SF 100-17334

San Francisco T-2, of known reliability, advised on October 7, 1949 that on that date ROY HUDSON contacted the subject. The reason for this contact was not known to T-2. San Francisco T-3, of known reliability, advised that in 1949 ROY HUDSON was West Coast Maritime Coordinator for the Communist Party.

San Francisco T-4, of known reliability, advised on November 3, 1949 that the subject planned to meet on that date with ARCHIE BROWN. T-3 stated that in 1949 ARCHIE BROWN was Trade Union Director, Communist Party, District 13.

On September 28, 1950 San Francisco T-5, of known reliability, advised that WILLIAM SCHNEIDERMAN would meet with the subject on that date. San Francisco T-6, of known reliability, advised on October 6, 1950 that WILLIAM SCHNEIDERMAN contacted the subject. The purpose of these contacts was not known to T-5 and T-6.

T-3 advised that WILLIAM SCHNEIDERMAN is Chairman of the Communist Party, District 13.

San Francisco T-7, of known reliability, advised that NORMAN LEONARD once stated, "We never admit that we are Communists." T-7 stated that NORMAN LEONARD is a member of the Communist Party.

The Daily People's World on August 25, 1950, page 3, columns 1-2, carried an article stating that Norman Leonard, San Francisco attorney active in civil rights cases, will speak at the California Labor School where the film "Hollywood Ten" is to be shown. T-3 advised that the Daily People's World is a West Coast Communist dominated and controlled newspaper. The California Labor School has been cited by the Attorney General as a subversive organization within the purview of Executive Order 9835.

The ILWU Dispatcher, a newspaper published by the International Longshoremen's and Warehousemen's Union, on September 1, 1950, page 5, columns 2-5, carried an article stating that a Bridges-Robertson-Schmidt Defense Committee conference was held on August 22, 1950. This article stated that Defense Attorney NORMAN LEONARD spoke on the legal aspects of the "frameup case." It is to be noted that in April 1950, HARRY BRIDGES [continued on page 20]

Page 20:

SF 100-17334

[continued from page 19] was convicted of perjury in a U.S. District Court, in San Francisco, for denying Communist Party affiliation at the time of his naturalization. JAMES R. ROBERSTON and HENRY SCHMIDT were convicted of conspiracy-perjury in connection with this matter.

San Francisco T-8, of known reliability, advised on October 19, 1950, that Norman Leonard spoke at the California Labor School on October 17, 1950. T-8 stated that LEONARD spoke on the California Loyalty Oath and claimed that this loyalty oath was unconstitutional and violated one's civil rights.

The Daily People's World on October 10, 1950, page 9, columns 1-2, carried an article entitled, "How to Defend Yourself," which was to be given as a California Labor School Workshop course. This article stated that NORMAN LEONARD will participate in the course. Subjects to be covered were listed as "arrest or search without warrant," "illegal breaking up of street meetings," "arrests for failure to move on," "frameups," "loyalty oaths," and "registration under the McCarran Act."

San Francisco T-9, of known reliability, advised on November 16, 1950, that LEONARD spoke on the McCarran Act at a meeting of the Interim Northern California Committee for the Protection of the Foreign Born, which was held at 160 Grand Avenue, Oakland, California. San Francisco T-11, of known reliability, advised that the Northern California Committee for the Protection of the Foreign Born is affiliated with the American Committee for the Protection of the Foreign Born.

The American Committee for the Protection of the Foreign Born has been cited by the Attorney General as a subversive organization within the purview of Executive Order 9835.

T-1 advised on November 22, 1950, that NORMAN LEONARD attended a party on November 11, 1950, at the residence of Mr. and Mrs. FRANCIS McTERNAN. T-1 stated that this party was held for the benefit of the Independent Progressive Party to pay election expenses.

San Francisco T-10, of known reliability, advised on October 18, 1950, that FRANCIS McTERNAN would speak to a class concerning the rights of arrested persons. T-10 stated that this class is to be sponsored by the Civil Rights Congress and the California Labor School and would be held on October 24, 1950. The Civil Rights Congress and the California Labor School have been cited by the Attorney General as being within the purview of Executive Order 9835. T-11 advised that the leadership of the Independent Progressive Party in San Francisco is communist dominated and controlled.

Page 21:

SF 100-17334

San Francisco T-12, of known reliability, advised on November 12, 1948 and on September 22, 1949 that NORMAN LEONARD subscribed to the Daily People's World. San Francisco T-13, of known reliability, advised on September 27, 1950 that LEONARD continued to subscribe to the Daily People's World.

T-1 advised on April 26, 1951 [redacted]

-CLOSED-

Page 28:

SAC San Francisco September 20, 1951

Director, FBI CONFIDENTIAL

DETCOM-SEARCHES
INTERNAL SECURITY – C
San Francisco file 100-28810-B

Reurlet dated July 24, 1951.

There are enclosed herewith two copies of the data which has been forwarded to the Department to be attached to the Master Search Warrant for search of the premises occupied by the law firm of Gladstein, Andersen and Leonard, 240 Montgomery Street, San Francisco, California, at the time the Emergency Detention Program is placed in operation.

The enclosures should be maintained in the list of places to be searched under authority of the Master Search Warrant

Enclosure

Bufile 100-356062-sub 47
PLC: mjt

cc—Bufile 100-8174
cc—Bufile 100-2865
cc—Bufile 100-352241
cc—Bufile 100-374320
cc—Bufile 100-331968
cc—Bufile on [redacted]

Page 32:

Office Memorandum UNITED STATES GOVERNMENT

TO: Director, FBI DATE: November 13, 1951

FROM: SAC, Los Angeles

SUBJECT: Norman Leonard
SM—C

NORMAN LEONARD was sworn in as a defense attorney at the bail hearing conducted in Los Angeles District Court on November 12, 1951, in connection with the Smith Act defendants.

Information received at this time indicates Mr. LEONARD is from the San Francisco area of northern California.

The San Francisco Office is requested to conduct an immediate investigation regarding the background of LEONARD, in accordance with previous Bureau instructions.

ETC: MJM
100-new
cc-San Francisco

Page 38:

FEDERAL BUREAU OF INVESTIGATION

THIS CASE ORIGINATED AT SAN FRANCISCO

REPORT MADE AT	DATE WHEN MADE	PERIOD FOR WHICH MADE
SAN FRANCISCO	JUN 2 1954	5/13, 14, 17, 18, 20/54

REPORT MADE BY

[redacted] fd

TITLE	CHARACTER OF CASE
NORMAN LEONARD	SECURITY MATTER - C

NORMAN LEONARD born 2/27/14, New York City, and married MARJORIE HELEN FRIEDMAN 6/12/37. MARJORIE LEONARD identified as CP or CPA member from 1943-1945. Subject is attorney with firm of Gladstein, Anderson [sic] and Leonard, 240 Montgomery Street, SF, and resides 750 Sanchez Street, SF. GLADSTEIN and ANDERSON [sic] have been identified as CP members and San Francisco T-13 has reported that anyone employed by the law firm must be a CP member. LEONARD identified as CP member in 1950 by San Francisco T-13 and San Francisco T-17. LEONARD's name appeared in a document of the CP Underground in 1950, although informant was unable to explain significance of document. LEONARD was a defense attorney for Communists in Los Angeles Smith Act trials in 1952, and was a defense attorney in SF in 1954 for persons charged with harboring [redacted] LEONARD's association or contact with the following organizations is set forth: ARI, American Veterans Committee, Committee to Secure Justice for the Rosenbergs, CLS, IPP, JAFRC, ILWU, [redacted] Northern California Committee for the Protection of Foreign Born.

Leonard was "PW" subscriber in 1940, 1941, 1945, 1947-1953. Description set forth.

Page 42:

SF #100-17334

his spouse that RICHARD GLADSTEIN was a member of the Communist Party.

San Francisco T-8 reported in March, 1954 that NORMAN LEONARD continued his affiliation as an attorney with the firm of Gladstein, Anderson [sic] and Leonard, 240 Montgomery Street, San Francisco.

San Francisco T-13 advised in 1950 that anyone employed by the law firm of Gladstein, Anderson, [sic] Resner and Leonard necessarily must be a Communist Party member.

T-8 advised in 1950 that the law firm of Gladstein, Andeerson, [sic] Resner and Sawyer occupied the fifth floor at 240 Montgomery Street on the eastside of Montgomery, between Bush and Pine Streets. This source stated that the law firm was primarily concerned with labor relations, ie., their most important clients being right wing and left wing labor unions. This source stated that the firm has represented Communist Party officials in various types of litigations.

San Francisco T-36 advised that in April or May, 1950, HAROLD M. SAWYER went into semi-retirement, and his place as a new partner was taken by NORMAN LEONARD.

Records of San Francisco T-1 disclosed that LEONARD advised T-1 prior to 1943 that he was employed as a research assistant to PHILIP C. JESSUP, Columbia University, from 1934 to 1938; as research assistant to NOEL T. DOWLING, Columbia University in 1937; and as a Reader for the California State Bar Association from 1940-1942. He advised that from July, 1938 to September, 1941 he was employed as an attorney for the law firm of Gladstein, Grossman, Margolis and Sawyer, and that he was taken in as a partner in the above firm in September, 1941.

(g) Residences

T-1 has advised the LEONARD stated on September 21, 1942 that he had resided at the following addresses in San Francisco:

- July, 1938 to April, 1939 – 1234 Jones Street
- April, 1939 to January, 1941 – 1840 Larkin Street
- March, 1941 to August 15, 1942 – 160 Carmel
- August 15, 1942 to September 21, 1942 – 267 Liberty Street
- Records of the Voters' Registration Office, San Francisco,

Page 47:

SF #100-17334

wanted any resolution by the AVC and the nature of the resolution. JENKINS indicated that he wanted "a blast at these anti-labor legislation bills which are directed to behead the advancement of education in the state," and indicated that these bills were directed at the California Labor School. JENKINS said that he would like to have a representative of the AVC "to sit in on the Board of Directors of the California Labor School."

San Francisco T-21 advised that LEONARD stated that he thought he could get the resolution passed without any trouble at the State Executive Board meeting and that there would be someone there to sit in on the California Labor School Board. He advised that the AVC had a delegation in Sacramento which could work on the anti-labor bills.

HOWARD RUSHWELL, a former CP member, stated in 1948 that the CP had captured large forces of the AVC.

Committee to Secure Justice for the Rosenbergs

San Francisco T-22 advised in 1953 that "an all-day conference in the Rosenberg-Sobel Case" was held in San Francisco on July 18, 1953 under the sponsorship of the Bay Area Rosenberg Committee. This source reported that LEONARD was present at the conference.

San Francisco T-23 advised in 1953 that LEONARD made a plea for money at a reception held at 570 El Camino Del Mar, San Francisco, in honor of EMANUEL H. BLOCH, attorney for JULIUS and ETHEL ROSENBERG.

San Francisco T-24 advised in December, 1952 that the CP leadership in District 13, CP, USA, directed that full support of the activity of the Committee to Secure Justice for the Rosenbergs be afforded by CP members.

California Labor School (CLS)

The CLS has been designated by the Attorney General of the United States pursuant to Executive Order 10450.

The "Daily People's World" newspaper of August 25, 1950, page 3, columns 1 to 2, contained an article which reflected that NORMAN LEONARD, San Francisco attorney active in civil rights cases, would speak at the CLS where the film "Hollywood Ten" was to be shown.

Page 48:

SF #100-17334

San Francisco T-20 made available in 1951 an announcement issued by the CLS which set forth the fall term schedule of the school for 1951. The schedule reflected that a seminar would be conducted on the subject "Defend Your Rights," and LEONARD was identified as a speaker before the seminar.

San Francisco T-25 made available in 1951 a handbill disseminated by the CLS which reflected that LEONARD would lecture on September 27, 1951 before the second session of the "Defend Your Rights" class.

San Francisco T-26 reported in October, 1951 that HOLLAND ROBERTS, Director of the CLS, expressed a desire on October 9, 1951 that a record be made of NORMAN LEONARD's recent talk before the CLS for circularization purposes.

San Francisco T-27 made available in July, 1951 the summer bulletin of the CLS. This bulletin reflected that NORMAN LEONARD was one of the various attorneys scheduled to participate in a program entitled "Democracy in Danger," to be held on July 18, 1951. The fee for this class was $2.00, according to the bulletin.

The "Daily People's World" newspaper of October 10, 1950, page 9, columns 1 and 2, contained an article captioned "How to Defend Yourself," which reflected that a course was to be presented by the CLS which would include subjects such as "Arrest or Search Without Warrant," "Illegal Breaking up of Street Meetings," "Arrests for Failure to Move On," "Frame-Ups," "Loyalty Oaths" and "Registration Under the McCarran Act." The article reflected that NORMAN LEONARD would participate in the course.

T-20 advised in 1950 that LEONARD spoke before the aforementioned class at the CLS on October 17, 1950.

Civil Rights Congress (CRC)

The CRC has been designated by the Attorney General of the United States pursuant to Executive Order 10450.

San Francisco T-28 made available in 1948 a document issued by the CRC which reflected that HUGH BRYSON and DAVID JENKINS, witnesses before the Kersten Committee, or NORMAN LEONARD, their attorney, were available to speak before various organizations to explain why they had refused to answer questions before the committee.

San Francisco T-29 made available in 1948 a CRC bulletin, [continued on page 49]

Page 49:

SF #100-17334

[continued from page 48] Volume 1, No. 8, dated December, 1948, issued by the San Francisco Chapter of the CRC. The bulletin primarily reported a CRC conference held in San Francisco on December 4, 1948 and reflected that various panels reported to the conference. One panel was described as "Legislative Committees and People's Organizations," and the reporter of this panel was identified as NORMAN LEONARD.

San Francisco T-30 advised in 1949 that NORMAN LEONARD was a prominent leader of the CRC conference held on December 4, 1948 at 255 Ninth Street, San Francisco.

San Francisco T-31 advised in 1950 that NORMAN LEONARD was active in the CRC.

San Francisco T-32 advised in 1952 that LEONARD was a speaker at a banquet sponsored by the CRC at the Leamington Hotel, Oakland, California on November 21, 1952 in honor of HARRY BRIDGES.

Independent Progressive Party (IPP)

The 1949 Report of the California Committee on Un-American Activities, Page 136, reflects that the CP launched the (Independent) Progressive Party in 1948 as its above-ground political and legislative apparatus.

Records of the Voters' Registration Office, San Francisco, disclosed in May, 1954 that NORMAN LEONARD, 750 Sanchez, registered as affiliated with the IPP on September 10, 1949 and that he had no subsequent registration.

San Francisco T-33 made available in 1933 a list of names contained in the files of the IPP, San Francisco. This source advised that the individuals listed therein were members but had not signed up as yet for 1953. Included therein under a subheading "Mission" was the name of NORMAN LEONARD.

Joint Anti-Fascist Refugee Committee (JAFRC)

The JAFRC has been designated by the Attorney General of the United States pursuant to Executive Order 10450.

Page 50:

SF #100-17334

San Francisco T-34 advised in 1953 that NORMAN LEONARD was then a member of the Executive Board of the JAFRC, San Francisco, although LEONARD did not attend meetings. This source stated that special appeal letters were sent out by the JAFRC in 1953, and Executive Board members were asked to attend a "full dress" meeting to develop ways to financially support the JAFRC, but that LEONARD did not attend the meeting.

International Longshoremen's and Warehousemen's Union (ILWU)

The 1948 Report of the California Committee on Un-American Activities, Page 475, identified the ILWU as a Communist dominated union. The Bridges-Robertson-Schmidt Defense Committee has been designated by the Attorney General pursuant to Executive Order 10450.

The ILWU "Dispatcher," a newspaper published by the ILWU, on September 1, 1950, page 5, columns 2 to 5, contained an article stating that a Bridges-Robertson-Schmidt Defense Committee conference was held on October *August* 22, [Italics denote handwritten] 1950. The article stated that Defense Attorney NORMAN LEONARD spoke on the legal aspects of the "Frame-Up Case." It is noted that in April, 1950, HARRY BRIDGES was convicted of perjury in the US District Court, San Francisco for denying CP affiliation at the time of his naturalization, and that JAMES R. ROBERTSON and HENRY SCHMIDT were convicted of conspiracy-perjury in connection with this matter.

San Francisco T-35 made available in 1953 data regarding the Bridges-Robertson-Schmidt Defense Committee of Local 10, ILWU. Data provided by this source reflects that NORMAN LEONARD reported on the legal aspects of the Bridges-Robertson- Schmidt Defense Committee. LEONARD related that illegal and unethical methods of gathering evidence had been used against HARRY BRIDGES, and that the alleged violation of the law by Bridges was, in fact, no violation at all and had no bearing on the Bridges-Robertson-Schmidt Case. LEONARD explained that the defendants did not have a fair trial and that the record was replete with errors committed by the prosecution and Federal Judge HARRIS.

The October 22, 1948 issue of the "San Francisco Call Bulletin" newspaper contained an article captioned "Three Witnesses Threatened by Crowd" and "Red Quiz Calls Extra Cops." The article reflected that a Congressional hearing regarding Communism in the maritime strike was conducted on that date at the US Post Office Building, San Francisco, by US Representatives CHARLES KERSTEN and O. CLARK FISHER. NORMAN LEONARD, according to the article, identified himself as counsel for the ILWU, and stated how he had been in [continued on page 51]

Page 51:

SF #100-17334

[continued from page 50] frequent communication with HARRY BRIDGES, head of the ILWU, over the past ten years. The article reflected that LEONARD was one of two attorneys who were physically removed from the hearing room by agents of the US Marshal's Office after a series of interruptions during the testimony of DAVID JENKINS, in which the attorneys loudly and angrily charged that JENKINS' constitutional rights were being violated.

The May 19, 1951 issue of the "Daily People's World," page 3, columns 1 to 2, contained an article captioned "ILWU Will Appeal 750 Thousand-Dollar Verdict," which reflected that the ILWU would appeal a $750,000.00 damage verdict against the union. NORMAN LEONARD was identified therein as ILWU Counsel.

The "M.C.S. Voice," dated October 18, 1952, page 8, column 2, a publication of the Marine Cooks and Stewards Union, contained an article captioned "Request Bridges Rehearing." The article reflected that a rehearing of the Harry Bridges Case by the Ninth Circuit Court of Appeals had been requested and that "Attorney NORMAN LEONARD told the MCS New York membership last week that in the Bridges Case the jury was under terrific pressure to bring in a verdict of guilty." LEONARD further mentioned "the acquittal of two defendants in the present Smith Act case in New York and said that this is the first crack in the wall of these frame-ups."

The March 18, 1953 issue of the "People's World," page 3, columns 2 to 3, reflects that NORMAN LEONARD, attorney for HARRY BRIDGES and two union associates, left San Francisco that date for New York to help prepare briefs and arguments for the US Supreme Court in connection with the appeal of the Bridges Case.

[redacted]

The records of San Francisco T-16 reflect that LEONARD advised that source in 1942 [redacted] and San Francisco T-8 advised in 1951 [redacted]

Northern California Committee for the Protection of the Foreign Born (NCCPFB)

San Francisco T-3 has advised that the NCCPFB is affiliated with the American Committee for the Protection of the Foreign Born, an organization designated by the Attorney General of the United States as within the purview of Executive Order 10450.

Page 52:

SF #100-17334

San Francisco T-36 advised in 1950 that NORMAN LEONARD spoke before a meeting of the NCCPFB at the CIO Hall, 160 Grand Avenue, Oakland, on November 15, 1950 on "The McCarran Act." This source reported that LEONARD stated that the McCarran Act was so contradictory that he did not think it was constitutional. LEONARD advised that it would probably be one and one-half years before the court passed judgment on the bill, and "so you Communists will not need to worry about registration for at least one and one-half years." T-36 advised that LEONARD indicated that "he thought we would be fools if we did register at any time."

San Francisco T-37 reported in 1954 that NORMAN LEONARD was one of various attorneys to be honored at a dinner held on April 30, 1954 at the Hotel Bellevue, San Francisco, and sponsored by the NCCPFB.

"Daily People's World" (DPW)

The DPW newspaper is a West Coast Communist newspaper.

San Francisco T-38 advised in 1940 that NORMAN LEONARD, 1840 Larkin Street, was a PW subscriber. This source reported that NORMAN LEONARD, 160 Cornell Street, was a PW subscriber in 1941.

San Francisco T-1 has advised that NORMAN LEONARD was a PW subscriber in June, 1942.

San Francisco T-38 advised that LEONARD was a PW subscriber in 1945, and San Francisco T-39 has advised that NORMAN LEONARD was a yearly subscriber to the PW in 1947. This source reported that NORMAN LEONARD, 750 Sanchez Street, continued as a subscriber in 1948 and 1949.

San Francisco T-40 has advised that NORMAN LEONARD was a PW subscriber in 1950 and 1951, and T-38 reported that LEONARD was a subscriber in 1952.

San Francisco T-10 has advised that LEONARD was a PW subscriber in 1953.

Contacts with CP Officials

San Francisco T-41 advised on September 28, 1950 that WILLIAM SCHNEIDERMAN would meet with NORMAN LEONARD on that date for an unknown purpose.

Page 64:

Office Memorandum UNITED STATES GOVERNMENT

TO: Director, FBI (100-352241) DATE: 5/31/55

FROM: SAC, SAN FRANCISCO (100-17334)

SUBJECT: Norman Leonard
IS – C

SECURITY INDEX REVIEW

REFERENCE

SAC Letter 55-30.
SUCCINCT RESUME OF CASE

Subject, born 1914, in New York City, has been an attorney with the firm of Gladstein, Andersen, Leonard and Sibbett, Communist Party attorneys in San Francisco, for the past fifteen years. HERBERT RESNER, former member of above firm and an admitted CP member from 1935 to 1950, stated subject was known to him as a CP member as late as 1950.

Subject has furnished valuable assistance to the CP by defending, in court, HARRY BRIDGES, JAMES ROBERTSON and HENRY SCHMIDT in San Francisco in 1950 and 1953; the ILWU in a damage suit in 1951; the Smith Act defendants in Los Angeles in 1952 and in 1954; the persons convicted of harboring [redacted] in 1954; [redacted in May 1955 [illegible] violated the Taft Hartley Act.

Subject has been active: as a speaker of the CLS, 1950 according to [redacted] and the 8/25/50 issue of the "Daily People's World," and in 1954 according to [redacted] who have furnished reliable information in the past; as a board member of the JAFRC in 1953 according to [redacted] who has furnished reliable information in the past; in the Northern California Committee for Protection of the Foreign Born in 1950 according to [redacted] and in 1954 according to [redacted] both of whom have furnished reliable information in the past.

REGISTERED
JET: rk
(7)
cc: 100-28810D (Security Index Review)
3cc: 100-30591 (Thumbnail Sketch File)

Page 66:

DIRECTOR, FBI (100-352241)
SAC, San Francisco (100-17334)

LEONARD was a defense counsel in San Francisco in 1954 in the case involving persons convicted of harboring [redacted] [redacted] Smith Act subjects.

LEONARD was active in the defense of [redacted] who was judged guilty of violation of the Taft Hartley Act in May 1955. LEONARD's part in this trial was arguing the court's instructions to the jury.

DETCOM TABBING

1. Subject is not presently tabbed Detcom.
2. He has not been approved for Detcom tabbing under criteria in SAC Letter 55-12.
3. It is recommended that subject be tabbed Detcom on the basis that he is qualified as a key figure for the following reasons.

    a. He is an attorney who is known to furnish important assistance to the Communist movement, e.g., defense of Smith Act subjects.
    b. He is prominent at the CIS, in that he gives lectures there.
    c. He is the attorney for the ILWU which is a union important in transportation.

A separate communication is being forwarded to the Bureau stating that the subject is being considered a Key Figure of the San Francisco Office.

Page 76:

JET: fd
SF #100-17334

The August, 1955 issue of the San Francisco Telephone Directory also reflects the subject receiving service at 750 Sanchez Street and 240 Montgomery Street, San Francisco, California.

II. CONNECTION WITH THE COMMUNIST PARTY AND OTHER SUBVERSIVE ACTIVITIES

On June 23, 1955, HERBERT RESNER, 3460 Wilshire Boulevard, Los Angeles, California, advised SA [redacted] that he, RESNER, had been a member of the Communist Party (CP) from approximately 1935 to February, 1950 in San Francisco, California, and was also a former partner in the present law firm of Gladstein, Andersen, Resner and Sawyer.

RESNER advised that as a member of the Lawyers Group of the CP in San Francisco, he was cognizant of the fact that NORMAN LEONARD was an active CP member during the approximate period 1940 or 1941 until at least February, 1950, when RESNER left the party.

California Labor School (CLS)

The CLS has been designated by the Attorney General of the United States pursuant to Executive Order 10450.

San Francisco T-2, who has furnished reliable information in the past, advised on May 11, 1954 that NORMAN LEONARD was present at a play or recital held at the CLS, 321 Divisadero Street, San Francisco, on May 8, 1954.

San Francisco T-3, who has furnished reliable information in the past, advised on August 4, 1954 that an undated letter from HOLLAND ROBERTS, Director of the CLS, and addressed to "Dear Sustainer," advised that NORMAN LEONARD would be one of the speakers at the CLS on August 8, 1954 and that the subject would be "Shall Our Schools Teach the Truth?"

San Francisco T-4, T-5, T-6, T-7 and T-8, who have furnished reliable information in the past, advised that NORMAN LEONARD was present at a lecture at the CLS on August 8, 1954 and that NORMAN LEONARD, together with Dr. HOWARD SELSAM, Director of the Jefferson School of Social Science, New York City, were speakers in what amounted to a panel discussion or forum on the subject, "Dare Schools and Colleges Teach the Truth?"

Page 77:

JET: FD
SF #100-17334

The Jefferson School of Social Science, New York, New York, has been designated by the Attorney General of the United States pursuant to Executive Order 10450.

Northern California Committee for Protection of the Foreign Born (NCCPFB)

The American Committee for Protection of the Foreign Born has been designated by the Attorney General of the United States pursuant to Executive Order 10450.

San Francisco T-9, who has furnished reliable information in the past, advised SA [redacted] on April 6, 1955 that the NCCPFB executes the policy of the national organization in its own area.

San Francisco T-10, who has furnished reliable information in the past, advised on May 17, 1954 [redacted]

The "Daily People's World," a West Coast Communist newspaper, in the May 3, 1954 issue, page 6, columns 2-4, states that NORMAN LEONARD was one of the attorneys honored at a banquet last Friday (April 30, 1954) at the Hotel Bellevue, San Francisco. The banquet was sponsored by the NCCPFB and the attorneys were honored for defending the rights of the foreign born.

The paper further states that the other attorneys honored at the banquet were: GEORGE ANDERSEN, LLOYD MC MURRAY, DORIS WALKER,

FRANCIS MC TERNAN, ALLAN BROTSKY, BENJAMIN DREYFUS, RICHARD BANCROFT, EWING SIBBETT, and RUBIN TEPPER.

HERBERT RESNER, described above, advised SA [redacted] on June 23, 1955 that as a member of the Lawyers Group of the CP in San Francisco until February, 1950, he knew that all of the above attorneys, excepting RICHARD BANCROFT and RUBIN TEPPER, to have been members of the same Lawyers Group of the CP in San Francisco in the late 1940s.

Mrs. MARY STALCUP MARKWARD, a former CP and Communist Political

Page 89:

CONFIDENTIAL

FEDERAL BUREAU OF INVESTIGATION

Reporting Office	Office of Origin	Date	Investigative Period
SAN FRANCISCO	SAN FRANCISCO	4/2/57	3/29; 4/1/57

TITLE OF CASE	Report Made by	Typed By
NORMAN LEONARD	JAMES E. TARLETON, JR. #11	AMR

CHARACTER OF CASE
INTERNAL SECURITY – C

Synopsis:

NORMAN LEONARD resides at 750 Sanchez St., San Francisco and is a partner of the law firm of GLADSTEIN, ANDERSEN, LEONARD & SIBBETT, 240 Montgomery St., San Francisco, California. LEONARD was counsel for VICTOR ARNAUTOFF at HUAC hearing 12/11/56 at which ARNAUTOFF took 5th Amendment. Reliable informants report LEONARD counsel for [redacted] appellant in Smith Act harboring case before U.S. [redacted]

DETAILS:

I BACKGROUND

Residence and Employment

On March 12, 1957 San Francisco T-1, who has furnished reliable information in the past, advised that NORMAN LEONARD resides at 750 Sanchez Street, San Francisco and is a partner of the law firm of GLADSTEIN, ANDERSEN, LEONARD & SIBBETT, 240 Montgomery Street, San [continued on page 90]

Page 90:

JET: AMR
SF 100-17334

[continued from page 89] Francisco, California.

II SUBVERSIVE AND RELATED ACTIVITY

Communist Party (CP)

On May 3, 1954 [redacted] was convicted of violation of Title 18, United States Code, Sections 3, 371 and 1071, harboring, in the United States District court, Northern District of California, and was sentenced to three years in prison. He was released November 20, 1954 on bail of $40,000, pending appeal. On January 20, 1956, the Ninth Circuit Court of Appeals issued a Stay of Mandate until May 19, 1956 for [redacted] and the other appellants to petition the United States Supreme Court for Certiorari. This time was extended until June 18, 1956. The petition was filed with the Supreme Court on June 19, 1956 in the case of United States vs. [redacted] et al.

On October 8, 1956 the United States Supreme Court granted Certiorari in the matter of [redacted] et al, PETITIONERS vs United State of America.

On October 8, 1956 San Francisco T-2, who has furnished reliable information in the past, advised that on that date, at New York State CP headquarters, [redacted] referred to NORMAN LEONARD as being the attorney who was representing him in Washington, D.C.

The San Francisco Chronicle Newspaper of December 12, 1956, Page 8, Column 6, contained an article which stated that NORMAN LEONARD was the attorney representing VICTOR ARNAUTOFF at a hearing before the House Un-American Activities Subcommittee in San Francisco on December 11, 1956.

ARNAUTOFF was described by Committee Counsel [redacted] as an identified CP member and, during the hearing, ARNAUTOFF relied on the 5th Amendment to avoid answering any questions about the CP.

Page 94:

FEDERAL BUREAU OF INVESTIGATION

Reporting Office	Office of Origin	Date	Investigative Period
SAN FRANCISCO	SAN FRANCISCO	10/25/57	10/2, 10, 21-23/57

TITLE OF CASE	Report Made by	Typed By
NORMAN LEONARD	JAMES E. TARLETON, JR. #8	AKP

CHARACTER OF CASE
INTERNAL SECURITY – C

Synopsis:

Subject resides at 750 Sanchez Street, San Francisco, and is a partner in the law firm of Gladstein, Andersen, Leonard and Sibbett, 240 Montgomery Street, San Francisco, California. [redacted] Subject was counsel for three uncooperative witnesses at HCUA hearings in San Francisco, June, 1957 and counsel in a deportation case based on past CP membership.

-P*-

DETAILS: I. BACKGROUND

Residence and Employment

On October 10, 1957, San Francisco T-1 advised that NORMAN LEONARD resides at 750 Sanchez Street, San Francisco, California, and is a partner in the law firm of Gladstein, Andersen, Leonard and Sibbett, 240 Montgomery Street, San Francisco, California.

Page 95:

JET: AKP
SF 100-17334

II. ACTIVITIES OF THE SUBJECT
[redacted]

On May 22, 1957, San Francisco T-2 advised that
[redacted]

Hearings of House Committee on Un-American Activities (HCUA)

From June 18 through June 21, 1957, a subcommittee of the House Committee on Un-American Activities, chaired by Congressman FRANCIS E. WALTER of Pennsylvania, held hearings in San Francisco, California. These hearings were public and were televised. The main subject of the investigation was the extent, character and objects of Communist Party activities within the professions.

At these hearings, NORMAN LEONARD, who identified himself as a member of the Bar of the State of California and the Supreme Court of the United States, and gave his address as 240 Montgomery Street, San Francisco, was counsel for three witnesses who refused to respond to Committee questions relying on the self-incrimination clause of the Fifth amendment.

Miscellaneous

On August 8, 1957, San Francisco T-3 furnished a copy of the May-July, 1957 issue of "The Lamp", which is a pamphlet published by the American Committee for the Protection of the Foreign Born, 49 East 21st Street, New York 10, New York. On page 4 of this publication, under the heading of "Late Bulletins", was the item, "NORMAN LEONARD, San Francisco attorney, undertook to file a motion for rehearing with the U.S. Court of Appeals for the Ninth Circuit in the deportation case of [redacted] of Seattle. On June 26 the Court of Appeals sustained her deportation to Norway, on the charge of past Communist Party membership".

Page 96:

Office Memorandum UNITED STATES GOVERNMENT

TO: Director, FBI (100-342241) DATE: October 25, 1957

FROM: SAC, San Francisco (100-17334)

SUBJECT: Norman Leonard
IS – C

Rerep SA JAMES E. TARLETON, JR., dated October 25, 1957 at San Francisco, 4 copies of which are enclosed, along with four copies of memorandum describing informants.

Subject is on the Security Index and his card is current and accurate.

Subject is also a Key Figure because, while not known to be a CP member, he is a partner in the law firm of Gladstein, Andersen, Leonard and Sibbett, the other three members of which have been reported to have been

CP members. Further, Subject was the attorney representing seamen whose case against the U.S. Coast Guard "screening program" resulted in the decision that the screening had been carried out in an unconstitutional manner. Evidence that the Subject furnishes important assistance to the communist movement is shown by his contacts with ISADORE WOFSY and REUBEN TERRIS at CP National Headquarters in June, 1956 concerning $10,000.00 received by Subject from National Headquarters for the release of [redacted]. Also, Subject was counsel for a CP member who relied on the fifth amendment when questioned by the HCUA in San Francisco in December, 1956 and again for three known CP members before the HCUA in San Francisco in June, 1957 who also were uncooperative and pleaded the 5th Amendment. In the event of an emergency, it is not believed that he would be sympathetic with the aims of the U.S. Government.

Interview of the Subject is not recommended at this time because there is no evidence of defection or change in his communist sympathies.

Subject's file contains a suitable photograph.

Careful consideration has been given to sources concealed and T symbols used only where necessary.

2—Bureau (Encl-8) (100-352241) (REGIS)
3—San Francisco (100-17334)

JET: AKP #8
(5)

Page 116:

SF 100-17334

1. X Subject's name is included in the Security Index.
2. X The data appearing on the Security Index card are current.
3. Changes on the Security Index card are necessary and Form FD-122 has been submitted to the Bureau.
4. X A suitable photograph X is not available
5. X Careful consideration has been given to each source concealed and T symbols were utilized only in those instances where the identities of the sources must be concealed.
6. Subject is employed in a key facility and is charged with security responsibility. Interested agencies are .
7. This report is classified because (state reason)
8. X Subject was not reinterviewed because (state reason) there was no indication of any change in Subject's known communist sympathies.

Furthermore, he is an attorney, interview with whom might prove embarrassing to the Bureau.

9. This case no longer meets the Security Index criteria and a letter has been directed to the Bureau recommending cancellation of the Security Index card.
10. X This case has been re-evaluated in the light of the Security Index criteria and it continues to fall within such criteria because (state reason) he is an attorney who continues to furnish support to the communist movement.

Page 151:

A mail cover on all mail addressed to [redacted] *revealed correspondence from Gladstein, Andersen, and Leonard, Attorney-at-Law, 240 Montgomery St., San Francisco on 9/21/51.*

[redacted]

The "DPW" dated 9/25/51, page 7, column 1 announced that the second meeting of the Fall series of Workshop meetings of the California Labor School would be held (no date given) to help progressive people meet the attacks of employer-dominated courts and Un-American committees. According to the announcement, Norman Leonard was to conduct the workshop.*

100-326958-222 p. 5
(12)

**Possibly in San Francisco.*

Staff Report of the Committee on Labor and Public Welfare, US Senate, 82nd Congress, Second Session, concerning the Marine Cooks and Stewards Union, set out the case of the United States of America before the NLRB Division of Trial Examiners San Francisco, California, in the Matter of the National Union of Marine, Cooks and Stewards and [redacted] *the American President Lines, Ltd. and* [redacted] *the National Union of Marine, Cooks and Stewards and* [redacted] *the American President Lines, Ltd. and* [redacted] *The union was represented by Gladstein, Anderson* [sic] *and Leonard, with Norman Leonard as one of the participating attorneys. In connection with the above case, hearings were held on various dates from 4/9/51 to 9/25/51.*

Above report enclosed with Letter
to the Director from [redacted]

[redacted]

[redacted] *(protect identity), advised that by check dated 9/28/51, the Russian American Society (RAS) (100-38593) was paid $141.00 from the trust account of the law firm of Gladstein, Anderson,* [sic] *and Leonard of which Norman Leonard was a member. According to informant, this trust account was maintained in the main office of the above bank.*

(continued on next page)

Page 152:

It was to be noted that on 10/25/51, the RAS was also paid $115.71 out of the same trust account.

100-38593-37 p.5,12
(10)

[redacted] *(protect identity), advised that the law firm of Gladstein, Anderson* [sic] *and Leonard of San Francisco, had on 11/6/51 issued check # 661 in the amount of $154.67 to* [redacted]

[redacted] *on 12/3/43 described the above members of the law firm as members of the Lawyers Branch of the Professional Section of the CP in San Francisco.*

[redacted]

[redacted] *(protect identity) advised that during 1951 and 1952 [redacted] received monthly payments on a semi-regular basis from the firm of Gladstein, Andersen, and Leonard, 240 Montgomery St., San Francisco, of which Norman Leonard was a member.*

Additional information.

[redacted]

This reference set out conflicting information furnished by [redacted] to INS, Washington, D.C., and to Bureau Agents concerning the law firm of Gladstein, Anderson [sic] *and Leonard, 240 Montgomery St., San Francisco, Calif.* [redacted] *had been represented by above firm in a claim for damages for a head injury which she received during the Spring of 1951 while riding as a passenger in a Key System bus in Alameda, California. Reference states that Norman Leonard of the above law firm received payments during 1952 from this firm.*

[redacted]

Page 223:

UNITED STATES DEPARTMENT OF JUSTICE
FEDERAL BUREAU OF INVESTIGATION

Copy to:

Report of: SA JAMES E. TARLETON, JR.

Office: SAN FRANCISCO

Date: OCTOBER 11, 1961

Field Office File No.: 100-17334

Bureau File No.: 100-434842

Title: NORMAN LEONARD

Character: INTERNAL SECURITY – C

Synopsis:

LEONARD resides at 750 Sanchez Street, San Francisco, Calif., and is a partner in the law firm of Gladstein, Andersen, Leonard & Sibbett, 240 Montgomery Street, San Francisco. LEONARD spoke at a meeting sponsored by the San Francisco Citizens Committee to Preserve American Freedoms in May and August, 1961, and sponsored an affair of the East Bay Community Forum in August, 1961.

DETAILS:

I. BACKGROUND

A. RESIDENCE AND EMPLOYMENT

On September 25, 1961, SF T-1 advised that NORMAN LEONARD resides at 750 Sanchez Street, San Francisco, California, and is a partner in the law firm of GLADSTEIN, ANDERSEN, LEONARD & SIBBETT, 240 Montgomery Street, San Francisco.

Page 224:

SF 100-17334
JET: dd

II. ACTIVITIES OF SUBJECT

A. CITIZENS COMMITTEE TO PRESERVE AMERICAN FREEDOMS (CCPAF) (See Appendix Page)

On May 1, 1961, SF T-2 advised that the San Francisco CCPAF was held at the Longshoremen's Hall, 301 Beach Street, San Francisco, and that NORMAN LEONARD would be one of the featured speakers.

On May 16, 1961, SF T-3, and on May 15, 1961, SF T-5 advised that a meeting sponsored by the San Francisco CCPAF was held at the Longshoremen's Hall, 301 Beach Street, San Francisco, on May 12, 1961. SF T-5 further stated that one of the speakers was Attorney NORMAN LEONARD who spoke on behalf of the CCPAF.

On August 14, 1961, SF T-3 advised that NORMAN LEONARD was Chairman of a meeting sponsored by the CCPAF on August 9, 1961, at the Friends Service Center, 2160 Lake Street, San Francisco. SF T-3 advised that NORMAN LEONARD gave a lengthy talk pointing out the dangers to academic freedoms and to the freedom to speak and to write since people have been sent to jail for violating the First Ammendment. [sic] LEONARD pointed out that the Constitution says Congress can make no law prohibiting free speech but that such laws have been made by Congress and have been upheld by split decisions of the Supreme Court.

B. EAST BAY COMMUNITY FORUM (EBCF):
(See Appendix Page)

On August 22, 1961, SF T-4 advised that NORMAN LEONARD is listed as a sponsor of a testimonial dinner held under the auspices of the Teachers Defense Committee of the East Bay Community Forum, Berkeley, California. This list of sponsors numbered about 75 persons.

Page 239:

SF 100-17334
JET/sem

CCPAF sent notices from the organizations Executive Committee of an executive committee meeting of the CCPAF to be held November 16, 1961, at the home of NORMAN LEONARD, 750 Sanchez Street, San Francisco.

On November 14, 1961, SF T-6 advised that NORMAN LEONARD chaired the meeting of the CCPAF held on November 10, 1961, at 2160 Lake Street, San Francisco, attended by about 35 people. SF T-6 stated that NORMAN LEONARD announced that the purpose of the CCPAF is to abolish the HCUA and help those committee members jailed for contempt of the HCUA. SF T-6 added that another speaker at the meeting stated that if enough Congressmen are visited perhaps they will refuse the HCUA appropriation for the coming year.

On December 4, 1961, SF T-6 furnished a copy of a leaflet of the Emergency Civil Liberties Committee (ECLC) (See Appendix) advertising a reception for HARVEY O'CONNOR, Chairman of the ECLC, on December 16, 1961, at 750 Sanchez Street, the residence of NORMAN LEONARD, - this reception to be for the benefit of the CCPAF.

On December 5, 1961, SF T-6 advised that NORMAN LEONARD attended, with about eight other persons, a meeting sponsored by the CCPAF on December 4, 1961, at 321 Collingwood Street, San Francisco. SF T-6 advised that the meeting was held to plan for the reception of HARVEY O'CONNOR at NORMAN LEONARD's home on December 10, 1961.

On December 11, 1961, SF T-3 advised that on December 10, 1961, a meeting of the CCPAF was held at the home of NORMAN LEONARD, 750 Sanchez Street, San Francisco. SF T-3 advised that at this meeting it was stated that things looked great on the Civil Rights front since most attorneys admit that the McCarran Act question is still unresolved. At the meeting it was stated that the HCUA has been stopped from holding public meetings as a result of the San Francisco demonstrations and that Congress is becoming responsive to liberal elements.

On January 31, 1962, SF T-6 advised that at a meeting of the local chapter of CCPAF [redacted]

Page 250:

SF 100-17334
JGC/CJS

COMMUNIST PARTY (CP) AND RELATED ACTIVITIES

On May 11, 1962, NORMAN LEONARD, 750 Sanchez Street, held a San Francisco Citizens Committee to Preserve American Freedoms (SFCCPAF) (see Appendix) meeting at his residence. Approximately 50 persons attended and the purpose of this meeting was to heard [sic] a report from [redacted] who had been recently subpoenaed by the House Committee on Un-American Activities in Los Angeles. During her talk, [redacted] mentioned that the Los Angeles Office of the Citizens Committee to Preserve American Freedoms (CCPAF) (see Appendix) receives $800.00 per month in sustainers. At this meeting $36.00 was collected.

(SF T-2 on 5/14/62)

On May 25, 1962, the Ninth Testimonial sponsored by the Northern California Committee for Protection of Foreign Born (NCCPFB) (see Appendix) was held at the Sir Francis Drake Hotel, San Francisco, and one of the persons honored was NORMAN LEONARD. Admission was $2.50 per person. Approximately 200 people attended this meeting and $922.00 was collected. NORMAN LEONARD stated that instead of honoring him he felt he should be honoring the committee for having enough "guts and background" to have an organization which is fighting for constitutional rights. ELIZABETH GURLEY FLYNN was present and was introduced as Chairman of the CP National Committee. [redacted] for the Northern California District, was also present.

(SF T-2 on 5/28/62,
SF T-3 on 7/10/62

[redacted]

(SF T-4 on 6/7/62)

On July 19, 1962, [redacted] met with NORMAN LEONARD at LEONARD's office in San Francisco. Informant did not know the details of the meeting.

(SF T-5 on 7/19/62)

Page 251:

1.

NORTHERN CALIFORNIA COMMITTEE
FOR PROTECTION OF FOREIGN BORN

The "Daily People's World", now known as the "People's World," a West Coast Communist newspaper, of November 2, 1950, page 10, columns 1 and 2, contained an article entitled, "Northern California Committee for Foreign Born Planned." This article stated that plans for the organization of a Northern California Committee for Protection of Foreign Born would be made at a meeting on November 6, 1950, at 150 Golden Gate Avenue, San Francisco, California.

A source advised on April 25, 1962, that the Northern California Committee for Protection of Foreign Born, although an independent organization, carries out a program of activity in Northern California which coincides with the aims of the American Committee for Protection of Foreign Born (ACPFB).

The source further advised that the Northern California Committee for Protection of Foreign Born continues to be active in defending the foreign born in deportation proceedings and in securing support for the repeal of the Walter-McCarran Law.

The ACPFB has been designated by the Attorney General of the United States pursuant to Executive Order 10450.

APPENDIX PAGE

Page 259:

UNITED STATES DEPARTMENT OF JUSTICE
FEDERAL BUREAU OF INVESTIGATION

Copy to:

Report of: [redacted] Office: SAN FRANCISCO

Date: 5/14/63

Field Office File No.: 100-17334 Bureau File No.: 100-352241

Title: NORMAN LEONARD

Character: INTERNAL SECURITY – C

Synopsis:

LEONARD resides at 750 Sanchez Street, San Francisco, and is a partner in the law firm of Gladstein, Andersen, Leonard, and Sibbett, 240 Montgomery Street, San Francisco. LEONARD is Provisional Chairman of the San Francisco Citizens Committee to Preserve American Freedoms and attends meetings of this group.

-P*-

DETAILS:

AT SAN FRANCISCO, CALIFORNIA

RESIDENCE AND EMPLOYMENT

NORMAN LEONARD resides at 750 Sanchez Street, San Francisco, and is a partner in the law firm of Gladstein, Andersen, Leonard and Sibbett, 240 Montgomery Street, San Francisco.

CONFIDENTIAL

Page 271:

SF 100-17334 CONFIDENTIAL

CITIZENS COMMITTEE TO PRESERVE AMERICAN FREEDOMS

The Guide to Subversive Organizations and Publications, revised and published December 1, 1961, prepared and released by the Committee on Un-American Activities, United States House of Representatives, contains the following on Page 42 concerning "Citizens Committee to Preserve American Freedoms"

1. “The (Communist) party’s front operations in the Southern California District today are *** confined to four major organizations,” which include theCitizens Committee to Preserve American Freedoms.

“The Citizens Committee to Preserve American Freedoms *** specializes in propaganda aimed at abolishing the Committee on Un-American Activities and discrediting the Federal Bureau of Investigation. Created in Los Angeles in 1952, the front organization is run by Frank Wilkinson, an identified Communist who recentlyresumed the full-time, paid post of executive secretary after approximately a year’s leave of absence to assist in a similar campaign by another front in New York City, the Emergency Civil Liberties Committee.

“When the Committee on Un-American Activities held hearings in Los Angeles September 2-5, 1958, to inquire into the nature of the party’s recent organization in California, the Citizens Committee to Preserve American Freedoms sponsored a series of public meetings to protest the hearings and the very existence of the committee. Communists subpoenaed as witnesses were guests of honor.

“At this time, leaders of the party’s Southern California District were mobilizing Communists in the area for participation in an intensified campaign to abolish this committee of Congress. How the Citizens Committee to Preserve American Freedoms served the party in this effort was revealed by (Communist Party) District Chairman Dorothy Healey in a report to the party’s Southern California District Council on September 21, 1958. Mrs. HEALEY declared that the party preferred public protest meetings to be held by the Citizens Committee to Preserve American Freedoms rather than under party auspices because Communists could attend without danger of being exposed as members of the party. She also noted that Communists scheduled as congressional committee witnesses could not appear beforehand at openly Communist rallies without creating the impression that the party was conspiring with witnesses to withhold information from the committee.”

(Committee on un-American Activities, House Report 259 on the Southern California District of the Communist Party, April 3, 1959, pp. 7 and 8.)

APPENDIX
CONFIDENTIAL

Page 277:

SF 100-17334
JGC: mhb

COMMUNIST PARTY (CP) AND
RELATED ACTIVITIES

NORMAN LEONARD, representing the San Francisco Citizens Committee to Preserve American Freedoms (CCPAF), a characterization of which is in the Appendix hereto, was one of a group of sponsors advocating a civil rights' workshop held December 7, 1963, in Los Angeles. Suggested questions for the workshop were:

1. Can the Negro depend on the Constitution to protect his rights?
2. What do civil rights and civil liberties mean to a man without a job?
3. Can the method of nonviolence be effective unless civil liberties are guaranteed?
4. Will the civil rights' movement be declared subversive?
5. Whis [sic] is the cart and which is the horse?

SF T-2, 12/12/63.

On January 14, 1964, NORMAN LEONARD, acting as chairman, held a meeting sponsored by the San Francisco CCPAF at his residence, 750 Sanchez Street, San Francisco. At this meeting there was a discussion of the local election personnel and issues.

SF T-3, 1/16/64.

On January 17, 1964, a leaflet, bearing the letterhead of the San Francisco Citizens Committee to Preserver American Freedoms over the signature of Norman Leonard, urged residents of PHILIP BURTON's Congressional District to vote for BURTON in the forthcoming congressional primary, and stated that Burton had promised to do all in his power to abolish the House Committee on Un-American Activities.

Page 284:

UNITED STATES DEPARTMENT OF JUSTICE
FEDERAL BUREAU OF INVESTIGATION
CONFIDENTIAL

Copy to:

Report of: SA [redacted]	Office: SAN FRANCISCO
Date: December	
Field Office File No.: 100-17334	Bureau File No.: 100-352241

Title: NORMAN LEONARD

Character: INTERNAL SECURITY – C

Synopsis:

> LEONARD resides at 750 Sanchez Street, San Francisco, California, and is a partner in the law firm of Gladstein, Andersen, Leonard, and Sibbett, 240 Montgomery Street, San Francisco. He has participated in Communist Party front group activities.

-C-

DETAILS:

AT SAN FRANCISCO, CALIFORNIA

RESIDENCE AND EMPLOYMENT

NORMAN LEONARD resides at 750 Sanchez Street, San Francisco, California; is also a partner in the law firm of Gladstein, Andersen, Leonard, and Sibbett, 240 Montgomery Street, San Francisco.

SF T-1, 12/14/64

CONFIDENTIAL

Page 285:

SF 100-17334
JGC/rg

COMMUNIST PARTY AND RELATED ACTIVITIES

On April 11, 1964, LEONARD attended a meeting of the San Francisco Citizens Committee to Preserve American Freedoms, held at 570 El Camino Del Mar, San Francisco.

At this meeting LEONARD stated that the purpose of the meeting was to honor the sponsors for the abolition of the House Committee on un-American Activities.

SF T-2 on 4/16/64

A characterization of the San Francisco Citizens Committee to Preserve American Freedons [sic] (SFCCPAF) is contained in the appendix pages of this report.

[redacted]

SF T-3 on 6/5/54

[redacted]
[redacted]

SF T-4 on 6/16/64

On July 7, 1964, NORMAN LEONARD held a meeting of the San Francisco Citizens Committee to Preserve American Freedoms at his residence, 750 Sanchez Street, San Francisco. The purpose of the meeting was to mail literature, on a bulk quantity, against the House Committee on Un-American Activities.
Approximately ten persons were at this meeting.

SF T-2 on 7/28/64

Page 286:

SF 100-17334
JGC/rg

On July 14, 1964, LEONARD held a meeting of the SFCCPAF at his residence, 750 Sanchez Street. This meeting was held to mail additional literature concerning the House Committee on un-American Activities.

SF T-2 on 7/29/64

NORMAN LEONARD, as Chairman of the SFCCPAF, signed a letter which demanded the abolition of agencies such as the House Committee on un-American Activities. This letter was bulk mailing.

SF T-5 on 7/29/64

On November 6-8, 1964, LEONARD attended the regional meeting of the committee to abolish the House Committee on un-American Activities. This meeting was held at 3839 Washington Street, San Francisco. NORMAN LEONARD introduced the various speakers and the purpose of the meeting was to discuss various ways which could be used to abolish the House Committee on un-American Activities.

SF T-6 on 11/8/64

Page 288:

1
SF 100-17334

NATIONAL COMMITTEE TO ABOLISH THE
House Un-American Activities Committee

The "Guide to Subversive Organizations and Publications" issued December 1, 1961, by the Committee on Un-American Activities, U.S. House of Representatives, page 115, contains the following citation regarding the National Committee to Abolish the Un-American Activities Committee (NCAUAC).

"Cited as a 'new organization' set up in the summer of 1960 to lead and direct the Communist Party's 'Operation Abolition' campaign. Seven of the national leaders of this group have been identified as Communists.

(Committee on Un-American Activities, House Report 1278 on the Truth About the Film 'Operation Abolition,' Part 1, October 3, 1961, p. 5.)"

A source has advised that the NCAUAC changed its name on March 3, 1962, to include the word "House" in its name, thereby becoming known as the National Committee to Abolish the House Un-American Activities Committee.

APPENDIX

Page 304:

SF 100-17334
LHJ/res

Union (ILWU) Membership List. It was estimated that an ad to be placed in the newspaper on December 18, 1964, would cost approximately $1,000 and it was felt that after the ad appeared, they could secure approximately $750 from people who read the ad.

The treasurer's report showed that this organization as of this date had $276.00 in the treasury.

SF T-1 – 12/10/64

A characterization of the SFCCPAF
is contained in the appendix hereto.

[redacted]

[redacted]

SF T-2 – 1/15/65

[redacted]

[redacted]

SF T-3 – 4/13/65

[redacted]

SF T-4 – 5/4/65

The "People's World" (PW) newspaper sponsored its annual celebration known as the 27th Anniversary Celebration at the Jack Tar Hotel on January 30, 1965. NORMAN LEONARD was master of ceremonies of this event.

Page 305:

SF 100-17334
LHJ/res

NORMAN LEONARD introduced at this meeting the following individuals and described them as follows:

ALVAH BESSIE...A victim from the original Hollywood ten screenwriters persecuted as an alleged communist.

ARCHIE BROWN...Victim of the Landrum-Griffin Act, is a self-proclaimed member of the CP and Chairman of the CP of San Francisco.

[redacted]...Victim of Walter McCarran Immigration Act.

ROSCOE PROCTOR...Victim of the Subversive Activities Control Board. Proctor is a self-proclaimed member of the National Committee of the CP, USA

LEONARD then introduced BETTINA APTHEKER, a student at the University of California and one of the leaders of the University of California (UC) Free Speech Movement (FSM). APTHEKER bitterly criticized the past chancellor of UC, UC President CLARK KERR, the Berkeley Police Department, former Senator WILLIAM KNOWLAND, and the judges in Berkeley handling trials of sit-ins at the UC. She, also in her speech, opposed the investigation by various law enforcement agencies and stated that the students know more of what is going on than the investigators do. BETTINA APTHEKER is a self-proclaimed member of the CP, USA.

Another speaker at this program was FRANK WILKINSON, Executive Secretary of the National Committee to Abolish the HCUA.

SF T-1—2/4/65
SF T-5—4/5/65
SF T-6—2/3/65
SF T-7—2/3/65
SF T-8—2/12/65
SF T-9—2/1/65
SF T-10—3/3/65
SF T-11—2/2/65

Page 306:

SF 100-17334

LHJ/res

The PW is a west coast communist dominated and controlled weekly publication.

A characterization of the National Committee to Abolish the HCUA is contained in the appendix hereto.

Page 324:

SF 100-17334
LHJ/sms

1. X Subject's name is included in the Security Index.
2. X The data appearing on the Security Index card are current.
3. Changes on the Security Index card are necessary and Form FD-122 has been submitted to the Bureau.
4. X A suitable photograph X is is not available
5. Subject is employed in a key facility and is charged with security responsibility. Interested agencies are .
6. This report is classified CONFIDENTIAL because (state reason) information furnished by SF T-1 through SF T-6 could reasonably result in the identification of confidential informants of continuing value and compromise future effectiveness thereof.
7. Subject previously interviewed (dates) . OTHER Court Order X Subject was not reinterviewed because (state reason) as an attorney and [redacted] interview with him could prove embarrassing to the Bureau.
8. This case no longer meets the Security Index criteria and a letter has been directed to the Bureau recommending cancellation of the Security Index card.
9. X This case has been re-evaluated in the light of the Security Index criteria and it continues to fall within such criteria because (state reason) he lends aid to CP front groups.
10. X Subject's SI card is X is not tabbed Detcom. Subject's activities warrant Detcom tabbing because (state reasons)

- C*-
COVER PAGE

Page 326:

UNITED STATES DEPARTMENT OF JUSTICE
FEDERAL BUREAU OF INVESTIGATION

CONFIDENTIAL

Copy to: 1 – Secret Service, San Francisco (CLASS 3) (RM)

Report of: SA [redacted] Office: SAN FRANCISCO

Date: NOVEMBER 18, 1966

Field Office File #: 100-17334 Bureau File #: 100-352241

Title: NORMAN LEONARD

Character: SECURITY MATTER – C

Synopsis:

LEONARD continues to reside at 750 Sanchez Street, San Francisco, California and is employed as an attorney-at-law in the law firm of Gladstein, Leonard, and Sibbett. 1182 Market Street, San Francisco, California. [redacted] Meetings of the San Francisco Citizens Committee to Preserve American Freedoms (SFCCPAF) and the National Committee to Abolish the House Un-American Activities Committee (NCAHUAC) have been held in his home. LEONARD does legal work for the Northern California Committee for Protection of Foreign Born (NCCPFB). He has an annual subscription to the PW.

-C-

DETAILS:

AT SAN FRANCISCO, CALIFORNIA

I. BACKGROUND

A. RESIDENCE

NORMAN LEONARD continues to reside at 750 Sanchez Street, San Francisco, California.

SF T-1, 11/14/66

CONFIDENTIAL

Page 330:

SF 100-17334

1

NORTHERN CALIFORNIA COMMITTEE
FOR PROTECTION OF FOREIGN BORN

The Guide to Subversive Organizations and Publications, revised and published December 1, 1961, prepared and released by the Committee on Un-American Activities, United States House of Representatives, contains the following on pages 131-132 concerning the Northern California Committee for Protection of Foreign Born:

1. Cited as a "regional" organization of the American Committee for Protection of Foreign Born. "The Committee on Un-American Activities found that in early publications the local affiliates frankly identified themselves as chapters of the American Committee for Protection of Foreign Born; the representation of themselves as independent groups came only after enactment of the Internal Security Act which would have required them, as affiliates, to register as Communist-front organizations

"Control of the local organizations*** was made possible primarily by virtue of the fact that the leaders of the local groups were Communist Party members and therefore subject to the discipline of the party. ***The local affiliates*** were actually little more than administrative staffs, whose purpose it was to implement the program of the Communist Party in their respective areas."

The Northern California Committee for Protection of Foreign Born had headquarters in San Francisco. "The executive secretary was Mrs. Grace Partridge, a former member of the State central committee of the Communist Party of California."

(Committee on Un-American Activities, House Report 1182 on Communist Political Subversion, August 16, 1957, pp. 86, 87, 33, 34 and 64.)

The American Committee for Protection of Foreign Born has been designated by the Attorney General of the United States pursuant to Executive Order 10450.

APPENDIX

Page 334:

UNITED STATES GOVERNMENT
Memorandum

TO: Director, FBI (100-352241) DATE: 2/16/67

FROM: SAC, San Francisco (100-17334)
(100-21093)

SUBJECT: Norman Leonard
SM– C

MARJORIE HELEN LEONARD
SM – C

Enclosed for the Bureau are nine (9) copies of LHM concerning the proposed travel of NORMAN LEONARD and his wife, MARJORIE HELEN LEONARD.

The first source used in LHM is [redacted]
The second source used in LHM is [redacted]
[redacted]
The third source used in LHM is [redacted]
The fourth source used in LHM is [redacted]

4—Bureau (ENCLS. 9) (RM)
(2—100-352241)
(2—100-339927)
2—San Francisco
(1—100-17334)
(1—100-21903)
LHJ: yml
(6)

1. *CC – LHM – State*
2. *Xerox – LHM - CIA.*
3. *Bcs – LHM – Bern, Rome, Paris*

By Rs. For Info
2-28-67 [illegible signature]
[Italics denote handwritten]

Page 353:

SF 100-17334
ZJ/cab

California. Subject's name was mentioned as one who might be contacted to give the speech for donations at this celebration.

SF T-3
2/3/67

B. [redacted]

[redacted]

[redacted]

SF T-1
5/3/67

[redacted]

SF T-4
1/10/67

The program for a “Working Conference on Selective Service Laws” sponsored by the San Francisco chapter of the NLG, to be held June 17, 1967, at the Sheraton-Palace hotel, San Francisco, listed NORMAN LEONARD as one of the scheduled speakers. His topic was to be “Judicial Review of Selective Service Orders.”

SF T-5
6/8/67

C. VIETNAM SUMMER

Vietnam Summer is described in an extensive article in “The National Observer” issue of June 19, 1967, as an organization with headquarters at the Cambridge, Massachusetts, Friends School, which sets its two primary aims as: “to stop the war in Vietnam, or at least marshal protests against it, and to defeat LYNDON JOHNSON in 1968...otherwise [continued on page 354]

Page 354:

SF 100-17334
ZJ/cab

we don’t take organizational stands on anything.” The club has its object “to teach and involve numerous local groups in techniques of distributing leaflets, gathering petitions, calling on Congressmen to hold public hearings on Vietnam in opposing the draft and in planning to run anti-war candidates in local elections.” The project co-director is quoted as stating Vietnam Summer “is to organize new people, to coordinate but not to organize where there is already activity” and is “aimed at the ghetto; the Blue Collar districts; the middle class neighborhood as untapped reservoirs of anti-war sentiment.”

The August 3, 1967, issue of the “Independent Journal”, a San Rafael, California daily newspaper, reported in an article entitled “Vietnam Summer – Draft, War Opens Clash During Debate” that on August 2, 1967, approximately 130 people attended a talk about the draft and war sponsored by Vietnam Summer in Marin County at Mill Valley, California City Hall.

The announced topic for discussion was "The New Draft Law: What It Means To You." According to the article, NORMAN LEONARD of the NLG gave an explanation of the draft law and spoke in detail on exemptions, amendments, mechanics and changes in the draft law.

Page 364:

SF 100-17334
MTG/dp

II. ACTIVITIES

[redacted]

SF T-2, 11/26/67

B. People's World (PW)

The PW is a West Coast Communist newspaper published in San Francisco, California.

Source advised that NORMAN LEONARD, 750 Sanchez Street, San Francisco, California, had renewed his subscription to the PW.

SF T-3, 1/5/68

C. Selective Service Counseling

The "Concord Transcript," a daily newspaper published in Concord, California, in the edition of January 29, 1968 carried an article captioned, "Resisters to Draft In Need Of Counseling," over the by-line "CHARLES LEWIS, Editor, The Transcript." This article reported that a San Francisco attorney named NORMAL [sic] LEONARD addressed a group of about 120 persons and stated "...it is a long hard road...these young men need all the counsel they can get." The article reported LEONARD was referring to young males who plan to resist Armed Forces induction or plan to seek noncombatant service as conscientious objectors.

Page 365:

SF 100-17334
MTG/dp

Page 365:

The PW in the Saturday edition dated March 23, 1968 carried an article captioned, "Biggest Legal Broadside Fired Against the Draft." This article reported that the most comprehensive legal assault on the draft to date was launched here (San Francisco) last week by the newly formed Selective Service panel of 102 Bay Area attorneys. The panel headed by San Francisco attorneys AUBREY GROSSMAN and NORMAN LEONARD filed a series of 22 motions with Federal Judge ALFONZO ZIRPROLI which argued the draft is unconstitutional because it discriminates against young men between the ages of 18 1/2 and 26, forcing them to fight a war which the majority of their age group opposes.

D. Voter Registration

NORMAN LEONARD, 750 Sanchez Street, San Francisco, born February 22 (year not shown) in New York, lawyer, registered to vote on November 24, 1967 and showed his affiliation as Peace and Freedom Party.

Records of Voter Registration,
San Francisco, California
SA [redacted] 4/18/68

The Peace and Freedom Party is a political party which appeared on the State of California 1968 general election ballot

E. Travel Abroad

A confidential source abroad advised that NORMAN LEONARD and MARJORIE HELEN LEONARD visited Florence, Italy from May 4 to 8, 1968 and Rome, Italy from May 8 to 12, 1968. During their stay in these cities they lodged at AGIP Motels and were not known to have been engaged in any suspect activities.

750 Sanchez St. SF T-4, 5/31/68

San Francisco, Calif.

[Italics denote handwritten]

Appendix D

Richard Gladstein FBI File: HQ 100-8174 Section 3

Page 1:

FEDERAL BUREAU OF INVESTIGATION

Reporting Office	Office of Origin	Date	Investigative Period
SAN FRANCISCO	SAN FRANCISCO	9/17/57	8/23, 27; 9/7, 11,12/57

TITLE OF CASE	Report Made by	Typed By
ISRAEL RICHARD GLADSTEIN	JAMES E. TARLETON	yt

CHARACTER OF CASE

INTERNAL SECURITY—C

Subject resides at 168 Palm Street, San Rafael, California, and is a partner in the law firm of Gladstein, Andersen, Leonard & Sibbett, 240 Montgomery Street, San Francisco, California. Reliable informants report no known subversive activities by the Subject in the past 6 months. In August 1957, Subject stated to Bureau Agents that he has never endorsed the Communist Party line.

Page 2:

SF 100-650
JET/yt

DETAILS:

I. BACKGROUND

A. Residence and Employment

Subject was interviewed by Bureau Agents on August 23, 1957 at his home, 168 Palm Street, San Rafael, California, and again on August 27, 1957 at his place of business, the law firm of Gladstein, Andersen, Leonard & Sibbett, 240 Montgomery Street, San Francisco, California.

II. SUBVERSIVE ACTIVITIES

Confidential informants who are familiar with certain phases of Communist party and front group activities in the Bay Area advise that they know of no subversive activities by the Subject during the past 6 months.

III. INTERVIEW WITH SUBJECT

On August 2, and 27, 1957, the Subject was interviewed in connection with another investigative matter by Bureau Agents. During the interview on August 27, 1957, GLADSTEIN commented several times to the agents that his relations with his clients, both labor unions and otherwise, are strictly from the view point of an attorney, and he takes no part in the administration of labor unions and has nothing to do with the formation of their policy. Subject told the agents that if a union endorses the recognition of Red China, he will represent that union to the best of his ability, but if that union is against the recognition of Red China, he will also represent that union in the same fashion.

Page 3:

SF 100-650
JET/yt

GLADSTEIN also stated to the agents, "I am sure you fellows have a dossier on me higher than I could see over, but if you will review your file carefully you will discover that I have never endorsed the Communist party line."

SF T-1, a self-admitted former member of the Communist party in San Francisco, advised on June 23, 1955, that he knew the Subject to be a member of the Lawyers Group of the Communist Party in San Francisco from approximately 1936 to 1950.

Page 4:

Office Memorandum UNITED STATES GOVERNMENT

TO: Director, FBI (100-8174) DATE: 9/17/57

FROM: SAC, SAN FRANCISCO (100-650)

SUBJECT: ISRAEL RICHARD GLADSTEIN
IS – C

Reference is made to report of SA JAMES E. TARLETON dated September 17, 1957, at San Francisco, 4 copies of which are enclosed, along with 4 copies of memorandum describing informants.

Subject is a key figure, is on the Security Index, and his Security Index card is current and accurate.

This case has been re-evaluated, and continues to fit current SI criteria.

This report is classified confidential because it contains information which, if disclosed, could injure the security of the United States.

A suitable photograph of the Subject appears on his Security Index card.

An interview with the Subject is not considered advisable at the present time. The interview referred to in the referenced report was conducted by SAs MONTE A. HALL and RICHARD E. LUEBBEN, in connection with case entitled "Unsub; Richard Gladstein – Victim; Elsie Myrtle Jensen – Victim; Extortion." The above agents advised that, in general, Mr. GLADSTEIN was exceptionally pleasant in his dealings with the agents and on a number of occasions during the interviews expressed the highest respect for agents of the FBI and stated from past experience, the agents of the FBI constituted the most formidable witnesses from a defense stand point that he had ever encountered.

However, since Mr. Gladstein presently states that he has never endorsed the CP line, it is believed that an interview with him on specific communist matters would not be successful.

Page 8:

FEDERAL BUREAU OF INVESTIGATION

Reporting Office	Office of Origin	Date	Investigative Period

SAN FRANCISCO	SAN FRANCISCO	3/19/58	3/10-13/58

TITLE OF CASE	Report Made by	Typed By
ISRAEL RICHARD GLADSTEIN	JAMES E. TARLETON, JR.	BCC

CHARACTER OF CASE
INTERNAL SECURITY—C

SYNOPSIS:

Subject resides at 168 Palm Street, San Rafael, California, and is a partner in the law firm of Gladstein, Andersen, Leonard & Sibbett, 240 Montgomery Street, San Francisco, California. Reliable informants report no known subversive activities by the subject in the past 6 months. An admitted former CP member testified before the HCUA, June, 1957, that Subject attended meetings or gatherings within the Professional Section of the CP in San Francisco in the mid-1940s.

Page 9:

JET: BCC
SF 100-650

DETAILS

I. BACKGROUND

A. RESIDENCE AND EMPLOYMENT

On March 13, 1958, San Francisco T-1 advised that Subject resides at 168 Palm Street, San Rafael, California, and is a member of the law firm of Gladstein, Andersen, Leonard & Sibbett, 240 Montgomery Street, San Francisco, California.

II. SUBVERSIVE ACTIVITIES

Confidential informants who are familiar with certain phases of Communist Party (CP) and related front group activity in the San Francisco area, advised that they know of no activity by the Subject during the past six months.

On June 19, 1957, before a public session of the Sub-committee of the Committee on Un-American Activities held in San Francisco, California, Dr. JACK PATTEN, who stated he had been a member of the Professional

Section of the Communist Party (CP) in San Francisco from 1942 to 1947, testified that RICHARD GLADSTEIN, a member of the legal profession, was one of the persons with whom, at one time or another, he attended meetings of an educational nature or gatherings within the Professional Section of the CP in San Francisco. PATTEN stated that since GLADSTEIN was not a member of the particular club of the party to which he belonged, he could not positively state that GLADSTEIN was a CP member.

III. MISCELLANEOUS

The subject is the attorney representing 10 seamen once classified as waterfront security risks, who filed suit against the Government on October 25, 1957, to recover a minimum of $500,000 in wages allegedly lost by seamen while the Government delayed in appealing a reversal of the security program.

Page 14:

FEDERAL BUREAU OF INVESTIGATION

Reporting Office	Office of Origin	Date	Investigative Period
SAN FRANCISCO	SAN FRANCISCO	9/17/58	9/2, 15, 16/58

TITLE OF CASE	Report Made by	Typed By
ISRAEL RICHARD GLADSTEIN	JAMES E. TARLETON, JR.	fra

CHARACTER OF CASE
INTERNAL SECURITY—C

SYNOPSIS:

Subject resides at 168 Palm St., San Rafael, and is a partner in the law firm of Gladstein, Andersen, Leonard & Sibbett, 240 Montgomery St., San Francisco, Calif. Subject is alleged to have recruited a person into the CP in the 1940s. Reliable informant reports Subject to have attended "National Guardian" fund dinner in 4/58. Other reliable informants report no known CP activity during the past six months.

Page 24:

1. X Subject's name is included in the Security Index.
2. X The data appearing on the Security Index card are current.
3. Changes on the Security Index card are necessary and Form FD-122 has been submitted to the Bureau.
4. X A suitable photograph X is is not available
5. X Careful consideration has been given to each source concealed and T symbols were utilized only in those instances where the identities of the sources must be concealed.
6. Subject is employed in a key facility andis charged with security responsibility. Interested agencies are.
7. This report is classified Confidential because (state reason) data reported [from T-1 and T-3] could reasonably result in identification of confidential informant of continuing value and compromise future effectiveness thereof.
8. X Subject was not reinterviewed because (state reason) while Subject stated to FBI Agents in 8/57 that he had never endorsed the CP line, it is believed that an interview with him on specific Communist matters would not now be successful and might result in possible embarrassment to the Bureau.
9. This case no longer meets the Security Index criteria and a letter has been directed to the Bureau recommending cancellation of the Security Index card.
10. X This case has been re-evaluated in the light of the Security Index criteria and it continues to fall within such criteria because (state reason)

Subject is a key figure. He is an attorney who is known to furnish important assistance to the Communist movement.

Page 50:

SF 100-650
JET/hko

CONFIDENTIAL

II. SUBVERSIVE CONNECTIONS OF THE SUBJECT

Northern California Committee for
Protection of Foreign-Born (NCCPFB) (see Appendix)

On March 31, and April 4, 1960, San Francisco T-2 and T-3, respectively, advised that an announcement had been made of an affair to be held April 22,

1960, at the Empire Room of the Sir Francis Drake Hotel, Sutter & Powell Sts., San Francisco. This announcement stated that the affair was sponsored by the NCCPFB for the purpose of honoring, among others, RICHARD GLADSTEIN, for 25 years of service in behalf of Labor and Civil Liberties.

On April 20, 1960, San Francisco T-4 advised that the March-April, 1960, issue of "The Light", which is the official publication of the NCCPFB, carried an article stating that the NCCPFB would honor RICHARD GLADSTEIN at a testimonial affair on April 22, 1960, for 25 years of service to the struggle for Civil Liberties.

On April 28, and May 5, 1960, San Francisco T-5 and T-4, respectively, advised that RICHARD GLADSTEIN was honored by the NCCPFB at it's 7th Annual Testimonial evening, held April 22, 1960, at the Empire Room of the Sir Francis Drake Hotel, Sutter & Powell Sts., San Francisco.

On June 8, 1960, SF T-2 advised that the May-June, 1960, issue of "The Light" stated that nearly 300 persons attended the Testimonial Evening, held April 22, 1960, at the Sir Francis Drake Hotel, San Francisco. The article stated the affair was sponsored by the NCCPFB to honor, among others, RICHARD GLADSTEIN, for his 25 years of service to the cause of Civil Liberties.

Communist Party (CP)

On August 11, 1960, San Francisco T-6 advised that, at that time, it was contemplated by functionaries of the San Francisco County CP that in the coming financial drive for funds for the CP people such as RICHARD GLADSTEIN would be asked for substantial contributions. The functionaries were aiming this drive at persons who have shown a favorable attitude toward the CP and can be considered sympathetic toward the Party.

Page 78:

SAC, San Francisco (100-650)   October 11, 1962

Director, FBI (100-8174)—*131* [Italics denote handwritten text.]

ISRAEL RICHARD GLADSTEIN
INTERNAL SECUIRTY—C

Reference is made to your letter dated 10-1-62 requesting authority to interview captioned subject.

It is noted that this subject for many years has represented Communist Party (CP) members not only in California, but in New York. He was the attorney for Artie [sic] Brown during his recent trial for violation of the Landrum-Griffin Act which resulted in Brown's conviction. The case involving Brown is now on appeal and the Bureau is of the opinion that an interview at this time could well be used by Gladstein as a means of embarrassing the Bureau by stating that his interview was a means of intimidating him in his defense of Artie [sic] Brown, a publicly-known CP member. In view of the above, authority to interview Gladstein is denied at this time.

NOTE ON YELLOW:

Subject is a key figure of the San Francisco Office.

JAJ: peb

Page 79:

United States Government
Memorandum

TO: Director, FBI (100-8174) October 1, 1962

FROM: SAC, SAN FRANCISCO (100-650) (P)

SUBJECT: ISRAEL RICHARD GLADSTEIN
IS-C

Bureau authority is requested to interview Subject in accordance with existing instructions relating to interviews of security subjects. If this subject is cooperative, no affirmative steps will be taken during the initial interview to direct his activities and complete background investigation required by Section 107C of the Manual of Instructions will be conducted and Bureau will be requested to authorize recontact with Subject as a PSI.

a. GLADSTEIN resides at 168 Palm Street, San Rafael, California, and is a partner in the law firm of GLADSTEIN, ANDERSON, [sic] LEONARD and SIBBETT, 240 Montgomery Street, San Francisco. He is white, born December 28, 1908, at New Haven, Connecticut, (unverified). Health appears good but he reportedly had a heart condition in 1958.
b. Subject is married to CAROLINE DECKER, a housewife, white.
c. Subject was a member of the Communist Party from at least 1937, to at least 1947, and in January, 1951, allegedly admitted his membership in the CP as of that date. He has been an attorney for the CP is [sic] California and New York, and in April, 1962, unsuccessfully defended ARTIE [sic] BROWN in the Landrum-Griffin Act prosecution. He now has this case on appeal.

d. Subject's wife, who is on Reserve Index B, reportedly was a member of the CP in 1932, and a section organizer for the YCL in the mid-1930s. In 1934, she was indicted and convicted of Criminal Syndicalism and served two years in state prison. In 1938, her voter's registration indicated preference for the CP. In January, 1951, Subject allegedly said his wife "is also a member of the CP."
e. None known.

Page 80:

a. None regarding his wife, but Subject, in August, 1957, told Atents [sic] that he had never endorsed the CP line and expressed admiration for the FBI. On two occasions in 1959, he expressed admiration for the Bureau and referred at one time to his alleged 'pinkish attitude' of some years ago. He tries to convey the impression that he is only trying to do the best for his clients and that he really is not a Communist at all.
b. It is felt that Subject desires respectability now that he has wealth, and his children, some being young teen-agers, may have influenced this trend. If this is not the case, and Subject refuses to discuss his past activities, the interview can still result in impression on the Subject that we consider his past to amount to a good deal more than a "pinkish attitude." It would be possible to interview Subject away from his employment and residence in a manner which would not result in embarrassment to the Bureau. If cooperative, Subject could furnish valuable information concerning CP finances and membership in the professional section of the CP in San Francisco.

Page 81:

(SC) 100-8174
100-51949

Date: October 26, 1962

To: Deputy Assistant Secretary for Security Department of State

From: John Edgar Hoover, Director

Subject: ISRAEL RICHARD GLADSTEIN
INTERNAL SECURITY – C

CAROLINE GLADSTEIN

SECURITY MATTER—C

Enclosed for the information of your Department and the Central Intelligence Agency (CIA) is a copy of a memorandum regarding the captioned subjects.

Reports concerning the investigation of these subjects will be transmitted to your Department and the CIA by separate communication.

The travel of these subjects to France, Austria and Italy is being referred to the Legal Attaches at Paris, Bern and Rome, respectively, for contact with appropriate security services in order that they may be advised of any pertinent information developed. This Bureau, however, would appreciate any information your Department or the CIA may receive regarding these subjects in other areas where they may travel.

Enclosure

1—Director (Enclosure)
Central Intelligence Agency

Attention: Deputy Director, Plans
2—Paris (Enc.) (See note page 2)
2—Bern (Enc.) (See note page 2)
2—Rome (Enc.) (See note page 2)
2—San Francisco (See note page 2)
1—Foreign Liaison Unit (route through for review)

JAJ: cad
(16)

Page 82:

Deputy Assistant Secretary for Security
Department of State

NOTE LEGATS, PARIS, BERN AND ROME AND SAC, SAN FRANCISCO:

The San Francisco Office should follow this case closely and advise the Bureau by letterhead memorandum of the subjects' return.

Enclosed for each Legat is one copy of the memorandum regarding the captioned subjects which is self-explanatory.

For the additional information of the Legats the following is noted concerning Israel Richard Gladstein:

Gladstein joined the Communist Party (CP) in 1937 and remained active therein through the early 1950s. Since 1938 the subject has espoused in the CP line in numerous speeches and writings and has been active in defense of

CP leaders in the San Francisco and New York areas. Subject is currently a law partner in the firm of Gladstein, Anderson [sic] and Leonard. In 1952 he served a six-month sentence in Federal prison for contempt of court. In recent years he has not been reported to be a formal member of the Party but has been active in representing various CP members in Federal court in the San Francisco area.

With regard to Caroline Gladstein the following is noted:

In the mid-1930s this subject was active in organizing strikes and making speeches advocating the overthrow of the Government by use of force and violence. She was indicted under the Criminal Syndicalism Act on August 15, 1934, and was subsequently convicted of this offense to serve 1 to 14 years. She thereafter served 2 years in the Women's Penitentiary, Tehachapi, California. She was reportedly the common-law wife of Jack Johnston, CP functionary in the Pittsburgh, Pennsylvania, area in 1932 and was also the alleged common-law wife of John Warnick, a known communist in the San Francisco area in 1934. Prior to her marriage to Gladstein in 1941 she, in addition to her reputation as a communist, was also known as a woman of very loose morals. Subsequent to the early 1940s she was not reported to be engaged in communist activities.

Page 83:

Deputy Assistant Secretary for Security
Department of State

The above information may be furnished to your sources in order that you may be advised of any pertinent information developed during the subjects' travel in the areas covered by you. Any information obtained by you indicating travel of these subjects to areas not covered by your office should be immediately transmitted to CIA and/or the appropriate Legat. Israel Gladstein is a key figure of the San Francisco Office. His wife, Caroline Gladstein, is not included in the Security Index.

Page 127:

Re: ISRAEL RICHARD GLADSTEIN

Nationality	United States
Birthplace	New Haven, Connecticut
Fingerprint classification	
	23 L; R; IIO; 15
	L; 6; R; IOI

FBI Number	4103668
Residence	168 Palm Avenue, San Rafael, California
Employment	attorney, 240 Montgomery Street, San Francisco, California

2. BACKGROUND DATA

GLADSTEIN graduated from the University of California in 1928; received his law degree in 1931 and was admitted to the California Bar the same year. From 1933 to 1941, he was married to REBECCA MELNELSKY, who divorced him. He has claimed military experience but no military record for him has been found.

3. BACKGROUND DATA AND INFORMATION CONCERNING SUBJECT's AFFILIATION WITH AND PARTICIPATION IN A SUBVERSIVE MOVEMENT

GLADSTEIN is reported to have joined the Communist Party in 1937 and to have been active therein through the early 1950s. He has represented various Communist Party members in legal actions and in 1952 served a six-month sentence in Federal Prison for contempt of court arising from his actions during a Communist Party trial. Gladstein continues to advise and aid the Communist Party in the San Francisco area.

Page 132:

UNITED STATES DEPARTMENT OF JUSTICE
FEDERAL BUREAU OF INVESTIGATION

Report of: SA [redacted] Office: SAN FRANCISCO

Date: September 25, 1964

Field Office File No.: 100-650 Bureau File No.: 100-8174

Character: INTERNAL SECURITY—C

Synopsis:

> Subject is an attorney at 240 Montgomery Street, San Francisco, and resides 168 Palm Avenue, San Rafael, California. He was a member of the National Lawyer Guild March, 1964. He spoke at a testimonial dinner of the NCCPFB,

June 5, 1964, San Francisco. In his talk he identified himself with the radical movement, attributed progress in liberal causes to the U.S. Constitution and supported the continuing work of the NCCPFB. One informant reports he said the communists are on the right side.

DETAILS:

I. BACKGROUND

A. Residence and Employment

RICHARD GLADSTEIN continues to reside at 168 Palm Avenue, San Rafael, California, with his wife.

[Redacted] San Rafael, Calif.—
9/18/64

Page 133:

SF 100-650
APC/msl

Observation *by a Special Agent of the FBI* [Italics denote handwritten text.] on September 1, 1964, a the office building at 240 Montgomery Street, San Francisco, disclosed that GLADSTEIN still has his law offices there.

II. ACTIVITIES

RICHARD GLADSTEIN, 240 Montgomery Street, San Francisco, California, was a member in good standing, as of March 28, 1964, of the San Francisco Chapter of the National Lawyers Guild.

[SF t-1—4/9/64]

See appendix hereto on National Lawyers Guild.

RICHARD GLADSTEIN, Attorney, was listed as a speaker, in a printed invitation of an affair sponsored by the Northern California Committee for the Protection of the Foreign Born (NCCPFB), 942 Market Street, San Francisco, to be held June 5, 1964, at the Sir Francis Drake Hotel, San Francisco.
SF T-2—6/17/64
SF T-3— 5/21/64
SF T-4—5/21/64

See appendix hereto for characterization of the NCCPFB.

Richard Gladstein spoke at the 11th Annual Testimonial dinner of the NCCPFB, which was advertised by mail and in the 'Peoples World' (PW) on May 23, 1964. It was held at the Sir Francis Drake Hotel, San Francisco.

GLADSTEIN, in his remarks, said, 'Nowhere in the world but in this country could it happen that you and I of the radical movement do this work. With the help of the Constitution we are progressing but it is not yet a paradise.' This dinner was held June 5, 1964.

SF T-5—6/8/64

Page 134:

SF 100-650

APC/msl

The PW is a west coast communist weekly newspaper.

At this testimonial dinner there was a slight rumble among some of the audience because of GLADSTEIN's remarks that progress in the 'liberal cause' was made possible only because of our Constitution.

[SF T-6—6/8/64]

At this dinner, Gladstein said there are good laws in the U.S. but reactionaries are spoiling the use of them. He said such laws as the McCarran Act were just bubbles and would be swept away as not consistent with the American Constitution. He said even the communists are getting their rights restored. They can talk on campuses and travel, are winning and are on the right side.

SF T-7—6/17/64

During his speech on June 5, 1964, GLADSTEIN cited cases he had handled for the NCCPFB, pointing out the need for this committee and the need to help it defend itself against attacks of the Federal Government.

[SF T-8—6/18/64]

RICHARD GLADSTEIN spoke at the dinner referred to above.

SF T-9—6/9/64
SF T-10—6/11/64
SF T-11—6/12/64

Informants reporting on Communist Party membership and activity in the San Francisco, and San Rafael, California areas have provided no additional information on the subject.

Page 135:

NATIONAL LAWYERS GUILD
SAN FRANCISCO CHAPTER

A source advised on May 4, 1964, that the San Francisco Chapter of the National Lawyers Guild, which is affiliated with the National Lawyers Guild and follows its policies and directives, was organized in the summer of 1937, and is currently active in San Francisco, California.

Page 136:

NATIONAL LAWYERS GUILD

The Guide to Subversive Organizations and Publications, revised and published December 1, 1961, prepared and released by the Committee on Un-American Activities, United States House of Representatives, contains the following on Page 121 concerning 'National Lawyers Guild:'

1. Cited as a Communist front.

(Special Committee on Un-American Activities, House Report 1311 on the CIO Political Action Committee, March 29, 1944, p. 149.)

2. Cited as a Communist front which "is the foremost legal bulwark of the Communist Party, its front organizations, and controlled unions" and which "since its inception has never failed to rally to the legal defense of the Communist Part and individual members thereof, including known espionage agents."

(Committee on Un-American Activities, House Report 3123 on the National Lawyers Guild, September 21, 1950, originally related September 17, 1950.)

3. "To defend the cases of Communist lawbreakers, fronts have been devised making special appeals in behalf of civil liberties and reaching out far beyond the confines of the Communist Party itself. Among these organizations are the ***National Lawyers Guild. When the Communist Party itself is under fire these offer a bulwark of protection."

(Internal Security Subcommittee of the Senate Judiciary Committee, Handbook for Americans, S. Doc. 117, April 23, 1956, p. 91.)

Page 137:

NORTHERN CALIFORNIA COMMITTEE
FOR PROTECTION OF FOREIGN BORN

The "Daily People's World", now known as the "People's World", a west coast communist newspaper, of November 2, 1950, page 10, columns 1 and 2, contained an article entitled, "Northern California Committee for Foreign Born Planned." This article stated that plans for the organization of a Northern California Committee for Protection of Foreign Born would be made at a meeting on November 6, 1950, at 150 Golden Gate Avenue, San Francisco, California.

A source advised on April 22, 1964, that the Northern California Committee for Protection of Foreign Born, although an independent organization, carries out a program of activity in Northern California which coincides with the aims of the American Committee for Protection of Foreign Born (ACPFB).

The source further advised that the Northern California Committee for Protection of Foreign Born continues to be active in defending the foreign born in deportation proceedings and in securing support for the repeal of the Walter-McCarran Law.

The ACPFB has been designated by the Attorney General of the United States pursuant to Executive Order 10450.

References

PROLOGUE

Galliher, John F., Wayne H. Brekhus, and David P. Keys. 2004. *Laud humphreys: Prophet of homosexuality and sociology*. Madison: University of Wisconsin Press.
Jacoby, Susan. 2009. *Alger Hiss and the battle for history*. New Haven, CT: Yale University Press.
Keys, David Patrick, and John F. Galliher. 2000. *Confronting the drug control establishment: Alfred Lindesmith as a public intellectual*. Albany: State University of New York Press.
McGonigal, Kathryn, and John F. Galliher. 2009. *Mabel Agnes Elliott: Pioneering feminist, pacifist sociologist*. Lanham, MD: Lexington Books.

CHAPTER 1

Brody, Leslie. 2010. *Irrepressible: The life and times of Jessica Mitford*. Berkeley, CA: Counterpoint.
Cochran, Bert. 1977. *Labor andcommunism: The conflict that shaped American unions*. Princeton, NJ: Princeton University Press.
Cohen, Stanley. 1972. *Folk devils and moral panics*. Oxford, UK: Basil Blackwell.
Duberman, Martin B., Martha Vicinus, and George Chauncey, eds. 1989. *Hidden from history: Reclaiming the gay and lesbian past*. New York: Penguin Group.
Duffield, Mark R. 1988. *Black radicalism and the politics of de-industrialization: The hidden history of Indian foundry workers*. Brookfield, VT: Avebury.
Erikson, Kai. 1966. *Wayward Puritans: A study in the sociology of deviance*. New York: Wiley.
Frances, Raelene. 2007. *Selling sex: A hidden history of prostitution*. Sydney: University of New South Wales Press.
Galliher, John F., Wayne H. Brekhus, and David P. Keys. 2004. *Laud Humphreys: Prophet of homosexuality and sociology*. Madison: University of Wisconsin Press.
Glass, Charles. 2013. *Deserters: A hidden history of WWII*. New York: Penguin.
Goffman, Erving. 1963. *Stigma: Notes on the management of spoiled identity*. Englewood Cliffs, NJ: Prentice-Hall.
Greenberg, David. 2008. Just words. *New York Times*. February 24. http://www.nytimes.com/2008/02/24/weekinreview/24greenberg.html.

Keen, Mike Forrest. 1999. *Stalking the sociological imagination: J. Edgar Hoover's FBI surveillance of American sociologists*. Westport, CT: Greenwood Press.

Keys, David Patrick and John F. Galliher. 2000. *Confronting the drug control establishment: Alfred Lindesmith as a public intellectual*. Albany: State University of New York Press.

LeMay, Michael C. 2013. *Transforming America: Perspectives on U.S. immigration*. Santa Barbara, CA: Praeger.

The Library of Congress. From Haven to Home: A Century of Immigration, 1880–1924. 2010. http://www.loc.gov/exhibits/haventohome/haven-century.html

McGonigal, Kathryn and John F. Galliher. 2009. *Mabel Agnes Elliott: Pioneering feminist, pacifist sociologist*. Lanham, MD: Lexington Books.

Ortiz, Paul. 2005. *Emancipation betrayed: The hidden history of black organizing and white violence in Florida from reconstruction to the Bloody Election of 1920*. Berkeley: University of California Press.

Pontikes, Elizabeth, Giacomo Negro and Hayagreeva Rio. 2010. Stained red: A study of stigma by association to blacklisted artists during the "Red Scare." *American Sociological Review* 75: 456–78.

Rosenfeld, Seth. 2012. *Subversives: The FBI's war on students, radicals, and Reagan's rise to power*. New York: Farrar, Straus, and Giroux.

Rowbotham, Sheila. 1976. *Hidden from history: Rediscovering women in history from the 17th century to the present*. New York: Vintage Books.

Schrecker, Ellen. 1994. *The age of McCarthyism: A brief history with documents*. New York: Bedford Books of St. Martin's Press.

———. 2008. Mere shadows: The early Cold War. In *Security v. Liberty: Conflict between civil liberties and national security in American history*, ed. D. E. Farber, 67–94. New York: Russell Sage Foundation.

Smith, Michael S. 1998. *Modern American Poetry. About the Smith Act Trials*. www.english.illinois.edu/maps/poets/g_l/jerome/smithact.htm.

Tedford, Thomas L., and Dale A. Herbeck. 2009. *Freedom of speech in the United States*. 6th ed. State College, PA: Strata Publishing. http://www.bc.edu/bc_org/avp/cas/comm/free_speech/smithactof1940.html.

U.S. Bureau of the Census. 1950. Statistical Abstract of the United States: 1950. Washington, D.C.: United States Department of Commerce.

Weiner, Tim. 2007. Hoover planned mass jailing in 1950. *New York Times*. December 23. http://www.nytimes.com/2007/12/23/washington/23habeas.html?_r=1&scp=1&sq=FBI%92s%20Hoover%20had%20plan%20to%20jail%2012,000%20%91disloyal%92%20Americans&st=cse.

———. 2012. *Enemies: A history of the FBI*. New York: Random House.

Wenger, Beth S. 1999. *New York Jews and the Great Depression: Uncertain promise*. Syracuse, NY: Syracuse University Press.

Zieger, Robert H. 1994. *American workers, American unions*. 2nd ed. Baltimore, MD: The Johns Hopkins University Press.

CHAPTER 2

Abrams, Irwin. 2001. *The Nobel Peace Prize and the laureates: An illustrated biographical history 1901–2001*. Nantucket, MA: Watson.

American Bar Association Journal. 1955. What's new in the law: Bar associations . . . subversive listing. September, vol. 41: 855.

Appiah, Kwame Anthony, and Henry Louis Gates Jr., eds. 2004. *Africana civil rights: An A–Z reference*. Philadelphia, PA: Running Press.

Aronson, James. 1970. *The press and the Cold War*. New York: Bobbs-Merrill.

Auerbach, Jerold S. 1976. *Unequal justice: Lawyers and social change in modern America*. New York: Oxford University Press.

Barranger, Milly S. 2008. *Unfriendly witnesses: Gender, theater, and film in the McCarthy era*. Carbondale: Southern Illinois University Press.

Bayley, Edwin R. 1981. *Joe McCarthy and the press*. Madison: University of Wisconsin Press.

BBC. 2005. On this day 1950–2005. 1958: Arthur Miller cleared of contempt. August 7. http://news.bbc.co.uk/onthisday/hi/dates/stories/august/7/newsid_2946000/2946420.stm.

BlackClassicMovies.com. Lena Horne: Singer, Actress, Legend. http://blackclassicmovies.com/Artist_Profile/lena_horne.html.

BlackPast.org. Remembered & Reclaimed. Cox, Oliver Cromwell (1901–1974). http://www.blackpast.org/?q=aah/cox-oliver-cromwell-1901-1974.

Bontecou, Eleanor. 1953. *The federal loyalty-security program*. Ithaca, NY: Cornell University Press.

Brown, Jared. 1989. *Zero Mostel: A biography*. New York: Atheneum.

Brown, Ralph S. Jr. 1955. Loyalty-security measures and employment opportunities. *Bulletin of the Atomic Scientists: A Magazine for Science and Public Affairs* 11: 113–17.

———. 1958. *Loyalty and security: Employment tests in the United States*. New Haven, CT: Yale University Press.

Buckley, Gail Lumet. 1986. *The Hornes: An American family*. New York: Alfred A. Knopf.

Caltech Today. 2009. Tsien Hsue-Shen Dies. November 2. http://today.caltech.edu/today/story-display.tcl?story_id=39604.

Carey, Gary. 1982. *Judy Holliday: An intimate life story*. New York: Seaview Books.

Chang, Iris. 1995. *Thread of the silkworm*. New York: Basic Books.

Cogley, John, and Merle Miller. 1971. *Blacklisting: Two key documents*. New York: Arno Press.

Commission on Government, Report of the Commission on Government Security (1957). http://www.archive.org/details/reportofcommissi1957unit.

Crosby, Donald F., S. J. 1978. *God, church, and flag: Senator Joseph R. McCarthy and the Catholic Church, 1950–1957*. Chapel Hill: University of North Carolina Press.

Driscoll, Edgar J. Jr., and Mark Feeney. 1984. Playwright Lillian Hellman dies on Martha's Vineyard. *Boston Globe*, July 1.

Dunaway, David King. 1981. *How can I keep from singing: Pete Seeger*. New York: McGraw-Hill.

Frankel, Noralee. 2009. *Stripping gypsy: The life of Gypsy Rose Lee*. New York: Oxford University Press.

Freedland, Michael. 1987. *Leonard Bernstein*. London: Harrap Ltd.

Gardner, David P. 1967. *The California oath controversy*. Berkeley: University of California Press.

Gellhorn, Walter. 1950. *Security, loyalty, and science*. Ithaca, NY: Cornell University Press.

Goertzel, Ted, and Ben Goertzel. 1995. *Linus Pauling: A life in science and politics*. New York: Basic Books.

Goldstein, Robert Justin. 2006. Prelude to McCarthyism: The making of a blacklist. *Prologue Magazine* 38, Fall. http://www.archives.gov/publications/prologue/2006/fall/agloso.html.

———. 2008. *American blacklist: The attorney general's list of subversive organizations*. Lawrence: University Press of Kansas.

Harmetz, Aljean. 2010. Lena Horne, singer and actress, dies at 92. *New York Times*. May 10. http://www.nytimes.com/2010/05/10/arts/music/10horne.html.

Harvey, Brian. 2004. *China's space program: From conception to manned spaceflight*. New York: Springer-Verlag

Holden, Henry M. 2008. *FBI: 100 years: An unofficial history*. Minneapolis, MN: Zenith Press.

Hunter, Herbert M. 1983. Oliver C. Cox: A biographical sketch of his life and work. *Phylon* 44: 249–61.

Hyman, Paula E., and Deborah D. Moore, eds. 1998. *Jewish women in America: An historical encyclopedia*. New York: The American Jewish Historical Society.

IEEE Control Systems Magazine. 2010. Tsien Hsue-Shen. June: 109. http://www.ieeecss.org/CSM/library/2010/june10/18-Obituaries2.pdf.

IMDB: The Internet Movie Database. Biography for Paul Robeson. http://www.imdb.com/name/nm0732079/bio.

Kaufman, Burton I., and Diana Kaufman, eds. 2009. *Historical dictionary of the Eisenhower era*. Lanham, MD: Scarecrow Press.

Keeley, Joseph. 1969. *The China lobby man: The story of Alfred Kohlberg*. New Rochelle, NY: Arlington House.
Liukkonen, Petri and Ari Pesonen. 2008. Books and Writers. Lillian Hellman (1905–1984). http://kirjasto.sci.fi/lhellman.htm.
Lynn, Kenneth S. 1997. *Charlie Chaplin and his times*. New York: Simon & Schuster.
Martinson, Deborah. 2005. *Lillian Hellman: A life with foxes and scoundrels*. New York: Counterpoint.
Mason, Jeffrey D. 2008. *Stone tower: The political theater of Arthur Miller*. Ann Arbor: University of Michigan Press.
McCabe, John. 1978. *Charles Chaplin*. London: Robson.
McMahon, Glenn. No Dumb Blonde. http://wtv-zone.com/lumina/judy/ndb.html.
Miller, Arthur. 2000. Are you now or were you ever . . . ? *Guardian*, June 17. http://www.guardian.co.uk/books/2000/jun/17/history.politics.
———. 1987. *Conversations with Arthur Miller*. ed. Charles Roudané. Jackson and London: University Press of Mississippi.
———. 2000. *Echoes down the corridor: Collected essays, 1944–2000*. ed. Steven R. Centola. New York: Viking.
Newman, Robert P. 1989. *The Cold War romance of Lillian Hellman and John Melby*. Chapel Hill: University of North Carolina Press.
New York Times. 1965. Judy Holliday, 42, is dead of cancer. June 8.
NNDB: Tracking the entire world. Robert Oppenheimer. http://nndb.com/people/808/000047667/.
Noland, Claire. 2009. Obituary: Qian Xuesen Dies at 98. *Los Angeles Times*, November 1. http://www.latimes.com/news/nationworld/nation/la-me-qian-xuesen1-2009nov01,0,2865408.story.
Pahl, Ron H. 2007. *Breaking away from the textbook: Creative ways to teach world history volume II: The Enlightenment through the twentieth century*. Lanham, MD: Rowman & Littlefield Education.
Pauling, L.C. 2001. *Linus Pauling: Selected scientific papers*, eds. B. Kamb, L. P. Kamb, P.J. Pauling, and A. Kamb. River Edge, NJ: World Scientific.
Robeson, Paul. 1958. *Here I stand*. Boston: Beacon Press.
Robeson, Paul Jr. 2010. *The undiscovered Paul Robeson: Quest for freedom, 1939–1976*. Hoboken, NJ: Wiley.
Rosenbaum, Jonathan. 2007. *Discovering Orson Welles*. Berkeley: University of California Press.
Rosenfeld, Seth. 2012. *Subversives: The FBI's war on student radicals, and Reagan's rise to power*. New York: Farrar, Straus, and Giroux.
Sanders, Jane. 1979. *Cold War on the campus: Academic freedom at the University of Washington, 1946–64*. Seattle: University of Washington Press.
Sbardellati, J., and T. Shaw. 2003. Booting a tramp: Charlie Chaplin, the FBI, and the construction of the subversive image in Red Scare America. *Pacific Historical Review* 72: 495–530.
Schrecker, Ellen. 1986. *No ivory tower: McCarthyism and the universities*. New York: Oxford University Press.
———. 1994. *The age of McCarthyism: A brief history with documents*. New York: Bedford Books of St. Martin's Press.
Schweber, S. S. 2000. *In the shadow of the bomb: Oppenheimer, Bethe, and the moral responsibility of the scientist*. Princeton, NJ: Princeton University Press.
Scitable: By Nature Education. 2011. Linus Pauling: A Lifetime of Science. http://www.nature.com/scitable/topicpage/linus-a-lifetime-of-science-6539763.
Seldes, Barry. 2009. *Leonard Bernstein: The political life of an American musician*. Berkeley: University of California Press.
Sicherman, B., C. H. Green, I. Kantrov, and H. Walker, eds. 1980. *Notable American women: The modern period*. Cambridge, MA: Belknap Press of Harvard University Press.
Spartacus Educational. Alger Hiss. http://www.spartacus.schoolnet.co.uk/USAhiss.htm.
———. Arthur Miller. http://www.spartacus.schoolnet.co.uk/USAmillerA.htm.
———. Charlie Chaplin.http://www.spartacus.schoolnet.co.uk/USAchaplinC.htm.

Time. 1952. The theater: Meeting-goer. June 2. http://www.time.com/time/magazine/article/0,9171,857252,00.html.

Walsh, David, and Joanne Laurier. 2009. An interview with Joseph McBride, author of *What Ever Happened to Orson Welles?*: Orson Welles, the blacklist and Hollywood filmmaking—part 1. World socialist Web Site: Published by the International Committee of the Fourth International (ICFI). http://www.wsws.org/articles/2009/jun2009/mcb1-j16.shtml.

CHAPTER 3

Ann Fagan Ginger—US Human Rights Violations since 9-11. 2006. Interview by Grace Aaron. http://video.google.com/videoplay?docid=713215581291529425.

Auerbach, Jerold S. 1976. *Unequal justice: Lawyers and social change in modern America*. New York: Oxford University Press.

Bailey, Percival R. 1982. The case of the National Lawyers Guild, 1939–1958. In *Beyond the Hiss case: The FBI, congress, and the Cold War*, ed. A.G. Theoharis, 129–75. Philadelphia, PA: Temple University Press.

Becker, Daniel. 2001. Segregated City: Black Lawyers in the 1950s. DCBAR, September. http://www.dcbar.org/for_lawyers/resources/publications/washington_lawyer/september_2001/lawyers.cfm.

Boger, John Charles. 2008. Tribute: William P. Murphy: In memoriam. *North Carolina Law Review* 86: 305–10.

Brown v. Board of Education, 347 U.S. 483 (1954)

Carlin, Jerome E. 1962. *Lawyers on their own: A study of individual practitioners in Chicago*. New Brunswick, NJ: Rutgers University Press.

Egelko, Bob. 2009. Doris Walker—fought to acquit Angela Davis. *SFGate.com*. August 19. http://articles.sfgate.com/2009-08-19/bay-area/17178005_1_national-lawyers-guild-ms-walker-afghanistan-and-iraq

Galanter, Marc, and Thomas Palay. 1995. Public service implications of evolving law firm size and structure. In *The law firm and the public good*, ed. R. A. Katzmann, 19–58. Washington, DC: The Brookings Institution.

Ginger, Ann Fagan. 1993. *Carol Weiss King, human rights lawyer, 1895–1952*. Niwot: University Press of Colorado.

Haskins, James. 1992. *Thurgood Marshall: A life for justice*. New York: Henry Holt.

Heinz, John P., and Edward O. Laumann. 1994. *Chicago lawyers: The social structure of the bar*. (Rev. Ed.). Evanston, IL: Northwestern University Press.

Helen Cirese Papers. n.d. An inventory of the collection at the University of Illinois at Chicago. http://www.uic.edu/depts/lib/specialcoll/services/rjd/findingaids/HCiresef.html.

Hoffman, Paul. 1973. *Lions in the street: The inside story of the great Wall Street law firms*. New York: Saturday Review Press.

Kunstler, William M., and Shelia Isenberg. 1994. *My life as a radical lawyer*. Secaucus, NJ: Carol.

Nader, Ralph, and Wesley J. Smith. 1996. *No contest: Corporate lawyers and the perversion of justice in America*. New York: Random House.

Sandefur, Rebecca L. 2001. Work and honor in the law: Prestige and the division of lawyers' labor. *American Sociological Review* 66: 382–403.

Sander, Richard H. 2004. A systematic analysis of affirmative action in American law schools. *Stanford Law Review* 57: 367–483.

———. 2006. The racial paradox of the corporate law firm. *North Carolina Law Review* 84: 1755–1822.

Shamir, Ronen. 1995. *Managing legal uncertainty: Elite lawyers in the New Deal*. Durham, NC: Duke University Press.

Smigel, Erwin O. 1964. *The Wall Street lawyer: Professional organization man?* New York: The Free Press of Glencoe.

Smith, Selma M. 1999. A century of achievement: The centennial of the Association of Women Lawyers. *Women Lawyers Journal* 85: 18–33.

Sugar, Maurice. 1988. The birth of the guild, 7–9 in *The National Lawyers Guild: From Roosevelt through Reagan*, eds. A.F. Ginger and E. M. Tobin. Philadelphia, PA: Temple University Press.
Thurgood Marshall, Supreme Court Justice. http://chnm.gmu.edu/122/hill/marshall.htm.
Tushnet, Mark V. 1996. *Making civil rights law: Thurgood Marshall and the Supreme Court, 1936–1961*. New York: Oxford University Press.
Wilkins, David B., and G. M. Gulati. 1996. Why are there so few black lawyers in corporate law firms? An institutional analysis. *California Law Review* 84: 496–625.
Wood, Arthur L. 1956. Informal relations in the practice of criminal law. *American Journal of Sociology* 62: 48–55.
Yale Law Journal. 1964. Notes and comments: The Jewish law student and New York jobs—Discriminatory effects in law firm hiring practices. 73: 625–60.

CHAPTER 4

ACLU of Northern California: Our History. http://www.aclunc.org/about/history/index.shtml.
A Timeline of San Francisco History—1950–Present. n.d. http://www.zpub.com/sf/history/sfh-3.html.
Burner, David. 1996. *Making peace with the sixties*. Princeton, NJ: Princeton University Press.
Calisphere: University of California. n.d. San Francisco General Strike. http://www.calisphere.universityofcalifornia.edu/themed_collections/subtopic4d.html
Fleming, Thomas. 1999. *Segregation and the Civil Rights Movement in San Francisco*. Interview by Chris Carlsson. Found sf. http://foundsf.org/index.php?title=Segregation_and_the_Civil_Rights_Movement_in_San_Francisco
Graves, Donna. n.d. National Park Service World War II: In the San Francisco Bay Area. *Tending the homefront: The many roles of Bay Area women during World War II*. http://www.nps.gov/nr/travel/wwiibayarea/womenatwar.htm
Humboldt Herald. 2007. The 1935 Humboldt County timber strike. June 21. http://humboldtherald.wordpress.com/2007/06/21/the-1935-humboldt-county-timber-strike/.
International Court System. n.d. Founder of the International Court System: Empress I Jose: José Julio Sarria. http://www.impcourt.org/icis/who/founder.html.
Issel, William. 1989. Business power and political culture in San Francisco, 1900–1940. *Journal of Urban History* 16: 52–77.
———. 1991. Liberalism and urban policy in San Francisco from the 1930s to the 1960.s *Western Historical Quarterly* 22: 431–450.
———. 2004. A stern struggle: Catholic activism and San Francisco labor—1934–1958. In *American labor and the Cold War: grassroots politics and postwar culture*, eds. R. W. Cherny, W. Issel, and K. W. Taylor, 154–176. New Brunswick, NJ: Rutgers University Press.
Luedtke, Carolyn Hoecker. 2000. On the frontier of change: A legal history of the San Francisco Civil Rights Movement, 1944–1970. *Temple Political and Civil Rights Law Review* 10: 1–47.
National Japanese American Historical Society. n.d. Media Advisory. Bay Area Day of Remembrance Press Conference. http://www.njahs.org/programs/viewdetails.php?id=305
Picture This: California Perspectives on American History. n.d. http://museumca.org/picturethis/.
Rorabaugh, W.J. 1989. *Berkeley at war: The 1960s*. New York: Oxford University Press.
Rosenbaum, Fred. 2009. *Cosmopolitans: A social and cultural history of the Jews of the San Francisco Bay Area*. Berkeley: University of California Press.
Taylor, Sandra. 1993. *Jewel of the desert: Japanese American internment at Topaz*. Berkeley: University of California Press.
Warren, Nancy. n.d. LGBT—Queer SF. *SFGate.com*. http://www.sfgate.com/living/gay/queersf/.

CHAPTER 5

Barnes, Bart. 1990. Obituaries; longshoremen's union leader Harry Bridges dies. *Washington Post*. March 31, p. B4.
Dispatcher. 1955a. The fifth frameup begins with a quick switch. June 24.
———. 1955b. Defense pleads for judgment that law abides. August 5.
Ginger, Ann Fagan. 1993. *Carol Weiss King: Human rights lawyer*. Boulder, CO: University of Colorado Press.
Ginger, Ann Fagan, and Eugene M. Tobin eds. 1988. Harry Bridges, the guild, and the FBI, In *The National Lawyers Guild: From Roosevelt through Reagan*, 51-53. Philadelphia: Temple University Press.
Kutler, Stanley I. 1982. *The American inquisition: Justice and injustice in the Cold War*. New York: Hill and Wang.
Larrowe, Charles P. 1972. *Harry Bridges: The rise and fall of radical labor in the United States*. New York: Lawrence Hill & Co. Publishers.
Leonard, Norman. 1986. *Life of a leftist labor lawyer*. Interview by Estolv Ethan Ward. Regional Oral History Office, the Bancroft Library. Berkeley, CA: University of California.
San Francisco Examiner. 1962. Brown gets jail in dock red case. May 5.
United States v. Brown 381 U.S. 437 (1965).

CHAPTER 6

California Historical Society. n.d. Biographical Record of Notable Living Men and Women of California. George R. Andersen.
Declarations of Candidacy. 1935. San Francisco General Municipal Election. November 5.
———. 1937. San Francisco General Municipal Election. November 2.
Dispatcher. 1966. George R. Andersen dies; devoted legal career to rights of workers. January 7, p. 3.
Memorial Meeting in Tribute to George Andersen. San Francisco, January 16, 1966.
People's World. 1966. A veteran of labor's battles: Attorney Andersen dies at 65. January 1, p. 12.
Raineri, Vivian McGuckin. 1991. *The red angel: The life and times of Elaine Black Yoneda*. New York: International Publishers.
San Francisco Chronicle. 1934. Attorney for radical gets death threats. July 20.
———. 1948. labor attorney is shot here. January 11.
———. 1949. Deportation hearing: Government witness reports on Communist doctrine in alien case. June 15.
———. 1956a. Lawyer Andersen was a red, witness says. January 1.
———. 1956b. "S.F. attorney denies he is a red." October 10.
San Francisco Examiner. 1933. Police trail killer of grower to Bay Area. October 7.
———. 1934. S. F. drive on Communists to continue. July 26.
———. 1936a. Ship murder defense given court rebuke. November 20.
———. 1936b. Attorneys wrangle: New ship murder jury fight: Defense hints pressure on prospective talesman. November 26.
———. 1943. Citizenship plea refused. May 7.
———. 1948a. Gunman shoots lawyer for reds. January 11.
———. 1948b. Andersen case: Shooting shocks mayor; attorneys offer reward. January 12.
———. 1965. George Andersen, 65, attorney dies. December 29.
Seldes, George H. 1937. *Freedom of the press and the 1934 general strike*. Garden City, NY: Garden City Publishing.
Selvin, David F. 1996. *A terrible anger: The 1934 waterfront and general strikes in San Francisco*. Detroit, MI: Wayne State University Press.
State Bar of California. Attorney Search. http://members.calbar.ca.gov/search/member.aspx.

U.S. Congress. House. Committee on Un-American Activities, 86th Cong., 2nd Sess., May 13, 1960.
U.S. v. Schneiderman 1957, Subversive Activities Control Board, Docket No. 1115–55, May 1.
Virtual Museum of San Francisco. n.d. "'Red' Suspects Demand Jury: Parade of 350 Arrested in Police Raids Starts before Lazarus." http://www.sfmuseum.org/hist4/maritime16.html.

CHAPTER 7

Costantinou, Marianne. 2006. Norman Leonard-noted labor, civil rights lawyer. *SFGate.com*, March 11. http://articles.sfgate.com/2006-03-11/bay-area/17284168_1_mr-leonard-norman-leonard-law-firm.
Leonard, Norman. 1950. "Analysis of the Internal Security Act of 1950 (McCarran Act)." November.
Leonard, Norman. 1986. *Life of a leftist labor lawyer*. Interview by Estolv Ethan Ward. Regional Oral History Office, the Bancroft Library. Berkeley: University of California.
San Francisco Chronicle. 1969. Answer to General Hershey. May 29.
San Francisco Examiner. 1965. Sit-in arrest tapes assailed by defense. April 14.
———. 1974. Top court aids lawyer in disbarment fight. July 11.

CHAPTER 8

Brotsky, Allan. 2005. Allan Brotsky oral history. Interview by Harvey Schwartz. Labor Archives and Research Center, SFSU. San Francisco, CA.
Civil Rights Congress. 1952. *Lawyers under fire*. New York.
Dispatcher. 1948. Reinecke case is part of battle against forces to destroy democracy. October 15, p. 8.
———. 1949. Gladstein withdraws from Bridges case to serve term for contempt. October 28, pp. 1, 12.
———. 1951. Immigration service stoolpigeon parade fails to prove charges against local 7-C's Mensalvas. April 13, p. 8.
———. 1952. Locals ask parole for R. Gladstein. July 4, p. 6.
———. 1974. ILWU attorney Gladstein suffers heart attack. August 30, p.1.
———. 1976. On the beam: By Harry Bridges. September 10, p. 2.
———. 1981. Richard Gladstein, ILWU attorney for 35 years, defended Bridges, Hall. June 5, p. 6.
Gladstein, Caroline Decker. 1978. Oral History. Ann Arbor: University of Michigan.
Gladstein, Richard. Supplement to Memorandum of Respondent. California District Court.
Honolulu Star Bulletin. 1999. Fear of communist infiltrators engulfed postwar Hawaii. October 18.
Kennedy, Dana. 1981. Counsel for Harry Bridges: Attorney was jailed but client was freed. *Los Angeles Times*. May 25, p. 18.
Kutler, Stanley. 1978. Interview with Richard and Caroline Gladstein. Bancroft Library. Berkeley: University of California.
Labor Arbitration Board. 1950. Cutter Laboratories, Berkeley. September 16.
Leonard, Norman. 1986. *Life of a leftist labor lawyer*. Interview by Estolv Ethan Ward. Regional Oral History Office, the Bancroft Library. Berkeley: University of California.
Recorder. 1950. Here are attorneys signing brief in contempt case. February 14.
San Francisco Chronicle. 1937. Anti-picket law invalid, judge rules. January 20.
———. 1941. Gladstein is almost in the army. May 11.
———. 1949a. Gladstein reported threatened in N.Y. June 28.
———. 1949b. Controversy in Berkeley over speech. November 10.
———. 1949c. Gladstein out as Bridges' defense attorney. November 25.
———. 1951. U.S. indicts 12 state red leaders. August 1.

———. 1952. Reds' lawyers go to prison. April 25.
———. 1955a. Gladstein disbarment action delayed. February 1.
———. 1955b. Gladstein wins fight against judge in Hawaii. April 9.
San Francisco Examiner. 1941. U.S. arrests Bridges in new ouster case. April 2.
Stein, Mimi. 1975. Notes on conversation with Richard Gladstein. *Bancroft Library*. Berkeley: University of California. February 6.
United States v. Brown 381 U.S. 437 (1965).
U.S. Congress. House. Committee on Un-American Activities. Communist Legal Subversion: The Role of the Communist Lawyer. 86th Cong., 1st Sess., February 16, 1959.
Wiececk, William W. 2006. *The birth of the modern Constitution: The United States Supreme Court, 1941–1953*. New York: Cambridge University Press.

CHAPTER 9

Aubrey Grossman. 1911–1999. A Militant Legal Crusader For Labor's Rights And the Rights of All People.
Auerbach, Jerold S. 1976. *Unequal justice: Lawyers and social change in modern America*. New York: Oxford University Press.
Bailey, Percival R. 1982. The case of the National Lawyers Guild, 1939–1958. In *Beyond the Hiss case: The FBI, congress, and the Cold War*, ed. A.G. Theoharis, 129–175. Philadelphia, PA: Temple University Press.
Brilliant, Mark. 2010. *The color of America has changed: How racial diversity shaped civil rights reform in California, 1941–1978*. New York: Oxford University Press.
Brotsky, Allan. 2005. Allan Brotsky oral history. Interview by Harvey Schwartz. Labor Archives and Research Center, SFSU. San Francisco, CA.
Chambliss, Elizabeth. 2010. Measuring law firm culture. *Law, Politics, and Society* 52: 1–31.
CliffsNotes.com. *The internal environment*. 15 Apr 2012. http://www.cliffsnotes.com/study_guide/topicArticleId-8944,articleId-8860.html.
Fortune, Don. 1977. Bridges, a labor legend. *San Francisco Examiner*. April 18.
Ginger, Ann Fagan, and Eugene M. Tobin, eds. 1988. The Rosenberg case In *The National lawyers guild: From Roosevelt through Reagan*, 96-98. Philadelphia, PA: Temple University Press.
Goffman, Erving. 1963. *Stigma: Notes on the management of spoiled identity*. Englewood Cliffs, NJ: Prentice-Hall.
Halberstam, David. 1993. *The fifties*. New York: Random House.
Harry Bridges: A Biography. http://www.ilwu19.com/history/biography.htm
Kerouac, Jack. 1957. *On the road*. New York: Viking Press.
Layman, Richard. 1994. *American decades: 1950–1959*. Detroit, MI: Gale Research.
Robin, Eugene Debs, ed. 1979. *Claude Bernard and the internal environment*. New York: Marcel Dekker, Inc.
San Francisco Chronicle. 1999. Obituary: Aubrey Grossman. December 10.
Schrecker, Ellen 1994. *The age of McCarthyism: A brief history with documents*. Boston, MA: St. Martin's Press.

Index

About the Authors

Colin Wark holds a PhD from Missouri University and is the author of two books and several journal articles. He is an associate professor of criminology and sociology at Texas A&M University-Kingsville.

John F. Galliher has a PhD from Indiana University-Bloomington and is the author of 14 books including two published by Lexington Books (2009, 2010), two by the University of Wisconsin Press, and two by the SUNY Press. He is a professor of sociology at Missouri University.

www.ingramcontent.com/pod-product-compliance
Ingram Content Group UK Ltd.
Pitfield, Milton Keynes, MK11 3LW, UK
UKHW041126071026
15587UKWH00009B/257